Annabel Karmel

COMPLETE
First Year Planner

Annabel Karmel

COMPLETE
First Year Planner

From the bestselling author of THE NEW COMPLETE BABY AND TODDLER MEAL PLANNER

How to enjoy a healthy pregnancy and a stress-free and healthy first year
including over 80 delicious recipes for you and your baby

About the author

Annabel Karmel is the UK's best-selling author on baby and children's food and nutrition. She is the number one parenting author and an expert in creating delicious healthy meals for children without spending needless hours in the kitchen.

Her books have sold more than 4 million copies worldwide and *The Complete Baby and Toddler Meal Planner* regularly features in the top 5 cookery titles.

Her popular website www.annabelkarmel.com has more than 120,000 members and around 200,000 visitors a month. It provides a wealth of parental information including eating during pregnancy through to weaning and first foods. Packed with recipes for babies, children and adults, the website also covers all aspects of nutrition.

Annabel was awarded an MBE in 2006 in the Queen's Birthday Honours for her outstanding work in the field of child nutrition.

Author's acknowledgements

▨ Many thanks to all the beautiful babies who modelled for my book: Bruno Black, Gabriel Calnan, Annie Dickinson, Joshua Lederman, Susanna Leigh, Sarah Schechter, Aleksander Squire and Harry Pedlow ▨ Rachel Franks and Jo Pedlow for the use of his hand ▨ Dr Margaret Lawson, Senior Research Fellow in Paediatric Nutrition, Institute of Child Health, Great Ormond Street Hospital ▨ Debby Gould, consultant midwife, Queen Charlottes and Chelsea Hospital ▨ Ruth Williams, NNEB home learning co-ordinator ▨ Peter Walker, baby massage expert ▨ Mark Johnson, Centre for Brain and Cognitive Development, Birbeck College, University of London ▨ Dr John Fysh, consultant paediatrician, Portland Hospital ▨ Dr Stanley Rom, consultant paediatrician, Portland Hospital ▨ Cheryll Adams, community practitioners' and Health Visitors Association ▨ Lynda Leach, midwife at St John and Queen Elizabeth Hospital ▨ Desiree Dorman, maternity nurse ▨ Lesley Wilson, play services manager, Great Ormond Street Hospital ▨ Sue Townsend, Mothercare ▨ Alison Alexander, consumer expert, *Prima Baby Magazine* ▨ Dawn Baran, registered health visitor and nurse ▨ Professor Brent Taylor PhD FRCPCH, Royal Free Hospital ▨ Lisa Schechter ▨ Peter Armitage, Au Pair Student Placement Agency ▨ Wendy Doyle ▨ Fiona Ford MSc FRD ▨ Gail Rees BSc SRDPhD ▨ Borra Garson ▨ Special thanks to Ann Herreboudt, midwife and child psychologist, St John and Queen Elizabeth Hospital for sharing her wealth of knowledge ▨ Tessa Evelegh for styling, Daniel Pangbourne for photography, Caroline Marsen for preparing the food for photography, Nadine Wickenden for the illustrations, my editor Emma Callery, Sue Miller for design, Amelia Thorpe and Grace Cheetham ▨ David Karmel, Jacqui Morley, Mary Jones and Evelyn Etkind ▨ Special thanks to Simon Karmel for all his support and encouragement

To Nicholas, Lara and Scarlett for the magical first years you each gave me and for reminding me what it's like to be little in a big people's world.

15 14 13 12 11

Published in 2003 by Ebury Press, an imprint of Ebury Publishing

A Random House Group Company

Text © Annabel Karmel 2003
Photography © Daniel Pangbourne 2003
Illustrations © Nadine Wickenden 2003

Annabel Karmel has asserted her right to be identified as the author of this Work in accordance with the Copyright, Designs and Patents Act 1988

The Random House Group Limited Reg. No. 954009

Addresses for companies within the Random House Group can be found at www.randomhouse.co.uk

A CIP catalogue record for this book is available from the British Library

The Random House Group Limited supports The Forest Stewardship Council® (FSC®), the leading international forest certification organisation. Our books carrying the FSC label are printed on FSC® certified paper. FSC is the only forest certification scheme endorsed by the leading environmental organisations, including Greenpeace. Our paper procurement policy can be found at www.randomhouse.co.uk/environment

Editor: Emma Callery ▨ *Designer:* Sue Miller ▨ *Photographer:* Daniel Pangbourne ▨ *Stylist:* Tessa Evelegh ▨ *Illustrator:* Nadine Wickenden

Printed and bound in China by C&C Offset Printing Co., Ltd

ISBN: 9780091888039

This book is not a substitute for health or medical information, and you are advised always to consult your doctor or other health professional for specific information. Great Ormond Street Hospital for Children cannot accept any legal responsibility for any injury, illness or harm sustained as a result of following recommendations in this book.

Contents

Introduction

Sometimes a personal tragedy acts as a catalyst and completely changes the direction of your life. This often happens when you least expect it and when everything seems to be going well. Fifteen years ago, I learned an important lesson: trust your own instincts when it comes to looking after your child, even if you feel you don't have the requisite experience – you are the best judge.

My first child Natasha was three months old and ready for her night-time feed but something was wrong. Her body was twitching and she seemed unusually sleepy and wouldn't breastfeed. I was concerned so I called a friend of mine, a doctor who lived in the same street. After some gentle persuasion he agreed to examine her. I remember him saying that first-time mothers worry and fuss unnecessarily but that I would learn to relax and he assured me that my baby seemed fine and that I should go to bed. I felt embarrassed that I had imposed on him but slept uneasily and woke early to see how she was.

Still sensing something was wrong, I bundled her into my car and took her to my GP who sent us straight to hospital. Five days later she died in my arms at Great Ormond Street Hospital. A viral infection had caused encephalitis and by the time she received treatment it was too late to save her.

I was devastated. I had a very successful career as a musician but I just lost my desire to perform any more and I cancelled all my engagements. I was very lucky to fall pregnant within a few months but when I went into labour one Saturday night my eminent obstetrician advised me to stay at home as the baby would 'take a long time coming'. Then, having assured me that he would not be going out, he proceeded to take his girlfriend to a restaurant. I called him on his bleep 30 minutes later and he repeated the same advice. As soon as I put down the phone my waters broke. I ran upstairs to get my things to go to hospital but I was horrified to feel the baby's head pressing down. My son Nicholas was delivered by my husband Simon on the staircase. It wasn't until two hours later that an ambulance arrived and even then they couldn't move me as I was still attached to the baby by the cord. My doctor, unable to display his impeccable bedside manner, albeit on the staircase, perhaps was otherwise engaged lingering over coffee and petit fours. His bleep was unobtainable but a desperate message awaited him on his answering machine at home.

It was fortunate that I had managed to drag my

reluctant husband to one antenatal class and he was able to do the business as a result of a 30-minute talk! Let that be a lesson to all errant husbands!

While it was pretty traumatic at the time, it turned out to be the easiest birth of all my children. We issued Simon with an honorary midwifery certificate but he subsequently hung up his forceps and moved us all to a house one street away from a hospital. Just as well as my next birth was a dramatically fast event and my new obstetrician (equally eminent) didn't have time to get there – probably a good thing as a year later he was struck off for life! I've been very unfortunate in my choice of obstetrician.

My first book, *The Complete Baby and Toddler Meal Planner*, was written after the birth of Nicholas, who was a terrible eater, and it was my memorial to Natasha. I felt that one of the most important factors that determines your child's health is their diet. My aim was to explain away the mystique of jars of baby food with their long lists of nutritional ingredients and a shelf life of over two years, and encourage parents to make their own fresh baby food, which is better for their baby and tastes 'real'. This book, now in its 19th edition, has become the definitive guide to feeding babies and is sold all over the world. I went on to write nine more books on all aspects of feeding children and this subject has become my passion.

My aim with this book, which branches into a wider area, is to help parents through the critical first year of their baby's life and demystify the abundance of expert advice on all aspects of babycare, much of which is conflicting. The book is designed as a practical hands-on guide and covers everything from getting your baby to sleep through the night to helping your toddler take his first steps and say his first words. I have drawn on my own experiences of bringing up three children (one who wouldn't sleep and another who wouldn't eat) and had the benefit of expert advice from many people, including the staff of the world-renowned Great Ormond Street Hospital with whom I have worked since my very first book.

Babies develop and grow more quickly in their first year than at any other time in their life. The unconditional love between you and your child is the most wonderful feeling in the world but being a parent is very demanding. You will need to learn how to do more than three things at once: you will need wisdom, you will need patience and you will need an unlimited supply of love, plus a back-up supply for use in the early hours of the morning when your baby is wide awake. I would like this book to help give parents the confidence to trust their own instincts and make an informed choice that is right for their individual child.

Annabel Karmel

CHAPTER ONE

PREPARING
for birth

EATING IN PREGNANCY

Even before conception it is important that you prepare your body as a healthy body is more likely to mean a healthy, happy pregnancy. It is during the time leading up to conception and the first three months of pregnancy that your baby will benefit the most from your eating a healthy diet. However, changing to a better diet at any time during pregnancy will help you cope with the demands of your developing baby and will help ensure that your baby is born strong and healthy.

Recommended weight gain

The amount of weight you should gain during your pregnancy depends on your height and how much you weighed around the time of conception. Body mass index (BMI) is an index of a person's weight in relation to height. It is calculated by dividing your weight in kilogams by the square of your height in metres and is the most accurate way of measuring your body fat. BMI charts are available at most clinics.

As a guide, a BMI of 19 to 25 is the normal range; 18 is underweight. If you are overweight when you conceive (BMI 25–29.9), you are more likely to face problems like hypertension and pre-eclampsia during your pregnancy. If you are underweight and gain too little weight in pregnancy, you run the risk of having a premature or low birth weight child. Women who gain less than 6 kg (13.2 lb) in pregnancy run the danger of giving birth to a premature or underweight baby, even if they are overweight at the beginning of the pregnancy.

Sometimes weight gain is not caused by eating too much. Some women have problems with fluid retention in pregnancy in which case you should consult your doctor.

Recommended weight gain
(American National Academy of Sciences)

Pre-pregnancy weight	Recommended gain
Underweight (below 19.8 BMI)	12.7–18.2 kg (28–40 lb)
Normal weight (19.8–26 BMI)	11.4–16 kg (25–35 lb)
Overweight (26–29 BMI)	6.8–9.1 kg (15–20 lb)
Obese (30–40 BMI)	6.8 kg (15 lb)

* Women who are 1.6 m (5 ft 2in) or smaller should use the lower end of the scale as a guide.

* If you are having twins, the average weight gain is 16–20 kg (35–45 lb).

* As a guideline, the healthy range for a baby's birth weight is between 3 kg (6 lb 8 oz) and 4.15 kg (9 lb 5 oz).

Excessive weight gain

It's bad news for mothers who feel they should be eating for two. Most women don't need any extra calories for the first six months of pregnancy and only about 200 extra calories a day for the last three months. That is equivalent to two slices of buttered toast.

Nor is pregnancy a good time to diet because you risk depriving your baby of the nutrients needed to

Good foods for 200 calories

- 1 slice wholemeal toast with a slice of cheese.
- Small jacket potato with 25 g (1 oz) cheese.
- 1 large banana.
- A bowl of cereal, e.g. Bran Flakes with skimmed milk.
- Tuna or salmon salad.
- Cup of soup and a slice of wholemeal bread.
- 2 tablespoons sunflower or pumpkin seeds.
- Grilled chicken breast.

develop properly. So if you are worried that you are gaining too much weight, take a look at your diet and the first foods that you should try to cut out are fatty or sugary ones. Also aim to eat more fresh foods as it is the processed convenience foods and snacks that tend to contain the most sugar and fat.

Pregnancy shouldn't be used as an excuse to binge on chocolates and cakes. It's fine to have occasional treats but if you put on too much weight, problems can result such as backache and varicose veins. Also it can be hard to shift the weight later and many women feel really depressed if they are still fat and can't fit into any of their clothes several months after they have given birth.

Exercise and health

Staying fit helps you cope better with pregnancy and labour so it's a good idea to do some gentle exercise every day, like yoga, swimming or walking. Exercise speeds up your metabolism. Yoga is excellent as it emphasises breathing and helps you relax, which is particularly useful for labour. Check the type of yoga offered is suitable as an antenatal class and make sure the instructor is qualified as some yoga postures may damage your back.

Sudden weight gain

If you have a sudden weight gain of more than 1 kg (2 lb 4 oz) per week, severe swelling of hands and face, headaches and/or blurred vision, call your doctor. This could be caused by pre-eclampsia, a pregnancy-related form of high blood pressure, which can be very dangerous. A little swelling or fluid retention is very common, especially in the third trimester, but if it gets worse or you are at all worried, contact your midwife, GP or obstetrician.

It is important that you avoid any exercise that puts strain on your joints, like high-impact aerobics. Your ligaments get softer when you are pregnant due to hormonal changes so they can be damaged more easily.

Healthy snacks to help you through the day

- Pitta bread pocket stuffed with salad.
- A bowl of fresh vegetable or lentil soup.
- Raw vegetables with dips, e.g. hummus or guacamole.
- A selection of dry roasted seeds.
- Sardines on toast.
- A bowl of fresh mixed salad.
- Cottage cheese with fruit.
- Mini bio-yoghurt drink.
- Natural yoghurt sweetened with fruit purée or honey.
- Fruit smoothie.
- Wholemeal biscuits, e.g. bran biscuit or oatcake.
- Wholemeal toast with Marmite.
- Rice cakes.
- Lightly salted popcorn.
- A bowl of cereal with skimmed milk.
- Fresh or dried fruit.

A balanced diet

Eating a balanced diet is all to do with choosing the right foods and eating them in the right proportion. Foods from the four largest groups illustrated on the food plate (opposite) should be eaten every day, while fat and sugar are best not eaten too often or in large amounts.

It is important to choose a variety of foods from each group, but in the right quantities, as illustrated. For most of us that will mean eating more starchy foods like wholegrain bread or cereals, pasta and rice and more fruits and vegetables.

Carbohydrates

Starchy foods like breads, cereals, rice, pasta and potatoes should form the main part of your diet. The carbohydrate contained in them is broken down in the body to release glucose, which gives us energy. Some carbohydrates will keep you going for a long time while others will only give short-lived energy.

There are two types of carbohydrate: complex (slow-burning) carbohydrates and simple (fast-burning) carbohydrates. Many people believe these foods are fattening but this is not true. It is how we cook or serve them that can pile on the pounds. For example, a slice of bread spread thinly with butter has twice as many calories as the bread on its own. A baked potato is not fattening but fried chips are.

Don't worry too much if you prefer white bread as it is fortified with vitamins and minerals like calcium and vitamin B1. Some white bread is also fortified with folic acid (look for the sign with the blue circle).

Q I'm worried that eating foods like bread and potatoes will make me gain a lot of weight and I was already overweight before I became pregnant.
A Starchy foods like potatoes, pasta and bread are low in fat and they are filling, which is fine provided they are not fried or served with creamy sauces or butter. Choose a baked potato, pasta with a tomato sauce or a bowl of wholegrain cereal. A large baked potato provides more than half your recommended daily amount of vitamin C.

Complex carbohydrates
Complex carbohydrates like wholemeal bread, brown rice, porridge oats, potatoes and pasta take longer to be broken down into glucose, which means that the sugar is absorbed more slowly and steadily into the bloodstream. Try to eat more complex carbohydrates as these give longer-lasting energy and satisfy your hunger better. Unrefined complex carbohydrates like wholemeal bread and wholegrain cereals are better for us because they retain more iron, natural vitamins and fibre. Including fibre-rich foods during pregnancy is important as during pregnancy women are more prone to suffer constipation. Remember to drink plenty of fluids with high-fibre foods.

Simple carbohydrates
Simple carbohydrates such as sugary breakfast cereals, sweet biscuits, cakes, fruit juice and soft drinks are made up of ingredients that are stripped of their natural fibre during processing and have lost most of their valuable nutrients. Eating these foods causes your

A healthy plateful

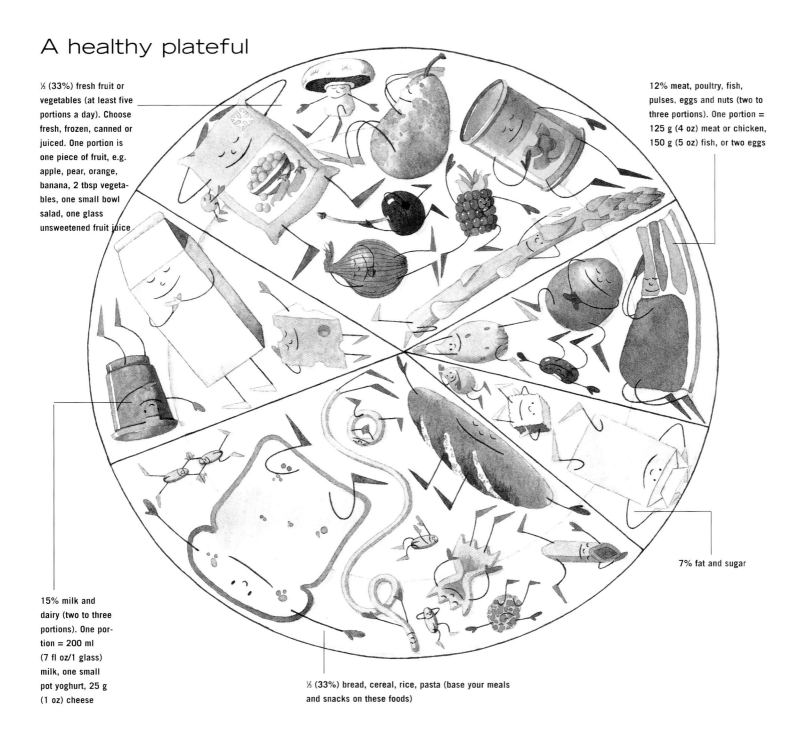

⅓ (33%) fresh fruit or vegetables (at least five portions a day). Choose fresh, frozen, canned or juiced. One portion is one piece of fruit, e.g. apple, pear, orange, banana, 2 tbsp vegetables, one small bowl salad, one glass unsweetened fruit juice

12% meat, poultry, fish, pulses, eggs and nuts (two to three portions). One portion = 125 g (4 oz) meat or chicken, 150 g (5 oz) fish, or two eggs

7% fat and sugar

15% milk and dairy (two to three portions). One portion = 200 ml (7 fl oz/1 glass) milk, one small pot yoghurt, 25 g (1 oz) cheese

⅓ (33%) bread, cereal, rice, pasta (base your meals and snacks on these foods)

blood sugar to rise rapidly but it would fall again all too quickly, leaving you feeling tired and hungry. These types of carbohydrate therefore only provide you with short-lived energy.

Fruit and vegetables

Fresh fruit and vegetables provide valuable vitamins and minerals plus fibre. A variety is important to make sure that you are including many different vitamins and minerals in your diet. You should aim for five servings a day. One serving of fruit is the equivalent of:

- 1 large fruit, e.g. apple, banana or orange.
- 2 medium fruits, e.g. kiwis or plums.
- Approximately 100 g (4 oz) strawberries or raspberries.
- Approximately 40 g (1½ oz) dried fruits.
- 1 glass of fruit juice.

One serving of vegetables is the equivalent of:

- Approximately 90 g (3½ oz) cooked green vegetables, 80 g (3¼ oz) cooked root vegetables or 75 g (3 oz) cooked peas or sweetcorn.
- Large bowl of salad.

Colourful fruits and vegetables tend to be more nutritious, so try to include some dark green and orange vegetables, berry fruits and orange fruits in your diet as these are rich in antioxidants. A diet rich in antioxidants may help prevent pre-eclampsia (see page 10).

There are two types of vitamins: water-soluble (C and B complex) and fat-soluble (A, D, E and K). Water-

Eating a whole fruit with skin or pith provides fibre and more sustained energy than a fruit juice.

Q Should I eat only organic fruit and vegetables?
A Organic fruits and vegetables may contain more minerals and as they are grown without pesticides they are an environmentally friendly option. It is safe to eat the skin, which contains natural fibre; however, you will need to wash fruit and vegetables carefully to remove any traces of soil or manure (used as fertiliser), which could cause infection by toxoplasmosis or E. coli. Organic produce is more expensive and you shouldn't feel worried about eating ordinary fruit or vegetables as there is no scientific evidence to show that pesticide levels in ordinary fruit and vegetables are harmful.

soluble vitamins cannot be stored by the body, so eat foods containing these each day. Vegetables and fruits are our main source of vitamin C and the need for vitamin C increases in pregnancy. Also vitamin C helps our bodies absorb iron from plant-based foods, so a glass of orange juice with your breakfast cereal or a salad with sandwiches is a good idea. Remember that boiling vegetables removes vitamins and minerals, so steam or stir-fry them or eat them raw.

Fibre

If you eat plenty of fruit (fruit with the skin left on and dried fruit are especially good), vegetables and complex carbohydrates like wholegrain cereals, oats and baked potatoes, you should get enough fibre in your diet. Bran is not such a good source of fibre as it can reduce the absorption of important minerals like calcium, iron, zinc and magnesium. Linseed is good added to breakfast cereals or salads as a source of roughage and also provides essential fatty acids.

To prevent constipation it is also important to drink plenty of water.

Vitamin & mineral supplements

■ A balanced and varied diet should supply you with all the vitamins and minerals that you need. However, if you think that you are not eating a good diet, it might be a good idea to take an antenatal multivitamin and mineral supplement during your pregnancy. You should always choose a multivitamin and mineral supplement because minerals like iron, zinc and calcium work more efficiently when taken together with other vitamins and minerals. For example, taking iron on its own will reduce your body's absorption of zinc.

■ You can continue to take a multivitamin and mineral supplement during breastfeeding as for many mothers it takes quite a long time to recover good nutritional status after pregnancy. For example, many mothers are deficient in iron after giving birth.

■ It is important to remember that vitamin supplements are not a substitute for a good, healthy diet as they contain only a small proportion of the nutritional benefits available from fruits and vegetables.

■ Talk to your doctor, midwife or a qualified nutritionist about choosing a suitable supplement. It must be specially formulated for pregnancy so that, for example, it contains no retinol (meat-derived vitamin A).

Protein

The major groups of foods containing protein are meat, poultry, fish, eggs, dairy products, pulses, nuts, cereals and grains.

Proteins are the building blocks of life but most people probably eat more than they actually need to. It is recommended that we eat two to three servings a day of protein foods. However, during pregnancy, protein requirements increase by about 5%, which is equivalent to the protein of an egg, a glass of milk or three slices of bread.

Meat and poultry

Meat and, to a lesser extent, poultry is high in protein and provides the best source of iron since it is most easily absorbed by humans. The need for iron increases during pregnancy because both mother and baby are busy creating new blood. However, you should avoid eating liver as the high levels of vitamin A can harm your unborn child. Choose lean meat, and it is best to ask your butcher to mince meat from good cuts rather than buying ready-prepared minced meat. Also remember that the dark meat of chicken or turkey is richer in iron than the white meat.

Undercooked and raw poultry and meat may be contaminated with harmful bacteria. The Department of Health advises cooking all meat and poultry thoroughly so that juices run clear and there is no trace of blood or pinkness. Be especially careful when eating barbecued food as this can often be cooked on the outside but still remain undercooked in the middle. Cook-chill poultry, if served cold, can contain listeria so is best avoided.

Q As I am a vegetarian, will my baby get all the nutrients that he needs if I don't eat any meat, chicken or fish ?
A If you are vegetarian, animal proteins, including dairy products and eggs, contain all the amino acids that the body needs. However, if you are vegan, soya (e.g. tofu) is the only plant-based food that contains all the amino acids so you should try to eat two vegetable protein groups each day to get all the amino acids. The groups are grains (e.g. rice, oats, wheat, bread, pasta), pulses (e.g. beans and lentils) and nuts and seeds.

Unless you are vegetarian, try to include red meat or chicken in your diet three times a week and also eat plenty of fresh fruit and vegetables because they contain vitamin C, which increases the absorption of iron from the food in your body.

Vegetarian pregnant women will probably be getting most of the nutrients that meat eaters receive except perhaps for vitamin B12 and iron. Vegetarians can obtain vitamin B12 from eggs and dairy produce, however. Many breakfast cereals are also fortified with vitamin B12. (See iron on page 17 and calcium on page 18 for vegetarian sources.)

Fish

A small portion (100 g/4 oz) of fish contains half of the recommended daily protein requirement. Oily fish like salmon, tuna, mackerel, sardines and trout are especially good to eat during pregnancy as they contain essential fatty acids (EFAs, see page 17), which are important for the development of a baby's brain, nervous system and sight, especially during the last three months of pregnancy.

Fish oils also substantially reduce the likelihood of suffering cardiovascular disease whether from heart attacks or strokes.

Current concerns over environmental pollutants in oily fish means pregnant and breastfeeding women are recommended to stick to just one portion of oily fish a week. The advice from the Foods Standards Agency (FSA) is to eat two portions of fish a week, one of which should be oily.

That said, there has not been much documented incidence of problems and any possible disadvantages of eating fish would have to be balanced against all the important nutritional benefits. For example, a recent study in the *British Medical Journal* showed that women who eat fish at least four times a week (two oily fish and two white) are less likely to have babies that are premature or with low birth weight.

Non-oily fish like cod, plaice, sole and sea bass are low in fat, which makes them easy to digest, and it is best to grill, griddle or bake them.

Fats and sugar

Fats and sugar should form the smallest part of the food plate – 7%. Foods like cakes, biscuits and crisps are high in fat or sugar and they contain very little goodness for you or your baby. Fats should make up about 30% of your total calories and the majority of these fats should come from nutritious foods like dairy produce, oily fish, meat, eggs, avocados, nuts and seeds. You should ensure that you restrict the amount of added fats like butter and oil in your diet. The best way to do this is to use low-fat methods of cooking like grilling, stir-frying or steaming.

It's fine to eat sugary foods in moderation but they will only give short-lived energy and too much sugary food can lead to weight gain and cause tooth decay. They will also cause the same sugar 'lows' experienced when eating too many simple carbohydrates. Pregnancy is not the time to load up your body with empty calories like those obtained from sugar.

Tinned tuna and salmon both contain lower levels of mercury than fresh fish. However, tinned tuna does not contain the valuable omega-3 oils that are found in oily fish such as mackerel, sardines and trout.

Pregnancy superfoods

Superfood	**Folic acid**
Status	Folic acid is needed for the development of your baby's organs and tissues and has been shown to reduce the risk of spinal defects such as spina bifida.
Intake	The Department of Health recommends that women who are planning to become pregnant should take a 400 mcg folic acid supplement a day and continue until the 12th week of pregnancy. Ideally you should have started to take these supplements before you became pregnant but it is not too late to start taking them afterwards. You should also try to ensure that you include plenty of foods that are rich in folic acid in your diet but even if you follow a healthy diet you should still take folic acid supplements. Some foods like bread or breakfast cereals have a sign to show that they are fortified with folic acid. The amount of folic acid in vegetables can be reduced in cooking, particularly if they are boiled for a long time or in a large amount of water, so steam, microwave or stir-fry vegetables instead. Alcohol and smoking can increase your need for folic acid.
Good sources	■ Green vegetables, e.g. spring greens, broccoli and brussel sprouts ■ Wholegrain cereals including fortified breads and breakfast cereals ■ Pulses, including baked beans ■ Yeast extract ■ Asparagus ■ Oranges ■ Nuts
Superfood	**Essential fatty acids (EFAs)**
Status	Your baby's brain starts developing even before you know you are pregnant so it's important to make sure that you are eating the right 'brain' foods to boost your baby's potential. EFAs are important for your baby's brain and visual development. They are called essential fats because they can't be made in the body. There are two types of fatty acids: omega-6 and omega-3. Most people already eat plenty of omega-6 from vegetable oils and spreads but omega-3 tends to be in short supply.
Intake	The richest source of omega-3 is oily fish like salmon, tuna, mackerel and sardines. EFAs are particularly important in the last three months of pregnancy when the unborn baby builds up a supply of omega-3 in the brain and nervous tissue. Tinned tuna is rich in vitamins and minerals but the processing removes most of the omega-3 fatty acids.
Good sources	**Good sources of omega-3** ■ Salmon ■ Fresh tuna ■ Trout ■ Sardines ■ Linseed oil ■ Walnut oil ■ Columbus eggs **Good sources of omega-6** ■ Sunflower oil ■ Safflower oil ■ Rapeseed oil ■ Grapeseed oil ■ Soft polyunsaturated margarine
Superfood	**Iron**
Status	Your unborn baby places huge demands on your iron reserves. Large amounts of iron are essential for the developing blood supply of the foetus and for the extra blood you need at this time. Iron is also important for placenta development and growth of the baby. Furthermore, you need to build up your baby's own store of iron for him to draw on in the first few months of life.

	If you feel washed out and exhausted or feel faint or dizzy during your pregnancy you could be suffering from low iron levels. A deficiency in iron may also lower your ability to cope with infection. Many women start their pregnancy already low in iron and become iron deficient. You probably won't experience symptoms until your condition is quite advanced or you may think that feeling so tired is just part of pregnancy, so your blood will be routinely tested at 12 weeks and again during your third trimester. When iron deficiency is severe, anaemia can be serious and has been linked to an increased risk of premature labour, stillbirth and low birth weight babies.
Intake	Iron from animal sources like red meat provides the best form of iron as it is much more easily absorbed into our bodies than non-animal forms of iron, present in pulses, spinach and dried fruit. To maximise the iron absorption from non-animal sources, you need to consume vitamin C-rich fruit and vegetables, e.g. kiwi fruit, strawberries, red peppers, tomatoes or a juice like orange or cranberry at the same meal as this will help your body absorb iron. If you are not a big meat eater, combining a small amount of animal protein with vegetable protein helps you absorb more iron from vegetables foods, e.g. spinach with meatballs. Try to avoid drinks like tea and coffee at meal times as they contain tannin, which inhibits the absorption of iron. It is much better to get iron from the food you eat rather than supplements. Iron supplements can cause constipation and can interfere with the absorption of other nutrients.
Good sources	**Good sources of iron that are well absorbed** ■ Red meat ■ Chicken or turkey, especially dark meat ■ Tinned sardines ■ Fish paste ■ Egg yolk **Other sources of iron** ■ If you include a source of vitamin C at the same meal or eat meat or fish with these foods it will help the iron to be absorbed ■ Breakfast cereals fortified with iron ■ Wholegrain cereals and breads ■ Dark green vegetables, e.g. broccoli and spinach ■ Pulses, including baked beans and lentils ■ Dried fruit ■ Wholegrain cereals and breads and fortified breakfast cereals
Superfood	**Calcium**
Status	Calcium is essential for strong bones and teeth and is an important nutrient during pregnancy particularly during the later stages when your baby's bones are hardening. A newborn baby's body contains 25–30 g calcium, most of which is absorbed from the mother in the final ten weeks of pregnancy. Dairy products provide the best and most easily absorbed source of calcium. If you do not eat dairy foods you will not get enough calcium from your diet and will need to take a supplement.
Intake	If you aren't getting enough calcium in your diet, your baby will draw on the calcium stored in your bones, which can lead to osteoporosis in later life, so a calcium-rich diet is essential in pregnancy and also later when breastfeeding. If you are worried about weight gain, switch to semi-skimmed or skimmed milk and reduced-fat cheese and yoghurts. They contain just as much calcium and protein as whole milk but less fat.
Good sources	■ Dairy produce, e.g. milk, cheese, yoghurt ■ Cereals/cereal products ■ Dark green vegetables, e.g. spinach ■ Fish with bones, e.g. tinned sardines, pilchards or salmon mashed up with the bones ■ White flour products and fortified breakfast cereals ■ Beans and lentils, including baked beans ■ Nuts, e.g. almonds ■ Tofu ■ Figs

Superfood	**Magnesium**
Status	Magnesium is essential for building strong bones, teeth and muscles.
Intake	Research shows that premature birth and the risk of low birth weight is increased with low intakes of magnesium early in pregnancy so make sure you have plenty of magnesium-rich foods at the beginning of your pregnancy.
Good sources	■ Seeds, e.g. pumpkin or sunflower ■ Leafy green vegetables ■ Nuts, pine nuts ■ Granary or wholemeal bread
Superfood	**Zinc**
Status	Zinc is essential for growth and for healthy foetal development. It helps to keep skin healthy, assists wound healing and boosts our immune system. Low levels of zinc can block folic acid absorption and can also affect fertility.
Intake	In general, dark red meat has a higher zinc content than white meat and fish has less than meat.
Good sources	■ Lean beef or lamb ■ Chicken or turkey, especially the dark meat ■ Wholegrain breakfast cereals ■ Brown and wholemeal bread ■ Pumpkin and sunflower seeds ■ Bananas
Superfood	**Vitamin E**
Status	A study conducted by Aberdeen University (December 2001) found that while genetic history and maternal smoking were influential factors in the development of allergies in children, maternal intake of foods containing vitamin E may be important in preventing allergenic development. Blood from the cords of 223 children was tested for responses to the common allergens, mite and grass pollen. The higher the mother's intake of foods containing vitamin E during the pregnancy, the lower the risk of the child's blood showing sensitivity to these allergens.
Intake	Vitamin E is fat-soluble so can be stored in the body and excessive amounts accumulate and can be toxic, so be careful of supplements containing vitamin E.
Good sources	■ Vegetable oils ■ Wheatgerm ■ Avocado ■ Nuts ■ Sunflower seeds

Drinks

The best drink is water. Our bodies are made up of 70% water and you should drink six to eight glasses of water (approximately 1.5 litres/2 pints) a day. Some of this can be made up of other fluids like fruit juice or herbal tea although water is best. Fruit juices are fine to drink and vitamin C-rich fruit juices like orange or cranberry help our bodies to absorb iron from food. The drawback, however, is that even pure fruit juice contains sugar in the form of fructose so drinking a lot of juice will pile on the pounds. Limit yourself to one or two glasses of pure, unsweetened juice a day.

Herbal teas and drinks

Herbal teas and drinks offer a good alternative to tea and coffee. However, some herbs, including black/blue cohosh, barbery, broom, rue, golden seal, feverfew, tansy and pennyroyal, can cause the uterus to contract.

■ Ginger tea can help alleviate nausea. Make a hot drink by boiling water and then add some grated fresh ginger. Allow to infuse and then strain and stir in a little lemon and honey to taste.

■ Peppermint tea can aid digestion and relieve flatulence. It can also help to ease nausea and heartburn.

■ Camomile tea can help with morning sickness and aids relaxation. Used tea bags soaked in boiling water and cooled and placed on your breasts can also help treat sore nipples.

■ Nettleleaf tea contains vitamins and minerals, including iron.

■ Dandelion tea is a natural diuretic and can help with water retention. It can also help relieve nausea.

Some of the foods that we eat, like fruit, contain a lot of water, in which case you can drink less. The problem is that the more you drink, the more you need to go to the loo, which is disturbing, especially when you want to sleep. So it is best to drink more during the day and less during the evening.

Raspberry leaf tea

■ Raspberry leaf tea strengthens the womb and may assist contractions. Many people believe that if it is drunk regularly in the second and third trimesters it can reduce the length of labour pains and make delivery easier. It may also reduce tearing and bruising.

■ It is best not to drink raspberry leaf tea during the first trimester because in early pregnancy it may cause miscarriage.

■ In the second trimester drink one to one-and-a-half cups a day and in the third trimester drink two to three cups a day.

Smoking and pregnancy
■ Cigarette smoke cuts down the amount of oxygen and nutrients passed to your baby. Mothers who smoke increase the risk of miscarriage. Their babies are more likely to be born prematurely and to be of low birth weight. Smoking also reduces fertility. Research shows that quitting smoking is the single most important thing you can do to improve the growth and long-term health of your baby.

Caffeine
Try to cut right down on drinks that contain caffeine such as tea, coffee and cola and don't forget that energy drinks like Red Bull also contain caffeine. The FSA advises that pregnant women should limit their caffeine intake to 300 mg of caffeine a day because high levels of caffeine can result in babies having a low birth weight or even lead to miscarriage.

Caffeine acts as a stimulant, raising blood pressure and making the heart beat faster. Also large amounts of tannin interfere with the absorption of certain vitamins and minerals. So limit your daily caffeine intake to the following:
■ 4 cups of instant coffee.
■ 3 cups of brewed coffee.
■ 6 cups of tea.
■ 8 cans of cola.
■ 1 can of energy drink.

Alcohol
The less alcohol you drink the better since alcohol passes through the placenta and affects your baby. No one knows how much alcohol is safe, but we do know that a high consumption of alcohol can affect his growth and interfere with your baby's ability to get enough oxygen and nourishment for normal cell development in the brain and other organs. Current government advice from the Department of Health is that pregnant women should have no more than eight to ten units of alcohol per week. Furthermore, of these units, no more than two should be in any one day, although the advice does state that it is better not to drink at all. Women who are having trouble conceiving should limit their alcohol intake to five units per week.

In 2002, a seven-year study involving nearly 25,000 women by Denmark's University of Aarhus found that women who drank five or more units of alcohol a week were 3.7 times more likely to miscarry in the first weeks of pregnancy compared with those who drank fewer than five.

Some doctors recommend avoiding drinking alcohol altogether during the first trimester when your baby's major organs are forming. In America, the US Surgeon General says that there is no safe limit for the consumption of alcohol during pregnancy and recommends that women should avoid it completely.

How much is a unit?
1 unit of alcohol =
■ 1 standard glass of wine.
■ 300 ml (½ pint) beer, larger or cider (normal strength).
■ 1 pub measure of spirits.
■ 1 pub measure of sherry or liqueur.

Drugs and medication
■ There are many drugs that, if taken during pregnancy, may seriously affect the health of your baby. Ask your doctor before taking any medication.

Diet and discomfort

It is suspected that the immune systems of you and your developing baby may not function as well as usual during pregnancy so take special care when preparing food as you may be more susceptible to germs.

Nausea and sickness

Feeling sick in the first 14–15 weeks of pregnancy is one of the most common early signs of pregnancy. Seven out of ten women suffer from it. The exact cause is unknown but the high levels of hormones and oestrogen coursing around a woman's body in the first three months is believed to play a major role. Although this is called 'morning' sickness, many women feel sick through the day. Don't worry unduly if you feel too sick to eat very much. Provided you were well nourished beforehand, your baby will get adequate nutrition from the reserves of vitamins, minerals, proteins and fatty acids stored in your body for a while. Reassuringly, for most women the last two-thirds of pregnancy are fine.

Ways to help ease your suffering

■ Try eating small, meals every two hours or so based on starchy carbohydrates, which are slow-burning foods that prevent your blood sugar dipping and help ease nausea.

■ Don't get up on an empty stomach. Having a plain biscuit and a warm drink before you get out of bed can help overcome morning sickness.

■ Try to rest whenever possible.

■ Avoid fatty foods as these can be difficult to digest.

■ Ginger is thought to reduce the nerve stimulation to the brain that prompts nausea or vomiting – try ginger beer, ginger biscuits or ginger tea (see page 20).

■ Dehydration is the biggest danger of morning sickness so make sure that you drink plenty of fluids like water, fruit juice, milk or herbal teas – peppermint, ginger or camomile herbal teas can be soothing.

■ Try to get some fresh air before eating. It's a good idea to go for a walk as gentle exercise can help relieve nausea and also helps to build up an appetite.

■ Acupressure wrist bands stimulate an acupressure point on your wrist, which can help relieve nausea.

Food poisoning

Salmonella is a fairly common cause of food poisoning. It can cause vomiting and diarrhoea and a high temperature but rarely causes damage to the unborn baby.

■ Ensure cooked-chilled meals are re-heated well.

■ Don't eat raw or undercooked meat or poultry.

■ Don't drink unpasteurised milk.

■ Cook eggs until the white and yolk are solid. Also avoid raw eggs in foods like homemade mayonnaise, soft meringue or chocolate mousse. Most bought mayonnaise and ice creams use pasteurised eggs, which renders the food safe.

■ Avoid all types of pâté.

■ Don't eat soft whip ice cream from ice-cream vans.

Listeriosis

This is a rare illness in pregnant women which has flu-like symptoms. The illness may be mild in the mother but it can severely affect her baby, resulting in miscarriage, still birth or major illness.

■ Avoid unpasteurised dairy products, e.g. sheep or goat's milk; soft cheeses with a surface mould and blue-veined cheeses; unwashed salad, fruit or vegetables.

Toxoplasmosis

This is a rare illness that is harmless in adults. There are few symptoms, usually no more than mild flu, but it may cause miscarriage or blindness in your unborn child. It is caused by a parasite that may be found in raw meat, cat faeces and contaminated soil.

■ Always wear rubber gloves when you are disposing of cat litter and when gardening.

■ Always wash your hands after contact with a cat.

■ Wash fruit and vegetables well.

Other foods to avoid

■ Peanuts, if you or your partner suffer from a diagnosed allergic condition like asthma or hayfever or if any other children in the family suffer from an allergy.

■ Shellfish like prawns and mussels are a major source of food poisoning so are probably best avoided.

■ Raw fish as in sushi; it may be a source of parasites.

Cheeses that are safe to eat include:

* Boursin * Caerphilly
* Cheddar * Cheese spread
* Cottage cheese
* Cream cheese * Edam
* Emmenthal * Feta * Gouda
* Gruyere * Mozzarella
* Parmesan * Port Salut

Constipation

This is common during pregnancy because the muscles of the intestine relax and cannot move the food through as quickly. Also, as the baby grows, your uterus gets bigger, which puts pressure on the bowel, making it work less effectively. Constipation can be relieved by increasing your intake of fluids and high-fibre foods, especially cereal fibre.

■ Aim to drink about six to eight glasses of water or other fluids a day (prune juice is good).

■ Increase your intake of fibre.

■ Drink hot water and lemon when you wake up.

■ Exercise like walking or swimming can also help.

Heartburn

Heartburn is an uncomfortable burning sensation in your oesophagus. It is more common during the last three months of pregnancy because progesterone relaxes the valve at the opening of your stomach, allowing stomach acid to travel back up into the oesophagus. Your growing baby aggravates the problem as he presses on your stomach. Heartburn often feels worse when you are lying down so don't lie down for an hour after eating and try to sleep propped up on several pillows.

■ Try eating smaller, more frequent meals.

■ Avoid fatty foods as they are more difficult to digest.

■ Avoid foods that might upset you like spicy and fatty foods, citrus fruits, fizzy drinks and caffeine.

■ Try drinking either before or after eating as drinking with a meal can aggravate indigestion.

■ Milk is good as it helps neutralise stomach acids.

Food cravings and aversions

The hormonal changes in pregnancy may alter your tastes and you may have a desire to eat strange foods or suddenly find that you can't bear to eat foods that you enjoyed before you became pregnant. This is normal and is most common in the first trimester.

Try to incorporate the foods that you crave into a balanced diet. Cravings for something sweet usually means a drop in blood sugar, which can happen if you don't eat often enough. Eating complex carbohydrates will help to keep blood sugar levels steady.

Some women crave non-food items like coal or ice. This is called pica and can stem from iron deficiency.

You and your baby during pregnancy

0–3 months

You

■ Hormones are flooding your body, which make your breasts larger and more tender and milk ducts develop in preparation for breastfeeding. The same hormones can cause morning sickness, so you may not feel like eating very much (see page 22).

■ Nature protects babies of mothers who feel too sick to eat well in the first trimester. At this stage, a baby does not need many calories and will develop perfectly well drawing on the vitamins, minerals, etc, from his mother.

■ Your enlarged uterus and developing baby press down on your bladder and the space for storing urine decreases, so it's quite normal to need the loo more often. After the 12th week your uterus moves up and the pressure may be relieved.

■ Your body begins to make almost twice as much blood for the developing blood supply of the foetus and placenta so it's important to include plenty of iron-rich foods in your diet.

■ Increased levels of progesterone affect your digestion and you may suffer from indigestion, wind or constipation. Pregnancy hormones also cause your gums to soften so you may get bleeding gums and are more likely to get an infection.

■ After the 12th week the risk of miscarriage falls significantly so you may want to start telling people your news.

■ You may feel as if you are on an emotional rollercoaster, up one minute and down the next. Don't worry, emotional highs and lows are normal and an increase in hormones is usually to blame.

■ Ideal weight gain: 1.4–1.8 kg (3–4 lb).

Your baby

■ The beginning of your pregnancy from the time of conception to the third month is when the most rapid changes occur as your baby's main organs are being formed. The heart starts beating at six weeks. By seven weeks your baby is the size of a pea. By the eighth week your baby's spine is well developed and he can flex it and move around, but you won't be able to feel this yet.

■ By the tenth week, a face with eyes, nose, mouth and tongue is forming. Your baby's limbs, fingers and toes are well developed and nails are starting to grow.

■ By 12 weeks your baby is able to yawn, suck, swallow and move his fingers. At the end of 12 weeks, the foetus is only about as long as your middle finger (7.5 cm/3 in) and weighs about 40 g/1½ oz.

■ Most of your baby's major organs are formed now although the sex organs are still not visible.

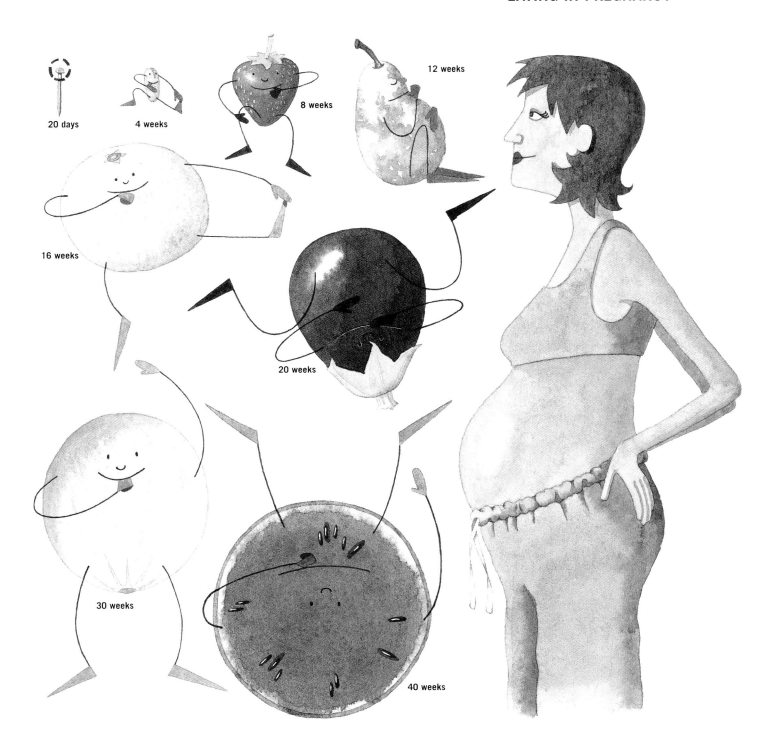

20 days

4 weeks

8 weeks

12 weeks

16 weeks

20 weeks

30 weeks

40 weeks

4–6 months

You

■ For many women this is the best stage in their pregnancy and a time when they feel radiant and full of energy. It you are feeling like this, it might be the time to do any essential shopping for your baby (see page 52).

■ Even if your energy levels are up, don't be tempted to skip meals. You still need to eat plenty of carbohydrates (see page 12) and help prevent swings in blood sugar levels.

■ You may notice that you are becoming constipated (see page 23). You may also suffer from heartburn (see page 23).

■ Your bump should be noticeable at around 17 weeks. Your tummy and breasts are starting to fill out. Around 18 weeks a dark line (linea nigra), which reaches from the navel to pubic hair, may appear. You should now be able to tell the sex of your baby by ultrasound scan.

■ By the end of the fifth month you should be able to feel your baby moving.

■ Your heart is beating at an amazing 14,000 extra times each day. This is necessary in order to pump the 40–50% more blood around your body.

■ Beware of developing anaemia. Your baby absorbs large amounts of iron to form muscles and blood, so it's important to continue to eat iron-rich foods (see page 17). Don't take iron supplements unless prescribed as they can cause constipation.

■ At around 24 weeks your breasts may leak colostrum (premilk), which is being made in preparation for feeding.

■ Vivid dreams are common.

■ Ideal weight gain: 3–6 kg (6 lb 8 oz–13 lb).

Your baby

■ Your baby's limbs are now forming as are tiny nails and eyelids, and tooth buds appear. Fine downy hair called lanugo starts to grow all over your baby's body to keep it at the right temperature

■ Although your baby's eyes are still fused shut at 15 weeks, he is aware of the difference between light and dark.

■ At 17 weeks you could easily hold your baby in the palm of your hand as he measures about 16 cm (6 in).

■ Your baby is becoming more active but in the first half of this trimester he's still thin and wrinkled and his blood vessels and skeleton are visible through his skin. By the end of the trimester your baby's skin is covered with lanugo and also vernix, a waxy coating that protects your baby's body from becoming waterlogged by the amniotic fluid.

■ Your baby needs calcium for strong bones and teeth (see page 18). This is a period of rapid growth so protein is also important as it is made up of amino acids, the building blocks of your baby's body (see page 15).

■ At 20 weeks your baby can kick his legs, wave his arms and grasp with his fists. He begins to hear and coexists with the pounding of your pulse and heartbeat and the murmuring of the placenta. His body has reached its correct relative proportions, which is why a foetal anomaly scan is done at this stage.

■ By week 22 your baby begins to recognise your voice and may respond to loud noises and music. If you massage your bump, your baby will feel it.

■ By week 24 your baby measures around 23 cm (9 in) and weighs less than 1 kg (2 lb). Your baby is developing a pattern of resting and waking, so at times you will feel lots of movement and at other times he will be still because he is sleeping.

7–9 months
You

■ Between 26 and 29 weeks is a time of major growth for your baby and you are putting on around 450 g (1 lb) a week.

■ At 31 weeks your womb is 500 times its normal size. Your baby now weighs about 1.6 kg (3 lb 8 oz), which is still less than half the average weight for a full-term baby. You may experience shortness of breath sometimes.

■ Keep your energy levels up or you will suffer from low blood sugar, making you weak and dizzy.

■ Hormonal changes mean mood swings are more common.

■ The increase in blood volume may cause your iron count to go down, so be sure to include some iron-rich foods in your diet.

■ It is common to suffer from constipation (see page 23).

■ If this is your first baby, by about 38 weeks your baby will probably drop into the pelvis, freeing up your lungs and making more room for your stomach. Breathing and eating become easier but this also causes more pressure on your bladder.

■ As pregnancy progresses and you get larger you may find that you suffer from backache. Avoid bending over and lifting heavy objects (including children).

■ Fill your freezer with home-cooked meals ready to enjoy when your baby is born.

■ If eating is a problem because your baby is pressing on your stomach, eat little and often. It may help to take liquid separate from meals to avoid feeling too full.

■ Rest as much as possible: don't stand if you can sit and don't sit if you can lie down. Only 3% of babies arrive on their due date but 80% are born within 14 days – so the end is in sight.

■ Ideal weight gain: 3.6–4.5 kg (8–10 lb).

Your baby

■ Your baby's brain is growing rapidly now, almost three-quarters of his brain develops in the last three months. To help brain and visual development, build up a supply of omega-3 fatty acids.

■ Weight gain speeds up, too, as your baby lays down fat stores under his skin in preparation for being born. If your baby is born at 28 weeks, he has a 95% chance of survival.

■ In this trimester, your baby will open his eyes for the first time. In the first half, your baby still has plenty of room to move around and this is his most active period. You can feel and see his strong kicks and you may even feel him moving rhythmically if he has hiccups.

■ By 31 weeks your baby's sense of taste has developed and he already has a sweet tooth.

■ At the end of 32 weeks your baby is beginning to store minerals such as iron, calcium and phosphorus. Babies' bones harden in the later stages of pregnancy and your baby will need to lay down calcium for strong bones and teeth. Your baby will also need to store a reserve of iron for the first five to six months of life after birth, when iron intake may be low.

■ The bones of your baby's skull can slide over each other for his head to go through your cervix at birth.

■ As your baby grows bigger he has less room to be active in the womb so you may feel less kicking. If this is your first baby, your baby's head should move down into your pelvis at around week 36 although sometimes this only happens when you go into labour.

■ By 37 weeks, your baby's lungs are maturing, getting him ready to breathe on his own. His body hair is disappearing, his face is filling out and his eyelids have eyelashes and he can open and close his eyes and suck his thumb.

■ At birth the average baby will weigh between 3.6 and 4.5 kg (8 and 10 lb).

Recipes

SUPERFOODS

Pumpkin seeds and **sunflower seeds are rich in minerals. They contain iron, zinc, selenium and vitamin E. A small bowl of roasted pumpkin and sunflower seeds makes a good snack during the day.**

Nina's glorious granola

Nina is a good friend of mine and she gave me a jar of this homemade granola as a present. I was completely hooked so she came over the next day and we cooked the recipe together. This makes a wonderfully nutritious breakfast. It's good on its own or with milk or yoghurt and fresh fruit. It will keep for several weeks in an airtight container.

Makes 10–12 portions
1 x 350 g (12 oz) jar honey
250 ml (8 fl oz) maple syrup
250 ml (8 fl oz) safflower oil
2 tsp pure vanilla essence
400 g (14 oz) jumbo organic rolled oats
75 g (3 oz) sunflower seeds
75 g (3 oz) pumpkin seeds

40 g (1½ oz) bran
40 g (1½ oz) wheatgerm
75 g (3 oz) sesame seeds
100 g (4 oz) flaked almonds
40 g (1½ oz) desiccated coconut
175 g (6 oz) raisins
75 g (3 oz) currants

■ Pre-heat the oven to 155°C /275°F/Gas mark 2.
■ In a saucepan, warm together the honey, maple syrup, safflower oil and vanilla essence.
■ Combine the rolled oats, sunflower seeds and pumpkin seeds and stir into the warm honey mixture.
■ Spread out onto a large baking sheet and bake for 10 minutes, stirring halfway through.
■ Remove from the oven, mix in the bran, wheatgerm and sesame seeds, return to the oven and bake for a further 15 minutes, stirring occasionally.
■ Remove from the oven again, spread the flaked almonds and coconut on top, return once again and bake for another 10 minutes, lightly stirring halfway through but still trying to keep the almonds on top. Finish off for a couple of minutes under a pre-heated grill, watching to make sure that it doesn't burn.
■ Add the raisins and currants and transfer to an airtight container.

Carrot and ginger soup

Carrots, coconut cream and ginger blend together to give this soup a wonderful flavour.

Makes 6 portions
✳ **Suitable for freezing**
25 g (1 oz) butter
1 large onion, peeled and chopped
1 clove garlic, peeled and crushed
1 kg (2 lb 4 oz) carrots, peeled and chopped

2 cm (¾ in) piece fresh root ginger, peeled and coarsely grated
1.5 litres (2½ pints) chicken or vegetable stock
75 ml (2½ fl oz) coconut cream or crème fraiche
2 tbsp chopped parsley
salt and freshly ground black pepper

▪ Melt the butter in a large, thick-based saucepan, add the onion and garlic and sauté for 5 minutes, until softened. Stir in the carrot and grated ginger, cover and cook for 3 minutes. Add the stock and bring to the simmer, cooking for 25 minutes until the carrots are tender.
▪ Transfer to a food processor and blend until smooth. Then stir in the coconut cream or crème fraiche, chopped parsley and seasoning to taste.

Garden vegetable soup

It's a good idea to cook and freeze some food for when you return home from hospital. This soup and the one above can be frozen in individual portions.

Makes 5 portions
✳ **Suitable for freezing**
2 tbsp olive oil
1 onion, peeled and chopped
1 clove garlic, crushed
100 g (4 oz) carrot, peeled and chopped
100 g (4 oz) cauliflower florets
2 potatoes, peeled and chopped

100 g (4 oz) courgette, chopped
100 g (4 oz) broccoli florets
1 leek, sliced
1 litre (1¾ pints) vegetable stock
100 g (4 oz) frozen peas
60 ml (2 fl oz) light crème fraiche
salt and freshly ground black pepper

▪ Heat the oil in a saucepan and sauté the onion and garlic for 2–3 minutes. Add the carrot, cauliflower and potato and sauté for 5 minutes, stirring to prevent them from sticking.
▪ Add the courgette, broccoli and leek and sauté for 2–3 minutes. Pour in the stock, bring to the simmer and cook for 15 minutes. Add the peas and cook for 3 minutes. Blend in a food processor until smooth. Stir in the crème fraiche and add seasoning, to taste.

SUPERFOODS

CARROTS are one of the best sources of beta-carotene, which is important for your baby's growth and for boosting your immune system. Eating carrots also helps with night vision, which will come in handy when you need to feed your baby in the middle of the night.

BROCCOLI is king of the healthy vegetable superstars and contains phytochemicals that can protect against cancer. It provides a rich source of vitamin C and betacarotene; the darker the florets, the higher the amount of antioxidants. Broccoli should be steamed or stir-fried as boiling almost halves its vitamin C content.

Pasta with roasted vegetables, balsamic vinegar and basil

You can make this recipe using either pasta or couscous. This makes a good complement to something simple like marinated chicken or beef skewers.

Makes 4 portions

150 g (5 oz) pasta shapes

4 baby or 1 medium courgette, cut into 2 cm (¾ in) pieces

4 plum tomatoes, cut into quarters

1 orange or red pepper, de-seeded and cut into 2 cm (¾ in) pieces

1 red onion, peeled and cut into 12 wedges

50 g (2 oz) extra-fine baby asparagus or button mushrooms, cut in half

2 sprigs of rosemary

1 clove of garlic, peeled and left whole

2 tbsp olive oil

salt and freshly ground black pepper

4 tbsp freshly grated Parmesan cheese

1 tbsp balsamic vinegar

2 tbsp fresh basil, torn into pieces

■ Pre-heat the oven to 180°C/350°F/Gas mark 4.

■ Cook the pasta in a large pan of lightly salted boiling water according to the packet instructions.

■ Place all the vegetables except the asparagus in a roasting tin. Lightly crush the rosemary and place among the vegetables together with the clove of garlic. Drizzle with oil and season. Place in the oven for 25 minutes. Turn halfway through and add the asparagus. Once cooked, remove the rosemary and garlic and stir in the pasta together with the Parmesan cheese, balsamic vinegar and basil.

Variation

Instead of mixing the roasted vegetables with pasta you could mix them with couscous. Pour 200 ml (7 fl oz) hot chicken or vegetable stock over 150 g (5 oz) couscous and leave to stand for about 5 minutes until all the liquid has been absorbed. Fluff up with a fork and stir in a generous knob of melted butter and 1 tbsp torn basil leaves.

Pasta with baby spinach and cherry tomatoes

This recipe is quick and easy to prepare. For best results, only lightly cook the vegetables and serve immediately.

Makes 4 portions

150 g (5 oz) pasta shapes
100 g (4 oz) small broccoli florets
1 tbsp olive oil
½ onion, peeled and chopped
14 small cherry tomatoes, cut in half

150 g (5 oz) baby spinach
handful of basil leaves, torn into pieces
100 ml (4 fl oz) light crème fraiche
5 tbsp grated Parmesan cheese
salt and freshly ground black pepper
2 tbsp walnut pieces (optional)

■ Cook the pasta in boiling salted water according to the packet instructions, adding the broccoli florets 3 minutes before the end of the cooking time.

■ Meanwhile, heat the oil in a large saucepan, add the onion and sauté over a low heat for 6–7 minutes, until softened. Stir in the tomatoes, spinach and basil and heat until the spinach is wilted.

■ Add the crème fraiche and Parmesan cheese and stir until heated through. Season to taste and mix with the cooked pasta and broccoli. Add the walnut pieces (if using). Serve straight away with a little extra freshly grated Parmesan cheese.

Penne with tuna, tomato and red onion

The red onion and semi-dried tomatoes give this pasta dish a lovely flavour.

Makes 4 portions

200 g (7 oz) penne
2 tbsp olive oil
1 red onion, peeled and sliced
4 plum tomatoes, quartered, de-seeded and roughly chopped

200 g (7 oz) can tuna in oil (drained)
75 g (3 oz) semi-dried tomatoes, chopped
1 tsp balsamic vinegar or 2 tsp lemon juice
handful of basil leaves, torn into pieces
salt and freshly ground black pepper

■ Cook the penne in boiling salted water according to the packet instructions.

■ Meanwhile, heat the oil in a frying pan, add the onion and and cook for about 6 minutes, stirring occasionally until softened. Stir in the fresh tomatoes and cook for 2–3 minutes until beginning to soften. Add the tuna, semi-dried tomatoes, vinegar or lemon juice, basil and seasoning and heat for 1 minute before stirring into the pasta and serving.

Spaghetti with plum and semi-dried tomatoes

This is very quick and easy to prepare and tastes delicious. For a good flavour you need to use ripe tomatoes. If the tomatoes are not ripe or lack flavour, add a little tomato purée.

Makes 4 portions
✳ **Tomato sauce suitable for freezing**
200 g (7 oz) spaghetti
2 tbsp olive oil
1 onion, peeled and chopped
1 clove garlic, peeled and crushed

8 plum tomatoes, skinned, de-seeded and chopped
100 g (4 oz) semi-dried tomatoes, chopped
1 tsp balsamic vinegar
handful of basil leaves, torn into pieces
pinch of sugar
salt and freshly ground black pepper

■ Cook the spaghetti in a large pan of lightly salted water according to the manufacturer's instructions.
■ Meanwhile, heat the oil in a saucepan, add the onion and garlic and sauté for 5–6 minutes. Add all of the remaining ingredients, cover with a lid and cook over a low heat for 10 minutes. Stir in the cooked spaghetti and serve.

Marinated chicken on the griddle

Serve with seasonal vegetables for griddling such as peppers, asparagus and parboiled new potatoes. Cut the vegetables into wedges, season with sea salt and pepper. Brush the griddle pan with olive oil and, when hot, cook the vegetables for about 5 minutes.

Makes 4 portions
Marinade
3 tbsp lemon juice
1 clove garlic, crushed
3 tbsp soy sauce
2 tbsp olive oil

2 tbsp runny honey
1 tbsp brown sugar
some freshly ground black pepper

4 chicken breasts
a little vegetable oil

■ In a bowl mix together all the ingredients for the marinade, add the chicken breasts and leave to marinate for at least 1 hour. Drain the marinade and reserve.
■ Heat the griddle, brush with a little oil and cook the chicken for 4–5 minutes on each side or until cooked. Strain the marinade, pour it into a small saucepan, bring to the boil and simmer for 1 minute (add a little water if necessary). Serve the chicken with the sauce.

SUPERFOODS
GARLIC helps to strengthen the immune system. A traditional European folk custom was to place a head of garlic in a small bag and tie it around a child's neck to ward off colds and flu. Indeed this was not so strange as some of the compounds found in garlic can be absorbed through the skin. Eating garlic also helps to improve circulation and lower blood pressure.

CHICKEN is an excellent source of lean protein and griddling is a good low-fat method of cooking. Chicken contains much less fat than other meats as most of the fat lies in the skin, which can be removed.

SUPERFOODS
FISH is packed with
vitamins, minerals
and protein, and oily
fish such as salmon
contains essential
omega-3 fatty acids
that cannot be made
in the body.

Glazed salmon with honey and soy on a bed of couscous

Marinating salmon gives it a wonderful flavour and a ridged, cast-iron griddle pan enhances the flavour of the salmon without having to add much fat.

Makes 2 portions
Marinade
1 tsp sesame oil
1 tbsp rice wine vinegar (or sherry vinegar)
1 tbsp honey
1 tbsp soy sauce

2 x 175 g (6 oz) middle cut salmon fillets, skin on

200 ml (7 fl oz) hot chicken or vegetable stock
125 g (4½ oz) couscous
25 g (1 oz) butter, melted
salt and freshly ground black pepper
1 tbsp chopped parsley
2 spring onions, finely chopped
1 tbsp vegetable oil

■ Put the ingredients for the marinade in a bowl, add the salmon fillets and leave to marinate in the fridge for at least 1 hour, turning occasionally.

■ Pour the stock over the couscous and leave to stand until all of the stock is absorbed (about 5 minutes). Fluff up with a fork and stir in the butter, seasoning, parsley and spring onions.

■ Lightly grease a cast-iron ribbed griddle pan by brushing it with vegetable oil and preheat the pan for 2–3 minutes on a medium heat. Remove the salmon from the bowl and reserve the marinade. Grill the salmon for 4–5 minutes, pressing down occasionally to get the seared parallel-line effect. If you don't have a griddle pan, you can heat a little oil in a frying pan and sauté the salmon for a few minutes on each side until cooked but still lovely and moist.

■ Pour the reserved marinade into a small saucepan and bring to the boil. Place the salmon on a bed of couscous, pour over the sauce and serve immediately.

Simply super salmon teriyaki

This is a simple, sophisticated and delicious way to cook salmon fillets.

Makes 4 portions
Marinade
90 ml (3 fl oz) soy sauce
100 ml (4 fl oz) sake (Japanese rice wine)
50 ml (2 fl oz) mirin (sweet Japanese cooking wine)
2 tbsp caster sugar

4 x 150 g (5 oz) thick salmon fillets, skinned
200 g (7 oz) basmati rice
4 tbsp vegetable oil
250 g (9 oz) button mushrooms, sliced
200 g (7 oz) beansprouts
3 tbsp finely sliced spring onion

■ Mix together the ingredients for the marinade. Place the salmon in a dish, pour over the marinade and set aside for at least 30 minutes.

■ When the salmon has finished marinating, cook the rice according to the instructions on the packet.

■ Heat half of the oil in a frying pan, add the mushrooms and sauté for 2 minutes. Then add the beansprouts and spring onions and cook for 2 minutes more. Drain the salmon, reserving the marinade, and pat dry. Heat the remaining oil in another frying pan, add the salmon and sauté for about 2½ minutes on each side or until slightly browned. Alternatively you can cook the salmon in a very hot griddle pan brushed with a little oil. Put the reserved marinade in a saucepan, bring to the boil and then simmer for 1 minute.

■ Arrange the beansprouts and mushrooms on a serving plate and place the salmon on top. Pour over the teriyaki sauce and serve with the rice.

Variation: teriyaki beef skewers
Makes 2 portions
175 g (6 oz) lean beef steak
Marinade
1 tbsp soy sauce
1 tbsp sesame oil
1–2 tsp caster sugar

1 tbsp rice vinegar
½ small garlic clove
½ tsp grated fresh root ginger

2 large spring onions cut into 1 cm (½ in) pieces or cubes of red pepper (optional)
wooden skewers soaked in water

■ Cut the beef into bite-sized pieces and mix together with the marinade ingredients. Cover and set aside for at least 1 hour, stirring occasionally. Thread onto skewers alternating with the pieces of spring onion. Pre-heat the grill to medium hot. Place the skewers under the grill for 10–12 minutes, turning occasionally.

Fillets of sea bass with spring vegetables

Makes 2 portions
1 tbsp olive oil
1 onion, peeled and chopped
100 g (4 oz) French beans
1 courgette, cut into thick batons
1 yellow pepper, cored, de-seeded and cut into strips
150 ml (5 fl oz) chicken stock

25 g (1 oz) butter
3 tomatoes, skinned, de-seeded and cut into pieces or 10 cherry tomatoes, cut in half
salt and freshly ground black pepper
2 x 150 g (5 oz) sea bass fillets, skin on
1 tbsp plain flour
1 tbsp vegetable oil

■ Heat the olive oil in a saucepan, add the onion and sauté for 4–5 minutes. Add the beans, courgette and yellow pepper and sauté for about 1 minute. Stir in the stock, bring to the simmer and cook for 5 minutes until the vegetables are tender. Drain, reserving the liquid into another pan. Bring the stock to the boil and allow to reduce by half. Stir in the butter and then the tomatoes and cook for 2 minutes. Add the vegetables and season.
■ Lightly season and flour the skin side of the fish. Heat the oil in a frying pan and sit the fish skin side down. Cook over a medium heat until the skin has become crispy and the flesh has just turned opaque. Place the fish on top of the vegetables and serve.

Tasty chicken fajitas

Makes 3 large or 4 small fajitas
1 tbsp olive oil
½ red onion, peeled and cut into strips
½ red pepper, cored, de-seeded and cut into strips
1 chicken breast, cut into strips
½ small green chilli, finely chopped

1 x 200 g (7 oz) can chopped tomatoes
1 tbsp fresh oregano, chopped
salt and freshly ground black pepper
3 large or 4 small tortillas
a little shredded iceberg lettuce
2–3 tbsp sour cream (optional)

■ Heat the oil in a frying pan, add the onion and red pepper and sauté for 5–6 minutes before adding the chicken and green chilli. Cook for about 3 minutes, then add the tomatoes, oregano and seasoning. Cook for a further 5 minutes until the mixture has thickened.
■ To assemble, heat the tortillas in the microwave according to the packet instructions. Place some of the chicken mixture along the centre of each tortilla, add some shredded lettuce and a little sour cream and roll up. Serve immediately.

SUPERFOODS
FISH is full of nutrients and low in fat. One small 100 g (4 oz) portion of fish contains half the recommended daily protein requirement. During pregnancy protein is needed for the growth of your baby and also for the growth of protein-rich tissues, including extra blood cells and the placenta. Unborn babies cannot make protein so it's important to include protein-rich foods in your diet.

RED PEPPERS have ten times as much vitamin A as green peppers. There are two forms of vitamin A: retinol found in animal foods like liver, and betacarotene found in plant foods like red pepper, and carrots. Betacarotene is fine but an excess of retinol is thought to increase the risk of miscarriage and birth defects, so it is best not to eat liver when you are pregnant.

SUPERFOODS

Spinach is a rich source of folic acid which is recommended for pregnant women to help prevent spina bifida. It is also a good source of vitamin C, especially if it is raw or only lightly cooked, and beta-carotene. Vitamin C and folic acid can be destroyed by over-cooking, especially by boiling in water, so eating spinach raw helps to preserve the nutrients.

Avocado is very nutritious and a good source of potassium.

Cheese is a good source of protein and a rich source of calcium which is important for the developing bones and teeth of your baby. Red onion contains high levels of quercetin a powerful antioxidant.

Fresh vegetable-filled tortilla wraps

Tortilla wraps taste delicious when filled with simple fresh ingredients – and they are very quick and easy to prepare. Each of these recipes makes 2 portions.

Cream cheese, spinach and tomatoes

150 g (5 oz) low-fat cream cheese
1½ tbsp chopped chives
salt and freshly ground black pepper

4 small flour tortillas or 2–3 large tortillas
8 sweet cherry tomatoes
50 g (2 oz) baby spinach leaves
squeeze of lemon juice

▨ Mix together the cream cheese and chives and season. Heat the tortillas according to the packet instructions. Spread the cheese mixture onto the centre of each tortilla. Slice the cherry tomatoes into quarters and sit on top of the cream cheese. Top each with spinach leaves and add some lemon juice onto each one. Roll up and cut in half before serving.

Avocado, tomato, pine nuts and basil

4 small tortillas
40 g (1½ oz) pine nuts, toasted
1 small avocado or ½ large avocado
2 ripe tomatoes, peeled and diced

10 basil leaves, torn
1 tsp lemon juice
1½ tbsp mayonnaise
few drops Tabasco sauce
small handful lamb's lettuce leaves

■ Toast the pine nuts in a dry frying pan over heat until golden, stirring occasionally. Mix together the avocado, tomatoes, pine nuts, basil leaves, lemon juice, mayonnaise and Tabasco. Heat the tortillas according to the packet instructions. Spoon the mixture into the centre of the four tortillas and top with a few lamb's lettuce leaves, then roll up and serve.

Caramelised red onion and mozzarella

4 small tortillas or 2 large tortillas
1 tbsp olive oil
2 medium red onions, peeled and thinly sliced
1 tsp balsamic vinegar

1 tsp brown sugar
salt and freshly ground black pepper
1 ball mozzarella
25 g (1 oz) rocket leaves
½ tsp balsamic vinegar

■ Heat the oil in a saucepan, add the onions and stir over a low heat for 10 minutes. Stir in the balsamic vinegar, sugar and seasoning and continue to cook for a further 5–8 minutes. Remove from the heat and leave to cool. Heat the tortillas according to the packet instructions. Divide the cooked onion mixture between the tortillas, slice the mozzarella and lay on top of the onions and season. Toss the rocket leaves with the balsamic vinegar and place on top of the mozzarella cheese. Roll up the tortillas and then cut in half before serving.

Yakitori chicken

I love Japanese food and yakitori chicken is a great favourite of mine.

Makes 4 portions
Marinade
7 tbsp soy sauce
4 tbsp sake (Japanese rice wine)
4 tbsp sugar

8 large chicken thigh fillets, skinned and boned, or 4 chicken breasts
1 green or red pepper, de-seeded and cut into chunks or use chunks of onion and shitake mushrooms

▉ Put the marinade ingredients in a small saucepan and boil rapidly until thick, syrupy and reduced to about one-third. Cut the chicken thighs or breasts into bite-sized chunks and trim off any fat. Marinate for 30 minutes to 1 hour.
▉ Soak 8 short bamboo skewers in water to prevent them from getting scorched. Thread chicken onto skewers, alternating with green or red peppers, or onions and mushrooms.
▉ Brush the chicken and vegetables with the yakitori sauce and arrange in a grill pan. Place under a pre-heated grill for about 8 minutes, turning and brushing with the sauce until cooked through.

Tender beef stir-fry

Tender strips of marinated beef with stir-fried vegetables and pasta makes a complete meal with protein, vitamins, carbohydrate and fibre.

Makes 6 portions
✳ **Suitable for freezing**
Marinade
1 tbsp soy sauce
1 tbsp sake (Japanese rice wine)
1 tsp sesame oil
350 g (12 oz) fillet, rump or sirloin steak, cut into strips
175 g (6 oz) pasta shapes
2 tbsp vegetable oil
1 clove garlic, peeled and crushed
1 onion, peeled and finely sliced

175 g (6 oz) carrots, peeled and cut into strips
50 g (2 oz) red pepper, cored, de-seeded and chopped
100 g (4 oz) green beans, topped and tailed and cut in half
100 g (4 oz) baby sweetcorn, cut in half
1 large spring onion, finely sliced
Sauce
300 ml (½ pint) chicken stock
2 tbsp oyster sauce
1 tsp brown sugar

■ Mix together the ingredients for the marinade in a bowl and marinate the beef for about 30 minutes. Cook the pasta in a pan of lightly salted water according to the packet instructions.

■ When the beef is marinated, heat 1 tbsp of the oil in a wok or large frying pan, add half the crushed garlic and then stir-fry the beef for about 4 minutes or until lightly browned. Remove the beef strips and set aside.

■ Heat the remaining oil in the wok, add the rest of the garlic and the onion and sauté for 2–3 minutes. Add the carrots, red pepper, beans and sweetcorn and stir-fry for about 6 minutes or until tender but still crisp.

■ Mix together all the ingredients for the sauce.

■ Return the beef strips to the pan together with the spring onion and sauce, cover and cook for about 4 minutes, stirring occasionally. Serve immediately.

SUPERFOODS
Beansprouts provide a good source of vitamins C and B.

Chinese-style minced beef wrapped in lettuce

A lovely combination of tasty minced meat with crunchy water chestnuts wrapped in crisp lettuce leaves. Water chestnuts are available in tins in supermarkets.

Makes 6 lettuce parcels

1 tbsp sesame oil	100 g (4 oz) water chestnuts, roughly chopped
½ small red and yellow peppers or 1 small red pepper, cored, de-seeded and chopped	75 g (3 oz) beansprouts
1 onion, peeled and chopped	2 tbsp oyster sauce
300 g (11 oz) minced beef	3 tbsp rice wine vinegar
	6 iceberg lettuce leaves

■ Heat the oil in a wok or frying pan, add the pepper and onion and cook for 5 minutes. Stir in the beef and cook for a further 3–4 minutes. Stir in the water chestnuts and beansprouts, cooking for 2–3 minutes. Stir in the oyster sauce and rice wine vinegar and stir fry for 2–3 minutes, until slightly thickened. Divide the mixture between 6 iceberg lettuce leaves, fold into parcels and serve immediately.

SUPERFOODS

GREEN BEANS have diuretic properties, they help to keep the kidney functioning and prevent water retention. Green beans also contain folic acid and vitamin A.

Avocados are rich in vitamin E. Often mistaken for a vegetable, they have the highest protein content of any fruit and are rich in monounsaturated fat, the 'good' type of fat which helps prevent heart disease. The essential fats found in avocados are the building blocks of beautiful skin. They also contain beta-carotene, fibre and folic acid together with high levels of folate, which helps the growth and reproduction of cells and reduces the risk of birth defects in pregnant women.

Mild chicken korma curry

Makes 4 portions
✳ **Suitable for freezing**
200 g (7 oz) basmati rice
1 tbsp vegetable oil
1 onion, peeled and roughly chopped
1 small red pepper, de-seeded and cut into
2 cm (¾ in) pieces
1 clove garlic, peeled and crushed

2 skinned chicken breasts, cut into bite-sized pieces
250 g (9 oz) French beans
3 tbsp mild Korma curry paste
4 ripe plum tomatoes, chopped
150 ml (5 fl oz) apple juice
100 ml (3½ fl oz) Greek yoghurt
salt and freshly ground black pepper

▨ Cook the rice according to the packet instructions.
▨ Heat the oil in a saucepan, add the onion, red pepper and garlic and cook for 6 minutes, until beginning to soften. Add the chicken and beans and cook for 4 minutes. Stir in the curry paste, tomatoes and apple juice. Bring to the simmer and cover. Cook until the beans are tender – 10 minutes. Stir in the Greek yoghurt and seasoning and cook for 4 minutes.

Avocado and pine nut salad

Makes 4 portions
50 g (2 oz) pine nuts
100 g (4 oz) French beans, halved
2 plum tomatoes, halved and cut into slices
or 100 g (4 oz) cherry tomatoes
200 g (7 oz) mixed salad leaves
1 medium avocado
2 hard-boiled eggs, each cut into 6 wedges

100 g (4 oz) sweetcorn (fresh, tinned or cooked from frozen)
Dressing
2 tbsp light olive oil
1 tbsp balsamic vinegar
1 tsp caster sugar
½ tbsp soy sauce
salt and freshly ground black pepper

▨ Lightly toast the pine nuts in a dry frying pan until lightly golden. Blanch the beans in boiling salted water for 3–4 minutes or until just tender.
▨ Make the dressing by whisking together the oil, vinegar, caster sugar and soy sauce and season, to taste. Stir in the blanched beans and the tomatoes and sweetcorn.
▨ Arrange the salad leaves in a dish, cut the avocado in half, remove the stone and skin, cut into thin slices and arrange on top of the salad leaves with the eggs. Spoon over the tomatoes, beans and dressing and finish by scattering over the pine nuts.

SUPERFOODS

WATERCRESS has a high vitamin and mineral content and is an excellent source of the antioxidants betac-arotene and vitamin C. It is one of the healthi-est fresh salad vegeta-bles. Watercress is a natural antibiotic and can help cleanse the system. Watercress leaves or juice can be applied to the skin to ease inflammation, help clear up spots and heal scars.

TINNED TUNA is a good storecupboard standby as it can be used in salads, with pasta or in sandwiches. It is rich in protein and vitamins but, unlike fresh tuna, tinned tuna is not a good source of omega-3 fatty acids.

Griddled pitta filled with chicken, avocado and salad

These filled pitta pockets are simply delicious and very easy to prepare.

Makes 4 pitta pockets
Marinade
1½ tbsp olive oil
2 tsp balsamic vinegar
1 tsp soy sauce
1 tsp chopped fresh oregano
1 skinless and boneless chicken breast

2 wholemeal or white pitta breads
40 g (1½ oz) watercress
¼ tsp balsamic vinegar
½ tsp olive oil
½ avocado, peeled and sliced
1 plum tomato, thinly sliced
salt and freshly ground black pepper

■ Mix together the marinade ingredients. Score the chicken three or four times with a sharp knife and place in the marinade for at least 1 hour. Drain and reserve the marinade.
■ Heat the griddle pan until very hot, brush with a little oil and put the chicken on it. Cook for 8–10 minutes, turning halfway through. Remove from the pan and slice into strips, seasoning to taste.
■ Cut each pitta bread into half and brush with any remaining marinade and place on the griddle for about 1 minute each side. Remove from the pan. Toss the watercress with the balsamic vinegar and olive oil and arrange the chicken, avocado, tomatoes and watercress into each of the pitta pockets. Add seasoning if desired and serve immediately.

Stuffed pitta pockets with tuna, egg and sweetcorn

Stuffed pitta pockets with a nutritious filling make a good snack or light lunch. This tuna mix is delicious.

Makes 2 portions
200 g (7 oz) can tuna in oil
100 g (4 oz) sweetcorn
2 tbsp mayonnaise
1 tsp white wine vinegar

4 spring onions, chopped
salt and freshly ground black pepper
few drops Tabasco sauce
2 eggs, hard-boiled
2 pitta breads

■ Drain the oil from the can of tuna and mix the flaked tuna together with the sweetcorn, mayonnaise, white wine vinegar, spring onion, seasoning and a few drops of Tabasco sauce. Roughly chop the hard-boiled eggs and add to the tuna mix, stirring well.
■ Toast the pitta breads, cut them in half to give 4 pitta pockets and divide the mixture between them. Serve immediately.

SUPERFOODS
A regular intake of
onions and leeks has
been linked to a
reduced risk of heart
disease and stroke.
They have a protective
action on your circula-
tory system, which
helps to prevent your
blood clotting.
Quercetin is a power-
ful antioxidant and the
highest concentration
of quercetin is found
in red onions.

Roasted vegetable enchiladas

These roasted vegetables wrapped in tortillas with a tomato sauce are divine. A tortilla is a traditional, circular, flat, unleavened Mexican bread made from corn or wheat flour and which you can buy in the supermarket. This recipe freezes very well so it's a good one to prepare in advance and have in the freezer for when you return from hospital.

Makes 4 portions
✳ **Suitable for freezing**
1 small red and yellow pepper, cored, de-
seeded and cut into bite-sized pieces
1 red onion, peeled and chopped
1 tbsp olive oil
1 tbsp balsamic vinegar
100 g (4 oz) mushrooms, quartered
1 courgette, chopped
salt and freshly ground black pepper

Tomato sauce
2 tbsp olive oil
1 onion, peeled and chopped
1 clove garlic, peeled and crushed
400 ml (13 fl oz) passata
1 tsp chopped fresh oregano or ½ tsp dried
pinch sugar

4 large or 8 small tortillas
125 g (4½ oz) grated Gruyere cheese

■ Pre-heat the oven to 190°C/375°F/Gas mark 5.

■ Place the peppers and onion in a roasting tray. Drizzle over the olive oil and balsamic vinegar and cook in the oven for 15 minutes, turning occasionally. Add the mushrooms and courgette and continue to cook for a further 10 minutes. Season to taste.

■ Meanwhile, to make the tomato sauce, heat the olive oil in a small saucepan, add the onion and garlic and sauté for 5–6 minutes. Stir in the passata, oregano, sugar and season, to taste. Bring to the simmer and then cook over a low heat for 8–10 minutes.

■ Before filling the tortillas, put them in the oven for 3–4 minutes or in a microwave for 40 seconds as this makes them more pliable and easier to fold. Divide the vegetables between the tortillas and roll up to form long cigar shapes. Place in an ovenproof dish, pour over the sauce and scatter over the grated cheese. Turn down the oven to 180°C/350°F/Gas mark 4. Place the tortillas in the oven for 10–12 minutes, until golden and bubbly, remove from the oven and serve immediately.

Rasberry, peach and amaretto brûlée

This is the most wonderful dessert and so easy and quick to prepare. You can also prepare it in advance. My favourite amaretto biscuits are the ones you buy wrapped in tissue paper, the Amaretti di Saronno. If peaches and raspberries are not in season you can use other fruits like mango, nectarines, grapes, kiwi, blackberries, etc.

Makes 4 portions

250 g (9 oz) raspberries
2 large ripe peaches, chopped
60 g (2½ oz) amaretto biscuits
200 g (7 oz) carton Greek yoghurt

200 ml (7 fl oz) carton low-fat crème fraiche
1 tbsp caster sugar
1 tbsp light muscovado sugar

■ Mix together the raspberries and chopped peaches and put them in a fairly shallow ovenproof dish. Before you unwrap the amaretto biscuits, crush them with a rolling pin, then sprinkle over the fruit.
■ Mix together the yoghurt and crème fraiche, stir in the caster sugar and spread this mixture over the fruit. Sprinkle over the muscovado sugar. Leave for a few minutes so that the sugar turns syrupy, then place under a pre-heated grill for a few minutes until golden and bubbling. Serve immediately.

Baked apples stuffed with figs and raisins

Makes 2 portions

2 large apples, e.g. Granny Smith or Pink Lady
15 g (½ oz) sugar

75 g (3 oz) raisins
6 ready-to-eat dried figs, chopped
15 g (½ oz) butter
150 ml (5 fl oz) apple juice

■ Pre-heat the oven to 180°C/350°F/Gas mark 4.
■ Score the skin of the apples around the middle using a sharp knife, which will stop the apple skin bursting, and removed the core. Place in a small baking dish and sprinkle with the sugar. Bake in the oven for 10 minutes and then remove the baking dish from the oven.
■ Mix together the raisins and chopped figs and pack into the part-baked apples, where the core was. Scatter any remaining raisins and figs over the top and place a dot of butter on top of each. Pour the apple juice into the dish and bake for 30 minutes.

SUPERFOODS

RASPBERRIES are rich in vitamin C, which is important for a healthy immune system. The body's requirements for vitamin C increase during pregnancy as this vitamin is needed for the production of new tissues. It also aids iron absorption. Vitamin C cannot be stored in the body so make sure that you eat vitamin C-rich foods every day.

FIGS are high in fibre and help to prevent constipation. Dried figs make a good snack for pregnant women. The drying process concentrates the nutrients and makes them a rich source of potassium and a good source of calcium and iron

Hot ruby fruit salad

This warm fruit compote has a wonderful flavour due to the rose water, and the pomegranates add a crunchy texture that complements the berry fruits beautifully.

Makes 4 portions

1 large ripe peach
2 large ripe red plums
20 g (¾ oz) butter
2 tbsp caster sugar

1 tbsp rose water or orange flower water
(can also use plain water)
75 g (3 oz) raspberries
50 g (2 oz) redcurrants
75 g (3 oz) blackberries
1 pomegranate, cut in half and de-seeded

■ Halve the peach and plums, remove the stones and cut each half into four pieces. Melt the butter in a large frying pan and place the plums and peach slices into the butter. Cook for 2–3 minutes before turning over and sprinkling with the sugar. Cook for a further 2–3 minutes and then pour over the rose or orange flower water. Gently stir in the remaining fruits and heat through for approximately 1 minute.

Apple, blackberry and pear crumble

A really good fruit crumble is one of my favourite desserts and is quick and easy to prepare.

Makes 6 portions
✳ **Suitable for freezing**
100 g (4 oz) butter
175 g (6 oz) plain flour
100 g (4 oz) demerara sugar
50 g (2 oz) porridge oats
25 g (1 oz) ground almonds

25 g (1 oz) butter
2 apples, peeled, cored and chopped
2 large pears, peeled, cored and chopped
60 g (2½ oz) caster sugar
finely grated zest ½ lemon
225 g (8 oz) blackberries

■ Pre-heat the oven to 200°C/400°F/Gas mark 6.
■ Rub the butter into the flour until it resembles coarse breadcrumbs. Stir in the demerara sugar, oats and almonds.
■ Melt the 25 g (1 oz) butter in a saucepan, add the chopped apples and pears and cook gently until just beginning to soften. Stir in the sugar, grated lemon zest and blackberries.
■ Transfer to a shallow ovenproof dish, sprinkle over the topping and bake in the oven for 30 minutes or until golden and bubbling. Serve hot on its own or with ice cream or custard.

Healthy snacks

Should you feel hungry between meals, make yourself one of these snacks rather than eating a biscuit or chocolate. Many of the nutrients in processed snacks like crisps have been destroyed so it is much better to have a healthy snack like raw vegetables with a dip, a pitta pocket stuffed with salad or cottage cheese, or yogurt and fruit

SUPERFOODS

Oats help to stabilise blood sugar levels and also give long-lasting energy.

Pumpkin seeds are packed with minerals – iron, zinc and selenium – and also vitamin E. Selenium is an antioxidant that helps protect cells against damage and studies have linked low levels of selenium with increased risk of miscarriage.

Raisin and sunflower seed cookies

These make a tasty and nutritious snack any time of the day.

Makes 12–15 biscuits
✱ Suitable for freezing
75 g (3 oz) butter
85 g (2½ oz) brown sugar
1 small egg, beaten
1 tsp vanilla essence

75 g (3 oz) raisins
50 g (2 oz) sunflower seeds
60 g (2½ oz) plain flour
60 g (2½ oz) porridge oats
½ tsp bicarbonate of soda
pinch salt

■ Pre-heat the oven to 180°C/350°F/Gas mark 4.
■ Cream together the butter and sugar until light and fluffy. Beat in the egg and vanilla and then stir in all of the remaining ingredients until completely combined. Shape into walnut-sized balls, place on two non-stick or lined baking trays and flatten slightly by pressing in the centre with your fingers. Place in the oven for 12–14 minutes until golden.

Honey and soy toasted seeds

This is very nutritious and tastes great. You can also add pecans or almonds or stir in raisins.

Makes 2–3 portions
1 tbsp sunflower oil
75 g (3 oz) sunflower seeds

75 g (3 oz) pumpkin seeds
1 tbsp soy sauce
1 tbsp runny honey

■ Heat the oil in a non-stick frying pan, add the seeds and cook, continuously stirring, for about 2 minutes or until the seeds are lightly browned.
■ Remove from the heat, add the honey and soy sauce, return to the heat for 1 minute and then leave to cool.

Fruit smoothies

When you don't feel like eating too much, fresh fruit smoothies can provide you with lots of nutrients.

Each makes 2–3 glasses
Cranberry, raspberry and blueberry breeze
250 ml (8 fl oz) cranberry juice
100 g (4 oz) fresh blueberries

100 g (4 oz) fresh raspberries
1 medium banana
100 ml (3½ fl oz) natural yoghurt
honey to taste

■ Blend together the cranberry juice, blueberries and raspberries. Pass through a sieve then blend together with the banana, yoghurt and a little honey to taste.

Kiss the peach
1 juicy peach
125 g (4½ oz) chopped mango
1 small banana

juice of 1 small orange
50 ml (2 fl oz) apple juice
2 passion fruit

■ Blend together the peach, mango, banana, orange and apple juice. Cut the passion fruit in half, scoop out the flesh and strain through a sieve. Stir the passion fruit juice into the peach mixture. You can also sprinkle some passion fruit seeds on top of the glass.

Spinach salad with mango

This is a lovely combination of flavours and is easy to prepare.

Makes 2–3 portions
75 g (3 oz) baby spinach, washed, or mixed salad leaves
25 g (1 oz) diced red onion
1 small or ½ large ripe mango, peeled and chopped
5 strawberries, hulled and sliced
2 tbsp dried cranberries

2 tbsp toasted pine nuts (toast in a dry frying pan)

Dressing
3 tbsp vegetable oil
1 tbsp balsamic vinegar
1 tsp sugar
salt and freshly ground black pepper

■ Combine all the ingredients for the salad in a bowl. To make the dressing, whisk together the oil, vinegar, sugar and seasoning. Toss with the dressing.

SUPERFOODS
CRANBERRY JUICE has long been used to help prevent and treat cystitis and other bladder and urinary tract infections. Research published in the *British Medical Journal* showed that women drinking cranberry juice halved their risk of succumbing to cystitis. Cranberries are also a good source of vitamin C.

MANGOES are very rich in antioxidants. One average sized mango provides the minimum daily requirement of vitamin C, two-thirds of the vitamin A, and nearly half the vitamin E. Ripe mangoes are easy to digest and are a good source of fibre.

Equipment planner: essentials for

During the last few months of your pregnancy you can be choosing much of the equipment that you will need once your baby is born. Here is a list to get you started for going into hospital. Information relating to other areas (see opposite) is given in further equipment planners that appear throughout the book.

What to take to hospital

Pack your bag for the hospital from the 36th week of pregnancy. Some hospitals ask you to take your own nappies and sanitary towels. If you need to go away overnight for work or are planning a last-minute break, remember to take your bag with you.

Essentials for you
- Front-opening nightie/shirt to make breastfeeding easy.
- Dressing gown and slippers.
- 1 pack sanitary towels ('maternity' or 'heavy flow').
- 1 pack sanitary towels ('medium' flow).
- 6 pairs of pants.
- 2–3 nursing bras.
- Disposable breast pads.
- Comfortable clothes to wear for going home (drawstring trousers are good).
- Toiletries and make-up.
- Glasses or contact lenses (if needed).
- Address book or personal organiser.
- Camera/video and film.
- Snacks to keep you going.
- You may want to take some alternative treatments like arnica tablets, which help your body recover from bruising.

Tea tree oil can be added to the bath and aids healing (about 4 drops) or maybe take some natural remedies for pain relief. Aconite is a homeopathic remedy for fear.

Essentials for your baby
- 4 cotton vests/stretchsuits.
- 4 babygros.
- 1 cotton or fine wool hat.
- 2 cardigans – cotton for summer, fleece or wool for winter.
- 1 pack newborn nappies and nappy sacks.
- 1 snowsuit or coat (for winter babies).
- Shawl or blanket for your baby's cot.
- Car seat (fitted to your car) – hospitals won't let you go home without one.

Once you get back home

Don't buy too many clothes in newborn size as you will be amazed just how quickly babies grow in the first few weeks and months. Also people are very kind when a baby is born and you will be surprised how many gifts the baby will be given.

Clothes for your baby
- 2 nightdresses, 100% cotton is best – nightdresses make it easier to change your baby at night.
- 6 stretchsuits.
- 6 wide-necked cotton vests/bodysuits with poppers underneath.
- 2 cardigans – cotton for summer, fleece or wool for winter.
- 2 hats – cotton hat with a brim for summer, fine wool bonnet for winter.

you and your baby

- 2 pairs of scratch mittens (optional).
- 3 pairs socks – simple socks made from cotton or wool are best.
- Shawl or blanket.
- 1 snowsuit for winter babies.
- 1 light jacket for summer babies.
- 4 bibs (optional but they do help to protect your baby's clothes).

Choosing baby clothes

- Choose stretchsuits with fastenings down both legs so you don't have to take the whole thing off every time you change a nappy.
- Try to choose clothes made of natural fibres, which allow your baby's skin to breathe.
- You will be changing your baby's clothes several times a day to begin with so look for clothes that are quick to put on and take off and are also easy to wash and dry.
- Avoid tight necks as babies hate things being pulled down over their heads. It's a good idea to choose clothes that do up at the front or side of the neck.
- Leave your baby's feet bare whenever possible and keep socks and booties loose.
- Make sure that the feet of all-in-one stretchsuits aren't too tight and uncomfortable.
- Remember that your baby will spend a lot of time on his back so it's best to choose clothes that open at the front so he's not lying on a seam.
- Frills around the neck tend to irritate babies and get covered in dribble.

- Check that clothes are both machine washable and colourfast.
- Some babies suffer a skin reaction from washing powder or fabric softeners. Be careful not to use too much detergent on clothes and try using a non-biological washing powder. Make sure that the clothes are thoroughly rinsed.

For washing and bathing
See page 67.

For going out and about
See page 80.

If possible, shop for the larger, heavier items like prams in mid-pregnancy. You may have to order these items and wait several weeks for delivery.

For bedtime
See page 94.

For sitting on and lying in
See page 109.

For breastfeeding
See page 121.

For expressing
See page 137.

For bottle feeding
See pages 144–7.

CHAPTER TWO

BIRTH
0–3 months

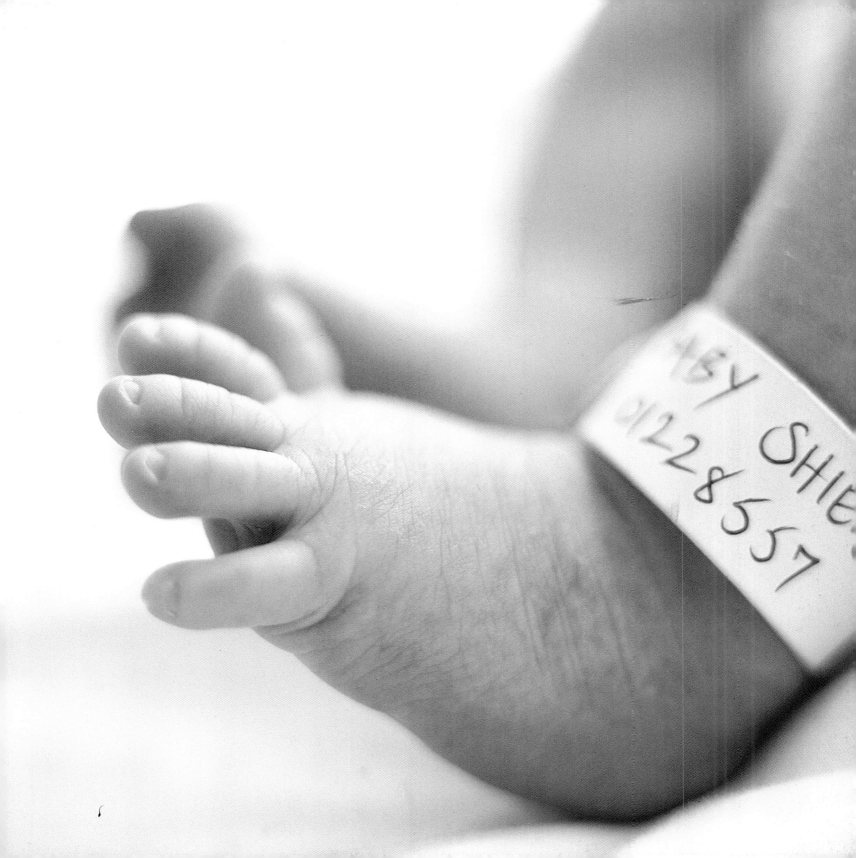

PRACTICALITIES

All women feel differently in the first few hours following the birth of their baby. Some women are elated and feel full of energy and want to examine their baby from top to bottom; some are exhausted and want to sleep; some want a quiet time alone with their baby and their partner; and others are a little stunned and report feeling 'numb' or being tearful. If you have had a long, difficult labour or Caesarean section, you may have low energy. All of these feelings are normal – just try do what feels right for you and your baby.

The birth of your baby

You may just want to rest and sleep and you may not want to hold or feed your baby for a few hours after the birth. This is normal and will change once you have rested and your energy is restored. However, it is important to remember that in the first two hours following birth babies are often very alert and are primed by the hormones of birth to be ready to get to know you, your partner and their environment. It is a crucial learning time, especially in regard to breastfeeding and getting to know each other. This does not mean that if for any reason you cannot share close contact with your baby at this time you will not form a close relationship with her in the future or will not be able to breastfeed. It simply means that soon after birth is an optimum time to do so.

Depending on how well you are, you will be offered a bath, shower or helped with a wash if you would like. You may feel hungry as birth uses up lots of energy.

It is best not to wash off the protective vernix as it will help moisturise your baby's skin. Instead your midwife can gently wipe your baby.

Your breasts will feel normal at first but this will change as more feeds are taken. Remember that following the birth of your baby you will loose blood, rather like having a 'heavy' period (see page 86).

After the placenta is expelled, your midwife or doctor will check your vagina for tears, which are normally repaired under local anaesthetic if necessary. Most of the stitches used today are dissolvable and do not need removing. It you are in any doubt, check with your midwife or doctor to see what will happen to yours. Furthermore, most stitching is now done just under the skin and so you may not see or feel the stitches from the outside.

Once you have had the opportunity to hold your baby skin to skin, your midwife may offer to clean and dress her. But if you are feeling well enough it might be a good thing for you or your partner to do this; just ask your midwife for a little help if you need it. However, don't let anyone rush you. All these things can wait while you have a chance to cuddle and get to know your baby. For the first hour or so after birth, babies are often wide awake and very eager to make eye contact to get to know you. It is a very precious time for you all.

Your baby's appearance

Your baby's appearance will depend on her birth experience. Many newborn babies look a bit squashed, wrinkled and red. Most babies are smeared with a slippery whitish substance called vernix, which protects and moisturises the skin in the womb, and there maybe traces of blood. Each baby has her own unique characteristics, unless she is an identical twin. Take time to look closely for the special distinguishing marks that make your baby unique from anyone else.

Most babies are born wet but quite clean. Those that are a little dirty, perhaps from meconium, just appear a tinge green. But there is hardly ever a time when a baby is born with a great deal of blood on them. It is best not to wash off the vernix as it helps moisturise your baby's skin. Instead, your midwife can gently wipe your baby. One of the key things after birth is to dry your baby and keep her from getting cold. This is why the labour rooms are usually so warm.

Genitals

Your baby's genitals, whether male or female, will appear larger in proportion to the rest of her body than at any other time before puberty. Also you have a rush of hormones just before birth, some of which may pass on to your baby, causing temporary extra swelling. Your baby may also have slightly swollen breasts in the first few days and may even contain a tiny quantity of milk. This swelling will soon settle down.

Skull

A baby's skull is designed to 'give' the skull bones overlapping under pressure to make the head smaller as it goes through the birth canal. The bones of the skull are not yet fused but joined together with fibrous tissue so

Q How long will I need to stay in hospital for?

A The length of stay in hospital for you and your baby can be anything from a few hours to a week and will depend on how labour and delivery went. If you had a Caesarean section, a forceps, a ventouse or breech delivery, you may need to stay longer than if you had a normal vaginal birth. Premature babies may need to be kept in an incubator. Some babies may require extra support for feeding and need to stay in hospital, although feeding support and help with caring for a healthy term newborn is available at home from your midwife.

don't worry if it seems a little pointed or mishapen. Usually by 24 hours the baby's head looks a more normal shape – in fact, even in the first few hours there is a remarkable difference.

Babies born with the help of ventouse extraction may have strangely pointed heads because of the suction cap that is placed on the scalp. The swelling usually subsides very quickly and at least within 24 hours. The suction creates a small swelling known as a 'chignon' and the baby looks as though she has a bump on her head. There is sometimes some bruising or redness around this but this will go within a few days. If your baby is born by forceps there are sometimes small marks on the baby's face but these will also fade within a few days.

After birth the areas between the bones covered by the fibrous tissue can be felt as 'soft spots' known as fontanelles. The fontanelles may seem very fragile but they are, in fact, covered with a tough membrane and there is no danger of damaging them with normal handling. The back fontanelle has usually gone by the time your baby is six weeks old and the front fontanelle usually closes around the age of 18 months.

'Stork marks'

Commonly babies are born with pinkish-red, flame-shaped marks over the skin on their eyelids, nape of neck, forehead or upper lip. These are normal and will fade during the coming months. They are traditionally known as 'stork marks' but their medical name is capillary naevi. Capillary naevi found elsewhere on the body may not fade. These are known as 'port wine' stains and may be birthmarks. If you are unsure, ask your midwife or doctor.

Eyes

Most Caucasian babies are born with blue/grey eyes, but these may change. Darker-skinned babies tend to have darker eyes at birth. Some babies are born with bloodshot eyes. This is also common but a little disturbing if it is your baby. However, it is nothing to worry about and the redness will quickly fade.

Hair

Some babies are born with a mass of dark hair, others with none, or any combination in between. Don't be surprised if this falls out in the first week or so and is then replaced with stronger hair, which may even be a different colour.

Mongolian blue spots

Darker-skinned babies may have a temporary blue discolouration on the lower back and bottom.

> **It may take a while for your baby's circulation to get going properly and her hands and feet may look a little blue at the beginning. This is normal.**

Babies' weight loss

■ Nearly all newborn babies lose weight in the first few days. Generally babies lose about 10% of their birth weight due to fluid loss from the baby's body post delivery and through passing meconium. Newborn babies also take time to learn to suck properly. Furthermore, if you are breastfeeding you produce only very small amounts of colostrum (see page 119) and babies need to take only a few millilitres of milk to begin with.

Umbilical cord

The cord will be clamped and cut. You or your partner may be allowed to cut the cord. If you would like to do this, ask your midwife about it. You will be left with a cord stump about 2–3 cm (1 in) long. Initially this is soft to touch and a creamy white colour with dark-bluish vessels passing through it. There may be some fresh spots of blood in your baby's nappy from the stump of the cord soon after birth. The cord slowly dries up, turns black as it decays and falls off. This is a normal process, so do not worry about it.

The first feeds

Soon after birth it is good to bring your baby to your breast. She is born with a reflex to root and suck. Ask your midwife to help with breastfeeding as much as possible as latching on properly will reduce damage to your nipple. More detailed information on a good breastfeeding position is given on pages 124–5. Don't worry if you and your baby aren't successful the first few times you try breastfeeding; it's quite normal and it will take time to get the hang of it. However, if you can, it's good to try and feed your baby frequently as this will stimulate your milk to come in. Naturally if you choose not to breastfeed, you can give your baby a bottle instead.

It's a good idea to bring your own baby clothes into the delivery room for your baby to wear after the birth. In summer your baby might just wear a nappy and a vest with poppers and in winter a babygro.

Handling your baby

Your baby's skin is very sensitive to being touched. The sudden sense of space and air next to her skin after she has been in the womb for nine months will feel very strange to your baby and each time she wakes she will want to be held and cuddled as it is very important that she feels loved and secure.

There is ample research evidence that having your baby put skin to skin with you soon after birth will help you and your new baby to adjust quickly to life together. Lay your baby on your chest between your breasts and place your hands around her back and ask someone to cover you both with a blanket or sheet. The research shows that skin-to-skin contact helps to regulate your baby's breathing and heart rate soon after birth. It promotes feelings of attachment between you and your baby and helps establish breastfeeding. Skin-to-skin contact with you can also help to protect your baby from hospital bugs. Even if you are feeling tired it is worth considering holding your baby in this way while you are waiting for your placenta to be expelled from your uterus. Discuss this with your midwife before your baby is born so she knows your preferences. If for any reason this cannot happen, you can enjoy skin-to-skin contact later or your partner could hold your baby skin to skin.

She will enjoy lying on your chest, feeling your heartbeat as you gently stroke your hands over her back. It is natural to feel nervous about handling your baby at first – the important thing to remember is that

Introducing your new baby

■ It is very common for a first child to show resentment and jealousy towards a new baby; after all, now he has to share you with someone else so you have to be careful how you handle the situation. A child can feel angry that his mother has seemingly left home and abandoned him. It is important to get brothers and sisters to visit as soon as possible and when he first sees you, it's best if you are not holding the baby. When I had my second child we couldn't make up our mind what to call her so we put three names in a hat and let Nicholas, our son, pick one out – so in the end it was Nicholas's choice! Try to involve your older child as much as possible in the care of your new baby. For example, he can help with feeding her and choosing her clothes.

■ It is a good idea if your partner arranges for your older child to bring a gift for the baby and have a gift ready for your first child from the baby.

■ It's a nice idea to place a photo of your older child in the baby's cot.

■ Take a photo of your child holding the baby, which can be made into a badge for your child to wear. He will be proud to tell his mates that the photo is of his new brother or sister.

she has no neck control so her head is very floppy, which means you need to support your baby's head at all times (see page 64).

Try to ensure that the cuddling time with your baby is unhurried and you are not pressured into moving the baby by hospital routines. There is no reason why weighing and dressing your baby cannot wait.

The special care baby

Each year 1 in 10 babies born in Britain require special hospital care and 1 in 50 require the highest neonatal intensive care. Each day, 100 babies are born too small or too soon. If this happens to you, your baby may need to spend time away from the postnatal ward in a special care baby unit.

Premature baby: A baby born before 37 weeks is technically pre-term, although most babies born between 35 to 37 weeks do not need special care. However, a baby born before 35 weeks may need monitoring and help with breathing and feeding. Around 1 in 18 babies is born prematurely in the UK each year. Often doctors have no idea why a baby is born prematurely but many cases happen because the membranes have ruptured early or if there is an infection.

Low birth weight: A baby who weighs 2.5 kg (5½ lb) or less at birth is considered to have a low birth weight. About 6–7% of babies born in the UK are low birth weight and 70% will weigh between 2 and 2.5 kg (5 and 5½ lb). Low birth weight babies can be premature or full term but have grown more slowly than normal. These babies are known as 'small for dates' or 'small for gestational age' and they usually stay in hospital until they are feeding and gaining weight satisfactorily.

Twins and multiple births: Due to the advances in fertility treatment, about 1 in 70 pregnancies are twins and 1 in 5500 are triplets. These babies are often born early and are often smaller and lighter than an average

If your baby is born prematurely you will produce a different type of milk to begin with that is higher in protein and sodium, specifically meeting your baby's needs.

Feeding premature babies

■ Premature and 'small for dates' babies need to be fed frequently. Breast milk is especially important as they miss out on the natural immunity that is usually passed from mother to baby via the placenta during the last weeks of pregnancy and are particularly vulnerable to infection. Breast milk provides antibodies to help protect them and can reduce the risk of life-threatening gut disease. If you are unable to breastfeed, your baby will be given a formula milk designed for premature babies.

■ If a baby is too tiny to suck she can be fed expressed milk via a tube into her tummy or via a cup that allows you to trickle milk into her mouth without her having to suck. If you are finding it difficult to express, try doing it next to your baby's cot or incubator as just being near her helps stimulate your left-down reflex.

■ Some babies may be too ill to be fed directly and will need to be given nutrients and fluids intravenously through a drip. The sooner you start to express your milk the better, freezing and storing it for when your baby is ready to feed. It will keep for three months. As soon as your baby gets stronger she can be fed your expressed milk via a tiny tube through her nose into her stomach.

newborn baby so may need special care to begin with.
Health problems: A baby may have had a difficult birth or may have picked up an infection. Alternatively, the baby may have a birth defect or simply need more expert observation by trained nurses.

Why an incubator?

After birth, warmth is critical for premature and low

birth weight babies as they lose heat and moisture rapidly and have few fat reserves for insulation. Very small babies aren't able to control their body temperature effectively – they can't sweat or shiver and the smaller they are the higher the temperature of their surroundings needs to be. An incubator provides a warm, humid environment for your baby, a sort of halfway home between your womb and the outside world. If your baby is premature, it may help you to regard this period as an extension of your pregnancy.

Your baby may not be capable of independent life quite yet. She may not be able to suck or swallow and may need to be fed through a tube passed down her nose into her stomach.

If your baby is born before 28 weeks, almost certainly her lungs will not be fully developed and she will need extra help with breathing. A ventilator takes over your baby's breathing, getting air into and out of her lungs. Babies on ventilators require intensive care and will need to be in a special care baby unit.

Seeing lots of equipment attached to your baby can be very frightening but many of the machines aren't actually doing anything to your baby; they are there to gather information so that the doctors know how to treat her. Apart from a ventilator your baby may need tubes for feeding, suction to clear the lungs and lines to monitor breathing, oxygen tension and temperature.

The importance of touch

As a parent you are longing to hold your baby and so it feels unnatural that she is parted from you and lying in a machine. However, some incubators are open, with heated mattresses and an overhead heater, so it is easy to touch your baby. Even in a closed incubator there are portholes through which you can touch your baby.

Jaundice

■ Over 70% of full-term babies appear jaundiced two to four days after birth and it is even more common in premature babies. Jaundice is caused by high levels of a substance called bilirubin in the blood, which gives the skin and whites of the eyes a yellowish tinge and is usually due to immaturity of the liver. Jaundice is more common in breastfed babies since to begin with formula-fed babies get more milk, which encourages bilirubin to be expelled from the body in the faeces.

■ For mild cases putting a baby in the sunlight at home is all that is required. Premature babies often feed less and so have fewer bowel movements, which means it takes longer to clear the bilirubin from the system. In more serious cases, a baby may need phototherapy lamp treatment or may be placed on a biliblanket, a mat made up of fibre optic tubes placed underneath your baby, which emits light onto the skin.

Although being handled can be stressful for a premature baby, an incubator can also be a lonely place. Providing your baby is just small and frail and not sick, you will probably be able put your hand into the incubator and gently stroke and caress her with the palm of your hand. Don't expect feedback. This will come in time, but your touch will reassure your baby of your loving presence. Maintain this kind of contact as much as possible every day.

Once your baby is allowed to be taken out of the incubator, you and your partner can hold her skin to skin. This is a great comfort to your baby as it helps stabilise her breathing, lets her get to know your smell and it encourages her to root for the nipple. Skin-to-skin comfort, known as kangaroo care, is very important for premature babies and it helps to boost the mother's milk production. Premature babies have been found to thrive on this method of care.

Going home

This is the day that will change your life forever. When you left home in labour you were a couple expecting a baby. When you return home, which may only be a few hours later, you will be parents. It's an amazing but at times scary prospect. The responsibility of caring for your baby will be yours alone.

Make sure you have the following:

■ A letter for your GP, health visitor or community midwife.

■ Information on how and where to register your baby's birth.

■ Any medicines or creams that you may have been given for yourself or your baby.

■ Your six-week post-natal check appointment may be given to you if you are to return to the hospital for this; otherwise you need to make an appointment at your GP's surgery for yourself and for your baby's six-week check.

■ If driving, your baby must by law be taken home in a car seat suitable for a newborn baby.

If you have the choice, leave the hospital around lunchtime as this helps you to get home and settled before bedtime. It also means that the daytime heat will be at its highest so the house will not feel too cold compared to the overwhelming heat of the hospital.

When you arrive home, don't be surprised if you feel

It's good to keep your baby close and involve her in your day-to-day life – you could set aside a small cosy space in each room that you spend time in. Your baby can sleep in her moses basket during the day and you could use a mat or blanket for her to lie on and perhaps a bouncy chair when she is awake.

worn out and possibly overwhelmed by the journey and what lies in front of you. As soon as you get home your baby may need feeding so find somewhere comfortable to do this. It will take you time to work out where to put your baby down safely. Some people use a Moses basket or carrycot that they carry around with them or leave it in a permanent daytime place, taking it to the bedroom at night-time. Some people have a crib where the baby sleeps, which may be put in their bedroom for the first few months and then moved to the baby's own room. Others let their baby sleep in the pram (provided it goes flat) during the day. For many parents the bedroom feels too far away for daytime naps.

From the baby's point of view, at this stage comfort and security comes from routine and familiarity of their sleeping area, not in the bigger sense of the room in which they are sleeping.

Establishing a routine

Some babies sleep for quite long stretches of time while others cat nap. It is a good idea to have a special place that is calm and quiet where you feed your baby.

A newborn baby will spend an average of 16 hours in 24 asleep. Of course some babies will sleep far less and some will sleep longer. To begin with, a baby will sleep about eight hours during the day and eight hours at night. Your day will probably be divided into two- to four-hourly stretches while your baby sleeps and then feeds. However, within a month, babies begin to sleep less during the day and more at night, still averaging about 15 hours. One of the hardest things about being a parent are the disturbed nights. Many people assume that their baby will fit in with them, but for most the reality is that they will have to fit in with their baby. Your baby will be able to catch up with sleep the next day but you will not always get the chance. If you keep your baby's cot by your bed, you won't need to disturb yourself too much when you give your baby a night-time feed. For ways of getting more rest, see page 91.

Visitors

You may prefer to try to stem the flow of visitors in the first few days to find your own feet and time with just your baby and partner.

If friends want to come and visit, encourage them to phone first as you will probably want to nap during the day. Don't be afraid to ask friends for help as maybe they could pop over to the shops on their way and bring something you need.

Pets

Pets can become jealous when you bring home your baby, so you must find time to make a fuss of your dog or cat and allow your pet to get used to this new member of the family. If you have a dog, he will enjoy going for walks with you when you take your baby out.

■ However well behaved your dog is, never leave him alone with your baby.
■ Don't let your dog or cat lick your baby or lick any of your baby's equipment.
■ Keep a close eye on your dog, buy extra treats, bones and dog biscuits to distract him.
■ Buy a cat net to prevent your cat climbing into your baby's cot or pram.
■ Make sure that you keep your pet vaccinations up to date.
■ Always keep your baby higher than your dog, i.e. don't put your baby on the floor to change her with your dog standing over the baby. This makes the dog feel dominant to the baby and you want the baby to seem dominant to the dog.

Professional help

■ There is good professional help on hand to get you through the first few weeks so make the most of it: health carers usually have a wealth of experience.

Midwives: Midwives have a professional responsibility for new mothers and babies from the onset of pregnancy until 28 days after the birth. You are usually given a list of phone numbers that you can call at any time during the day or night if you are concerned about you or your baby. Once you are home your midwife will visit you for a minimum of ten days but not necessarily every day. In some cases they will visit you for up to 28 days but usually after ten days they hand over to your local health visitor.

Health visitors: Your health visitor has the professional responsibility to look after you and your baby until she is five years old. She will advise you about feeding, inoculations, etc. and will regularly weigh your baby at your local health clinic. Your health visitor will also perform developmental and hearing checks (see page 262) to ensure that your baby is developing properly. Your health visitor will generally visit you at home 12–14 days after your baby is born.

Your GP: If you are worried about your baby's health, you should call your GP. Babies can become seriously ill quite quickly so it is important to seek medical help if you are at all worried. Even something like diarrhoea, which may seem quite minor, can lead to dehydration, which can cause serious problems.

Hospital emergency departments: It is important that you know how to get to your nearest hospital with an accident and emergency unit in case of problems.

Handling your baby

Your baby has already been with you for nine months so in the first three months after birth she needs lots of Mummy (or Daddy) contact. Babies love to feel secure; their heads flop easily so they will always need some support for their head to begin with.

Holding your baby

The more confidently you handle your baby, the more at ease she will feel. Babies don't like to be startled so make sure that your baby is aware of your presence before you go to pick her up. Young babies have an instinctive fear of being dropped because they can't control their head and if you allow your baby's head to flop back she will feel that she is going to fall and her whole body will jerk in fright (this is called the Moro reflex).

Dressing your baby

Dressing and undressing your wriggling baby can be tricky. On average, newborn babies will need about four changes of clothes a day so you're in for plenty of practice.

To begin with, you may find that your baby doesn't enjoy being dressed and undressed as she prefers to feel snug and warm. As she grows up, however, she will enjoy the feeling of kicking her legs without a nappy.

It is easiest to dress your baby on a flat surface like a changing table, which is high enough so that you don't get an aching back from bending over. Lay her on top of a padded changing mat covered with a soft towel. Have her clothes ready, be gentle but quick and make sure that the room is warm. Smile and talk to her as you change her.

If it's cold, you will probably want to dress your baby in a vest as well as a stretchsuit.

To put on a vest:

■ First scrunch it up and stretch the neck as wide as possible so that you can slip it on in one go.

■ Support your baby's head and then ease the vest over her head without touching her face, if possible.

■ Hold the armholes open wide and guide through your baby's arms.

■ If the vest has poppers, hold your baby's feet in one hand, lift her bottom up slightly and pull the back of the vest under her bottom, then do up the fastenings.

To put on a stretchsuit:

■ Lay your baby on top of the open suit.

■ Gather up each sleeve and reach your hand in through the sleeve openings to find your baby's hand and gently pull her arm through the sleeve.

■ Place your baby's legs and feet into the stretchsuit and fasten the poppers from the ankle up – in this way there is no chance of getting it wrong!

Similarly, when undressing your baby make it easier by rolling up the sleeves to slide her hand out and rolling up vests, T-shirts, etc. and pulling the neck wide before lifting them over your baby's head.

Carrying your baby in a sling

■ From the age of one week up to about a year, you can carry a baby around with you in a sling worn on your chest. This has straps that go over your shoulders and round your waist and it holds the baby in an upright position. Your baby has the comfort of being held close to your body and involved in what you are doing while you have the advantage of having your hands free.

Picking up and putting down your baby

1 Picking up As you pick up your baby, slide one hand under her neck and spread your fingers around the back of her head so you are supporting her neck in the palm of your hand and her head with your fingers.

Slide your other hand under her bottom so her bottom is in your hand and your fingers support her lower back. Once your baby feels safe in the security of your hands, lean over her and lift her slowly towards you and transfer her close to your body.

When you put your baby back down, lean forwards so you are close to her and supporting her neck, head and bottom. Lay her down and gently slip your hands out from under her body.

2 Cradling Your baby will enjoy resting against your chest with your arms wrapped securely around her head and lower back.

Cradle your baby in the crook of one arm with your hand supporting her upper leg and the other arm supporting her back and bottom. This is a good position for rocking your baby.

3 On the shoulder Resting your baby on your shoulder can be very comfortable for both you and your baby, but all babies posset small amounts of milk so you may want to protect your shoulder with a muslin cloth.

Lift up your baby with her body resting against your chest and her head looking over your shoulder. Have one hand supporting her bottom and one her head. Holding your baby close like this makes her feel secure. This is a good position for winding your baby after a feed.

Washing and bathing

I remember how nervous I was when it came to giving my first baby a bath. She looked so fragile and I was very wary of handling a wet slippery baby. No one had really explained to me how to clean around the cord stump or how to wash her hair. Consequently I was far more frightened about facing the ordeal of bath time than my baby was.

I soon learned that a tiny baby isn't as fragile as she looks so while you need to be careful, you don't need to handle her as if she is going to break. In fact, the more confidently you hold and handle your baby the safer she will feel and the more content she will be. There are many different ways to wash your baby – for example, taking a bath with your baby is lovely and intimate – but however you choose to go about it, it should be loving, warm, safe and fun.

It's important to bear in mind that, in reality, newborn babies don't get very dirty and you don't need to bath your baby every day. There is some evidence that over-washing can lead to skin irritation and eczema developing.

Some parents bath their baby two or three times a week and massage on other days. However, your baby's face may need a gentle wash more than once a day and you need to pay special attention to keep her bottom clean and dry at every nappy change.

Topping and tailing

There is no need to bath your newborn baby every day unless you both enjoy it. Once or twice a week is quite sufficient as long as you 'top and tail' on the other days. Before you undress your baby, gather together gauze, cotton wool, a bowl of warm water, a bowl of cooled boiled water or saline solution, a changing mat and a clean towel, a fresh nappy and a change of clothes.

Vernix
■ Babies may be born with vernix especially if they are premature. This is a soft sticky white cream that moisturises the skin in the womb. Vernix should be left on if possible as it will continue to moisturise the skin. However, you can still bath your baby as it won't come off during normal washing.

■ Cover your changing mat with a towel, undress your baby down to her nappy and lie her on the towel.
■ Leave your baby's eyes alone unless they are dirty or sticky. If you find that you do need to clean her eyes, wipe gently from the inner corner outwards with some cotton wool or gauze moistened with a little cooled boiled water or saline solution. Use a separate piece of gauze for each eye.
■ Clean your baby's face and creases around her neck and under her chin with some cotton wool moistened with cooled boiled water. Wipe over and behind her ears using a fresh piece of damp cotton wool for each ear. Don't be tempted to clean inside your baby's ears or inside her nose.
■ Remove the nappy and clean your baby's nappy area (see page 73).
■ Gently pat your baby dry, paying special attention to the area around her cord stump and the creases in her skin and finally dress your baby.

Care of the umbilical cord
The sight of a baby's clamped cord stump can be quite unnerving and I know that a lot of parents are worried about how to look after it. The clamp on your baby's

Equipment planner:
washing and bathing

Baby bath

For the first few months you can bathe your baby in a specially designed plastic baby bath. These are not essential but they have the advantage of using much less water than an adult bath and you can use them in any room. You can buy baby baths that you can place on a surface at about hip height so you don't need to bend down too much. You can also buy a foldaway stand that holds a bath at waist height. The disadvantage is that you still have to lift a bath full of water.

Some baby baths fit over an ordinary bath, which makes them easy to fill and empty. Alternatively, you can bath your baby in the big bath right from the start and you can use a non-slip bath mat, foam bath support or specially shaped plastic chair for your baby to lie on.

Bath thermometer

You can buy bath thermometers – many of these are decorated with colourful cartoon characters and have heat-sensitive monitors, which indicate the water temperature when left in the bath for 15 seconds.

Changing mat

A changing mat on the floor is cheap and safe unless you have large dogs or a bad back. As a more versatile alternative you might want to look into changing units – see page 72 for advice.

Gauze

You can buy sterile, absorbent gauze from a chemist for cleaning your baby's eyes or umbilical stump.

Cotton wool

It's best to clean your baby's bottom using cotton wool and warm water rather than using baby wipes as this is less likely to irritate the skin.

Baby wipes

Try to use emollient-based baby wipes.

Saline solution

This is useful for cleaning your baby's eyes (although you could also use cooled boiled water) and is available from the chemist for contact lens wearers.

Towels and face cloths

Always make sure you have a fresh supply – you will find that you use them at an alarming rate.

Nappy bucket

Essential if using reusable nappies (see page 76).

Nappy wrapper bin

A nappy wrapper bin seals germs in anti-bacterial film. It provides a quick, hygienic way to get rid of dirty disposable nappies.

stump may be removed by a midwife after about three days once the stump has dried and hardened. Some parents prefer to hold the plastic clamp to clean the chord as they dislike touching it so some midwives leave the clamp on. Whichever you choose, it makes very little difference to separation times. Within a week or ten days the stump should turn black and fall off of its own accord, provided that you keep it clean and dry.

There is no need to delay your baby's first bath provided you dry the cord properly afterwards. Wipe gently around the dried stump using some gauze dipped in a little cooled boiled water or splash water over the stump in the bath. Pat dry with a soft towel and then leave it open to the air to dry. Parents used to be advised to dab the cord with an antiseptic wipe but this is now thought to lengthen the healing process.

When putting on your baby's nappy it is important to fold down the front so that the cord is exposed; this should keep urine away from the area and will allow the air to circulate.

Sometimes there is a bad smell coming from the stump as it separates and it may bleed a little but your baby should not feel any discomfort. Although this is nearly always normal, it may mean that an infection has developed. Ask your midwife to check, if she's still coming in, or see your health visitor or GP. If the area around the cord becomes red and inflamed or there is a lot of discharge, call your doctor.

Bath time

Bathing a slippery, squirming baby takes practice, but relax even if your baby cries to begin with, you will find that it gets easier every time and your baby will soon enjoy playing and splashing around in the water. Bath

Safety

■ Never leave your baby unattended in a bath, even for a short time, as a baby can drown in a few inches of water. Don't think that a baby bath seat means that you can leave your baby.

■ Have everything you need ready before you start.

■ Put cold water in the bath first and then hot, which reduces the chance of scalding. Always check the temperature of the water with your elbow before you put your baby in the bath.

■ Use a bath thermometer.

■ If you bath your baby in the big bath, don't sit her at the end of the bath nearest to the taps – there is a risk that she may be scalded if the tap is very hot.

■ Place a non-slip mat in the bottom of the bath.

time will become part of a regular routine, helping your child wind down ready for bed.

How often you bath your baby depends on how old she is. Newborns don't get very dirty, so two or three times a week is fine. A good time to bath your baby is before the last feed at night as this will help to settle her for bedtime. There is no need to wash your baby's hair every time you give her a bath.

Getting ready

Before you get your baby ready for her bath, make sure that the room itself is warm and that you have a changing mat, cotton wool, plastic jug or baby sponge to hand, together with a clean towel, face cloth, fresh nappy and change of clothes. It is a good idea to warm the towel on a radiator ready to wrap your baby in after the bath. As you run the bath, keep the water fairly shallow but just deep enough to cover your baby's body by about 12–20 cm (5–8 in). Put cool water in before hot and test the temperature of the water with your elbow or the inner side of your wrist. Your baby's

skin is more sensitive than yours and the water should feel warm but not too hot. Until you get a feel for the temperature you could use a baby bath thermometer – the ideal bath temperature is around 37°C (98°F). Never add hot water once your baby is in the bath. If you are intending to wash your baby's hair or face, make sure there are no bath additives in the water.

Washing your baby's hair
■ Undress your baby and clean her nappy area using cotton wool (see page 73) and wrap her in a towel. Hold her securely against your side with your arm under her back and her head supported in your hand.
■ To wash your baby's hair, lean her head gently over the bath and, using your other hand, take a jug of clean warm water or wet sponge and pour or squeeze a little water over her head. If your baby has a lot of

Cradle cap
■ A dry, scaly scalp (cradle cap) can be common among babies but it is quite harmless. Some babies get cradle cap on their foreheads or even in their eyebrows. Cradle cap is a build-up of dead skin cells on your baby's head and often has a yellowy, scaly appearance. Cradle cap shampoos work well or you could try very gently agitating the cradle cap with a soft flannel or very, very soft hairbrush.
■ One of the best ways to alleviate cradle cap is to rub olive or almond oil or E45 cream into the scalp (you may need to try several emollients until you find the one that works best for your baby. In the morning put a little baby shampoo (there are some baby shampoos specially formulated for cradle cap, eczema and other dry skin conditions) on your baby's head and massage in without any water. Move a damp flannel over her head, gently rubbing it in a circular movement. Rinse the head with warm water to remove loosened scales. Repeat the washing and rinsing every two to three days.
■ Don't be tempted to pick the scales off with your fingers as this can make the condition worse and can cause bleeding or infection. Generally the cradle cap will clear up within a few weeks. If it isn't responding to this treatment, then see your GP. Occasionally cradle cap can last for several months. Some toddlers still have patches of cradle cap but the hair grows over so that it's not visible. A small number of babies with excessive cradle cap may go on to develop eczema.

Cradle cap can occur when parents are too gentle when washing their baby's head. Be gentle but firm and massage the scalp as you wash the hair.

hair, you may want to use a mild baby shampoo. Rinse well and pat dry. Be careful not to get soap in your baby's eyes: stinging eyes can put her off bath time. If your baby has cradle cap (see box, page 69), brush or comb her hair, or if your baby has no hair, use a soft baby brush to gently massage the scalp.

Bathing your baby

■ To bath her, unwrap her from the towel and lower her slowly into the bath with both hands, one hand supporting her shoulders and head with your fingers under her armpit, and the other supporting her legs or bottom. Smile and talk to your baby as you do this.

■ Keep one hand under your baby's arm and around her chest with her head supported on your forearm and use your free hand to wash her. Start at the top and wash your baby's face then work down her body. Use soft clean flannels or a clean sponge to wash your baby. To wash her back and bottom, sit her forward or turn her over, keeping her face above water.
■ When she is clean, lift her out with both hands and wrap her in a towel. You will need to cover her head, so a towel with a hood is ideal. Lie her on a changing mat and pat her dry, paying special attention to skin creases in the neck, legs and arms. This could be a good time to give her a massage (see pages 82–5).

Washing from top to bottom

Ears: Some babies have very waxy ears but this is natural as long as the wax is semi-solid and yellow-brown in colour without smell. Never poke a cotton bud inside your baby's ears as this can introduce an infection or damage her eardrum. Wipe around the ears with damp cotton wool. If the wax is runny, smelly or changing in colour, see your GP as this could indicate an infection.

Eyes: Because of the risk of infection, there is no need to clean your baby's eyes unless there is a discharge or they are sticky. If there is a yellow discharge in your baby's eyes, this may lead to sticky eye (a mild form of conjunctivitis). This is made worse because the tear ducts are too small to drain the eyes. Use cotton wool moistened with saline solution or cooled boiled water and wipe the discharge from the inside outwards. Use a fresh piece of cotton wool for each eye.

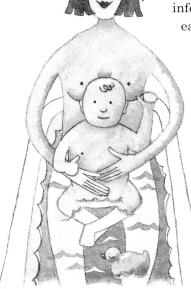

If your baby's eyes are slightly sticky but not red or inflamed, it is probably a blocked tear duct. Try massaging with a clean finger the skin just under the corner of your baby's eye. Massage in circles very gently for 30–60 seconds. If there is any redness or inflammation, contact a doctor.

Nose: All babies' noses will become blocked sometimes. There is no need to do anything unless your baby seems unwell or is finding it difficult to feed or sleep. In this case see your GP. A few drops of saline solution in the nose can soften up the blockage.

Neck: Dribble and old milk tends to collect in the creases of your baby's neck and as young babies aren't able to lift their head, the area doesn't get any air and it can become smelly or sore. Wipe the folds with cotton wool soaked in soapy water and then rinse with a clean, wet flannel and dry.

Armpits: Make sure that you dry your baby's armpits properly after a bath or they can become sore.

Nails

Even though a newborn baby's nails are fairly soft, they can still scratch her face quite badly so it's important to keep her fingernails well trimmed. You may need to do this every few days, particularly if your baby scratches her face a lot – it is surprising how

> Keep the time that your baby is undressed to a minimum, so don't leave your baby in the bath for more than a few minutes.

Dry skin

■ Some newborns, especially if they go past their due date, are born with very dry skin. Care needs to be taken to moisturise these babies daily. Some of them may need their skin moisturised more than once a day. Use a pure oil for this like olive, almond, grapeseed or linseed oil, or use aqueous cream.

■ Adding soap or bubble bath in bath water can make dry skin worse. Detergents may also increase the risk of eczema by stripping away layers of protective fats. Plain water is better or add a little bath oil such as Oilatum or Infacare. Alternatively, mix a few drops of almond oil with one or two drops of lavender, camomile or mandarin oil. Lavender oil is good if your baby has a stuffy nose, camomile helps if your baby suffers from colic and mandarin is a relaxant. There are also special emollient bath additives available for babies who have eczema.

■ On the whole, this dry skin will heal but for some babies it becomes part of their life or may develop into eczema. Lots of babies that develop very dry skin or eczema will grow out of this by three years of age.

quickly nails grow. Hold your baby's fingers one at a time between yours, gently pull the soft flesh back from the nail to reduce the risk of cutting her finger and trim the nail using special baby scissors with rounded tips. It may be difficult to get your baby to hold still so ask your partner to hold her hand while you cut the nails. If your baby is a sound sleeper you may be able to trim her nails while she sleeps. You could also try using an emery board to file down her nails. It is not advisable to bite off your baby's nails.

Cut toenails straight across as shaping them can cause them to become in-grown, and do not cut them too short. Any red or inflamed areas of skin around the nail indicate an infection that needs to be treated.

The joy of nappies

Your newborn baby will need her nappy changed whenever it is wet or soiled. The number of times will depend on your baby, but as a rule you will need to change her nappy when she wakes up in the morning, after every feed, including night feeds, after her bath and when you put her to bed at night. There is no need to wake your baby at night to change her nappy unless she has done a poo and she has a sore bottom. It has been estimated that you need to change your baby's nappy at least 4700 times before she is toilet trained.

There is a wide variation in how frequently your baby fills her nappy. Newborn babies will pass lots of stools a day, maybe as many as ten. As they approach three months, breastfed babies tend to settle down into their own pattern and pass fewer stools than bottle-fed babies. The normal range is about one to three poos each day but some babies can go without a bowel movement for several days and maybe only do a poo every two to five days. This is not a health or medical problem but it can cause bad wind and smelly poo. You will soon get used to the pattern of your baby's pooing.

As you will be changing your baby's nappies so frequently it's a good idea to invest in a changing unit. You will need somewhere where you can keep all the things that you need, like nappies, wipes and creams, in one place. Before you buy a changing unit, test that it's high enough not to cause you backache. Some units have casters, which makes them mobile, and some come with a bath, which may seem like a good idea but you will have to fill and empty it by hand. As a long-term investment you could think about buying a changing unit that doubles as a chest of drawers. A cheaper but also very practical alternative is to use a 'top changer', a changing unit that fits over the cot.

Changing a nappy

Before you change your baby's nappy make sure you wash your hands and that you have everything you need either beside the changing table or, if you are away from home, in your nappy bag (see page 79).

What you need
■ Changing mat or towel.
■ Cotton wool or washable wipes.
■ Bowl of warm water for babies under one month or baby wipes for an older baby.

Safety
■ Make sure that the sides of your baby's changing unit are high enough to prevent your baby from rolling off.
■ NEVER leave your baby alone on a changing mat that is not on the floor. Your baby is developing rapidly and can suddenly become mobile and roll over.

■ Clean towel for drying your baby's bottom.
■ Petroleum jelly or nappy cream (optional).
■ Clean nappy.
■ Nappy sacks/nappy wrapper bin.
■ Wipes for cleaning your hands when you are out.

■ Cover your changing mat with a towel. Unbutton your baby's vest and pull it up so it doesn't get soiled.
■ Use the existing nappy or liner to wipe away as much poo as possible. If you are changing a boy make sure his penis is pointing down towards his knees as it is likely that he will wee when his nappy is removed. It's also a good idea to place some cotton wool or tissues over his penis. For a girl you could place absorbent kitchen paper under her bottom to absorb any wee.
■ Using cotton wool moistened with warm water, clean your baby's genitals and surrounding skin, lifting up your baby's legs by holding both ankles so that you can clean her bottom. For girls, wipe from front to back to prevent bacteria from the anus getting into the vagina. For boys, work from the leg creases towards the penis and don't pull back his foreskin.
■ Gently dry your baby's bottom with a soft clean towel, making sure that you dry between the creases, and apply a nappy cream or Vaseline if necessary (see Barrier creams, page 74). Be aware that most nappy creams contain petroleum jelly, which can dry the skin.
■ Use one hand to gently raise your baby's legs and the other to slip a fresh opened nappy (tabs at the back if using a disposable one) under her bottom so that the top is in line with her waist.
■ Let go of your baby's legs and bring the front of the nappy up between her legs and tuck it around her tummy. Unpeel the tabs, pull them firmly over the front flap and press down to fasten or secure with pins if using reusable nappies. Make sure your hands are dry and not oily. If the cord stump is present, fold down the front of the nappy to keep the stump dry.

Handy hints
■ Dispose of soiled disposable nappies hygienically. If possible, drop any formed stool into the toilet, then put the nappy into a nappy sack, tie up and place in a tightly covered nappy bucket or a nappy wrapper bin.
■ Always wash your hands after changing your baby's nappy.
■ Nappy creams are not necessary with most modern disposable nappies. In fact, creams can hinder the effectiveness of the one-way dry liner.
■ Make sure there is enough room to put a finger down between your baby's tummy and her nappy so that it is not too tight.
■ Baby boys often get an erection when being changed, which is perfectly normal. There is no need to pull back the foreskin, this area is self-cleaning.
■ You can make your own baby wipe solution to use with cotton wool or reusable washable wipes. Make a pot of camomile tea and leave to cool. Add 1 tbsp of vegetable oil, a few drops of lavender essential oil, and a teaspoon of honey or a few drops of porpolis tincture. This solution will keep for two to three days and can be kept in a squeezy or pump bottle to use when required.

Nappy rash

Irrespective of the type of nappy you choose to use, if your baby is left in a wet or dirty nappy for too long, nappy rash will result. Urine is broken down into ammonia by the bacteria in your baby's stools and this, in turn, will burn and irritate her skin, causing redness around the genitals, which can lead to ulceration if not treated. This bacteria will thrive in both a disposable and washable nappy if left on for too long. If your baby's bottom looks red, use any of the following ways of treating it.

■ Keep your baby's skin dry and leave the nappy off whenever possible for at least ten minutes to air her bottom when changing a nappy.
■ Use a barrier cream to protect your baby's sensitive skin (see box, above right).
■ Don't wash your baby's bottom with soap and water as this can irritate and dry out the skin and don't rub her skin, rather pat it dry.
■ If using baby wipes, choose non-alcohol ones. Alcohol-based baby wipes can dry out your baby's skin.
■ A rash on the bottom can be caused as a response to allergens present in the mother's food passing into her breast milk so reduce potentially allergenic foods in your diet as well as spicy or acidic foods. This can also happen when your baby starts on solid food.
■ If using cloth nappies, line your baby's nappy with a layer of cotton soaked in camomile tea solution (see Handy hints, page 73). This is very soothing for the baby as well as healing.
■ You may need to change your baby more often or use more absorbent nappies. When putting on a nappy, don't secure it too tightly to allow air to circulate.
■ Some of the chemicals in disposable nappies can

Barrier creams

■ A wide variety of barrier creams is available, which can calm nappy rash.
Conventional creams: Some of the most popular and effective are Sudocreme, Morhulin, Vaseline and zinc and caster oil. Metanium is good for really sore bottoms, especially if your baby has had gastro-enteritis.
Calendula creams: Any calendula-based barrier cream is an ideal, soothing alternative.
Natural oils: The skin can be lubricated with small amounts of olive, almond, grapeseed or safflower oils, which are plant-based, nourishing and safe. In addition, tiny amounts of essential oils, such as tea tree, lavender or camomile can be added to natural oils.

irritate your baby's bottom so you could try using cloth nappies instead.
■ Nappy rash in cotton-nappy users can also be caused by a reaction to the washing detergents being used, even where it seems fine on the rest of the body. Try switching powders to a mild detergent and give an extra rinse to the wash.
■ Nappy rash can be caused by teething and weaning. If this is the case, see if you can establish which foods are causing the upset and try alternatives. Teething-induced nappy rash can sometimes be treated with homeopathic teething granules (available in chemists).
■ Thrush can often be the cause of nappy rash. If the nappy rash is not clearing despite your best efforts, seek medical advice. Your baby may also have thrush in her mouth. Typically this presents itself as white appears on the tongue or gums, which are present before a feed and cannot be wiped away. Your baby may need to be treated for both the nappy area and mouth. If you are breastfeeding, you will also need an appropriate cream for your nipples.

Nappy contents

A newborn baby's stools normally start off as a striking black and then progress to green, brown and finally, after about ten days, yellow.

In the first few days you will find that your newborn baby's bowel movements consist of a black, tar-like sticky substance, which is composed of amniotic fluid debris that has built up in her intestines. This is called meconium.

Some babies pass meconium during birth so your baby may not pass more stools on the day of birth. Most babies will pass meconium when they have either a breast or bottle feed, although it may take up to 24 hours for this to happen. When the baby sucks for a feed this initiates an action called peristalsis, which is a movement in the gut that moves waste products down and eventually out.

Your baby should have a meconium stool within 24 hours of being born. Your midwife will probably ask you if your baby has pooed and may well ask you what colour it was. The reason for this is that when meconium is passed, it shows that everything is in good working order for your baby.

Sometime in the first week, when all the meconium has been passed, your baby's stool will become less sticky and turn greenish-brown.

After about a week or ten days, your baby's stools will then turn a yellowish-brown colour. The stools of

If for any reason you want to be sure that your baby is passing urine, insert some cotton wool balls into your baby's nappy.

Mini periods
■ Newborn girl babies often have a thick white sticky vaginal discharge. This is normal. Simply clean what you can easily. Do not try and part the labia to clean. Also a few girl babies will have a bloody discharge from their vagina. This is also normal and a hormonal response. If there is not more than a tablespoonful of discharge, do not worry about it; it is simply like a small period and will stop after a couple of weeks.

breastfed babies tend to be softer as breast milk has a natural laxative effect. They also smell more pleasant (if this is ever possible) than the stools of formula-fed babies, which tend to be browner in colour and occur more frequently.

As for urination, babies have no bladder control for several years. It may be difficult in the early days to say how many wees your baby has had because they will get lost in the poo. The wee may also disappear into the absorbent lining of disposable nappies. You may have to touch the pad to feel that it's wet.

You may discover that the colour of your baby's urine changes from time to time. It may become dark and concentrated if your baby has not had enough fluid during the day. High temperatures can also cause concentration of urine because the baby sweats a lot. If you are worried that your baby is not urinating, either breastfeed more frequently or, for bottle-fed babies, give water to drink and also see your GP if you are concerned.

If your baby becomes dry because the amount of urine reduces, constipation may be one of the warning signs (see page 78).

The smell of urine can change, too, which could be a sign of dehydration. Urine can also be affected by the food eaten by breastfeeding mothers.

Choosing the right nappy

You have two main types of nappies to choose from: disposable and washable nappies. Both have advantages and disadvantages and it is up to you to weigh up the pros and cons of each system to see which will be best for you and your family. It might be a mixture of both.

Disposable nappies

There is a huge variety of disposable nappies on sale and the choice can be quite bewildering. Every baby is different so you will probably need to try out several brands until you find the one that suits your baby best. A nappy should fit snugly enough to prevent leaks but should not be so tight that it rubs. A good way to check is to make sure you can comfortably slide one of your fingers between your baby's nappy and her tummy.

Cloth nappies

I must admit that I used disposable nappies on my babies; I just assumed that cloth nappies would take too much time and effort. But designs have changed so much that cloth nappies are much easier to use than formerly.

Washable nappies come in a variety of shapes and sizes and vary considerably in their ease of use and cost. The easiest to use are shaped like disposable ones with elasticated legs and Velcro or popper fastenings at the waist. These nappies are for you to buy and wash at home. In general, the more shaped, fitted and easy to use a nappy is, the more expensive it is. On average you will need between 18 and 24 washable nappies at any one time and three to four waterproof wraps.

All-in-one nappies: These are most like a disposable nappy with a waterproof layer sewn onto the cotton nappy. This makes them very easy to use but means they are more expensive to buy and will take longer to dry than a two-part system.

Two-part system: This consists of a cotton nappy with a separate waterproof outer covering – a wrap, which comes in different sizes to ensure a good leak-proof fit and the nappy may come in one size or multiple sizes.

A one-size nappy is designed to fit from birth to potty training and is adjusted to the size required at any one time. This type of nappy can be a very cost-effective system. Multi-sized nappies usually come in two different sizes, starting with the smallest.

The waterproof layer of the two-part system is known as the wrap. This has taken the place of the rubber pants of old. Wraps are now made of modern durable fabrics laminated to make them waterproof while remaining breathable, and close with Velcro or poppers. Pure wool wraps are also available, which are totally breathable, waterproof and a natural alternative. They are usually more expensive and require

Laundry service

■ A nappy laundry service will deliver clean nappies to you at home, usually once a week and take away the dirty ones to wash for you. This way you have all the benefits of washable nappies without having to wash them yourself. A laundry service will not only provide clean nappies but will also usually let you rent or buy waterproof outer wraps and provide you with disposable paper liners and a bin to store the dirty nappies in (see Useful addresses, page 268).

Disposable vs washable nappies

	Adavantages	Disadvantages
Disposable nappies	■ Easy to use and save a lot of time and effort as no washing or drying involved. ■ Readily available and there is a huge choice of shapes, sizes and brands so you can shop around to find which best suits your baby. ■ Super-absorbent material rapidly absorbs moisture into the centre of the nappy helping draw it away from your baby's skin. ■ Easy to dispose of – simply pop them in the bin after use. ■ No initial outlay for nappies; you just buy them as you need them. ■ Ready to use at any time, no preparation or washing or drying involved in their usage.	■ More expensive than washable nappies in the long term. ■ Made from pulped wood and use up a lot of trees: four and a half trees are destroyed to keep one baby in disposable nappies. ■ Produce a lot of waste. In the UK, 4 million nappies a day are sent to landfill sites. Some parts of disposable nappies take 200–500 years to decompose fully so this means that nappies you throw away now could still be around when your great grand-children are born. ■ Disposal with household waste, which usually ends up in landfill, means the human excrement will end up there too and not in the sewage system so is not treated and safely broken down. ■ Some babies are allergic to the chemicals in disposable nappies. Some brands are worse than others.
Washable nappies	■ Soft, comfortable nappy made from natural fibres, which allow the skin to breathe. ■ Chemical-free layer next to your baby's skin. ■ Overall cost from birth to potty training is less than using disposable nappies all the time. ■ Some varieties can be adjusted or folded to fit any size. ■ More environmentally friendly. ■ Machine washable and dryable. If you have a washing machine, a 60°C wash is all that is required to sanitise nappies.	■ Need to be washed and dried and therefore more time consuming. However, there are some nappy laundering services available. ■ Larger initial outlay. ■ They are not always readily available although you can buy them by mail order. However, those who sell cotton nappies are usually highly knowledgeable about the products and can provide advice and information about their use. ■ They create a bulkier bottom for today's clothes, which are generally cut for the slimmer-fitting, disposable nappy. ■ Have to be taken home dirty if your baby is changed when out and about.

more looking after but are ideal for night-time as they keep a baby's bottom lovely and cool and fully aired.

The traditional terry nappies could also be considered a two-part system. They are not shaped and require folding prior to use. The main advantages over a shaped and fitted nappy are cost and speed of drying.

Nappy liners: In addition to the nappies and wraps, you may wish to use nappy liners. The main purpose of a liner is to make using washable nappies easier. It catches the poo and, depending on the type of liner used, can either be emptied into the toilet or flushed away. Paper liners are the most common and are flushed away when soiled. You may also wish to use a polar fleece or polyester layer to act as a stay-dry layer. Moisture passes through this layer into the absorbent layer of the nappy and helps to keep moisture off your baby's skin. These are then washed with the nappies.

Storage
You will need a bucket to store your nappies in between washes (1–3 days).

Constipation

If your baby is constipated, stools will be harder than normal, she may strain and cry when trying to pass a stool and she may get colic-type pains. Constipation is more common in bottle-fed babies because breast milk is very well absorbed whereas cow's milk formula leaves a baby with more waste to dispose of. It will only become a problem for breastfed babies if your baby is not drinking enough, particularly in hot weather or if she has a fever. Most formula-fed babies have daily bowel movements although for some this may be every two to three days. Breastfed babies sometimes have a bowel movement only once a week. Since formula-fed babies have firmer stools, this can sometimes cause constipation. To help prevent this from occurring:
■ Make your baby's formula to the right concentration.
■ Offer cooled boiled water between feeds.
■ Massage can sometimes help (see page 82).

If your baby becomes constipated once eating solids, give foods rich in fibre like fruit and vegetable purées. Dried fruits are good. Wholewheat cereals are good after six months. Cut down on rice and bananas.

Diarrhoea

Most children suffer with diarrhoea at some point. Possible reasons include: too much fibre or sugar, food sensitivity, or a side effect of drugs, particularly antibiotics. Infections of the intestinal tract by bacteria or viruses, including food poisoning, are a common cause, when vomiting may accompany the diarrhoea.

Diarrhoea in small babies is potentially very dangerous as they can become dehydrated and lose vital salts from the body very quickly. This is particularly so if the baby is also vomiting or shows signs of having pain in her abdomen. If your baby has several watery stools and is vomiting for more than 4–6 hours or seems distressed, seek urgent medical advice.

Diarrhoea on its own in babies, or mild diarrhoea and vomiting in babies over the age of a year, is not as serious, but if your child passes more than six watery stools in 24 hours, seek medical advice. Signs of dehydration requiring urgent attention at any age include:
■ Less frequent urination.
■ More concentrated, dark yellow urine.
■ Dry mouth and lips.
■ Sunken eyes.
■ Lethargic behaviour.

If there is diarrhoea and vomiting, make sure your child maintains her fluid intake. Do not stop milk in babies under the age of a year, continue with breast or bottle feeds and try to offer feeds more frequently than usual. Between feeds you can also offer cool boiled water or special oral rehydration fluids, available from your chemist. If your baby is vomiting and is unable to keep fluids down, she needs to be seen by a doctor. For older children offer small drinks of water or very dilute fruit juices every 1–2 hours. If your child wishes to continue to eat even through the diarrhoea and vomiting, you can let her have small quantities of what she fancies, but avoid very fatty, spicy or sugary foods.

Sometimes when a baby has had diarrhoea for an extended period, she may develop a secondary lactose intolerance, meaning she may have difficulty digesting the sugar in milk. This is usually a temporary condition and will clear within a few days. There are low-lactose baby milks available from the chemist, but do not stop breastfeeding or discontinue your usual formula milk without seeking medical advice first.

Getting organised for going out

Going out with your baby, whether it is for a walk to the park or out for the day, is more likely to be a positive experience if you have got yourself well organised beforehand. Take a look at the list below and decide what else you could add to your changing bag.

Try to get into the habit of making sure that your changing bag is always ready – replace any used nappies or baby clothes as soon as you come home. If you are out shopping, try to find out beforehand which of the shops have a mother and baby changing room.

What to take on outings for your baby
- Nappies.
- Small packet of baby wipes or damp cotton wool in a plastic bag.
- Travel changing mat or towel.
- Small tub of nappy cream.
- 2 bibs and muslin squares for mopping up.
- Spare clothes for your baby.
- Small packet of tissues.
- A few small toys to keep your baby amused.
- Sun cream and sun hat for summer; wool hat for winter.
- Drink and snack for yourself.
- If you baby is bottle-fed, take ready-mixed bottles of milk in an insulated bag or 250 ml (8 fl oz) cooled boiled water in a bottle and a 225 g (8 oz) sachet of milk powder. Or use pre-sterilised bottles with cartons of ready-mixed formula.

Sun protection

Sunburn is bad for everyone but a baby's skin is especially sensitive and sun damage can increase the risk of skin cancer later in life. Keep your baby out of the sun completely while she is under six months and then keep her out of direct sunlight. Also, put a sun hat on

your baby's head and if you are outside on a hot day, apply a high-factor hypoallergenic sun cream (25 or higher) especially formulated for babies – do a patch test first. You can also buy special textile suits for your baby that protect her from the sun. If your baby is in a pushchair, use a large adjustable parasol to shade her.

Travel

- If you take your baby on a long car journey, don't leave her for too long in her car seat. Take her out regularly so she can stretch and kick.
- Ensure there is a sunshade in the car and never leave your baby in a hot car unattended.
- A baby dressed for a winter's day can soon become overheated when taken inside a warm building or car. You may need to remove some of her outer clothing.

Equipment planner: going out

The choices of equipment for carrying your baby, starting with a pram and moving onto a buggie when she is a little older, can be bewildering. Here is an outline of the pluses and minuses of what is available.

Pram/pushchair

For the first three months your baby will need a pram or a versatile pushchair in which she can lie flat. Newborn babies shouldn't sit upright or even semi-upright as their back muscles aren't strong enough. The traditional pram is very comfortable but it is expensive and too large for most households. It is also not easily transportable by car or public transport.

What to look out for when choosing

■ Is it easy to fold and put in the car? Try collapsing it.
■ Is it quite light to carry?
■ Are the brakes easy to operate?
■ Does it have multi-position seats? A pram or pushchair is only suitable from birth if it fully reclines.
■ Does it have a safety harness that is easy to fasten?
■ Does the car seat fit your car?
■ Is there a PVC hood and apron for rain and a sun canopy or parasol to protect your baby from the sun?
■ Does it have adjustable handles? This helps if you and your partner are very different heights.
■ Does it have swivel wheels?
■ Does it have a spacious shopping tray?
■ Are the covers easy to remove and wash?
■ Does it have good suspension? A gentle rocking motion will help send your baby off to sleep.

Three-in-one pram/pushchair: The three-in-one comes in three pieces: chassis, carrycot and pushchair. It converts from a pram, in which your baby can lie flat, to a rear/forward-facing pushchair.

Two-in-one pram/pushchair: The two-in-one combines the comfort of a pram with the versatility of a pushchair. However, there is no carrycot.

Travel-system car seat/carrycot/pushchair: This offers a baby car seat, carrycot and pushchair in one (some models do not come with a carrycot). The car seat attaches to the pushchair chassis to make a small pram. The advantage of this is that you do not need to wake your baby if she has fallen asleep in the car.

Pushchair: A typical pushchair has either a reclining bucket seat or a lie-back seat unit and folds for easy storage. Some designs are suitable from birth if the pushchair fully reclines. Some models have fully reversible seat units so that your baby can face you or face forwards.

Buggie/stroller: These tend to be the most lightweight and they are compact and easily transportable so may make a good choice if there are lots of stairs to negotiate or you only tend to go short distances and often need to fold up the pushchair and lift or carry it.

Three-wheelers: A robust three-wheeler offers added comfort on uneven surfaces and is ideal for off-road walking or pushing uphill It has a multi-position padded seat.

Double buggies: Suitable for two babies or a baby and toddler side by side or sitting one behind the other, but only one of the children can lie flat in the latter models.

and about

Car seats

Every year, thousands of children are involved in car accidents and most happen at an average collision speed of just 22 mph. Statistics indicate that a child car seat could have prevented two in three deaths or serious injuries to unrestrained children. Newborn babies must be carried in a rear-facing baby seat or infant carrier.

Make sure you have a baby car seat for your first journey back from hospital. They cannot travel facing forwards until they have the strength in their neck and back to sit up on their own for long periods. A rear-facing baby seat must never be used on the front seat of a car where a passenger airbag is fitted. In addition, it is illegal to carry a baby or child under three in the front seat of a car without using a baby or child car seat.

Car seats can be used to carry your baby to and from the car but are not suitable for long periods as they aren't good for the developing back. Falling from a car seat or bouncy chair is a major cause of head injury in babies under one so don't put baby seats on high surfaces like table tops.

What to look out for when choosing
■ Does the seat fit your car properly? Make sure it can be fitted exactly according to the manufacturer's instructions.
■ Is the seat easy to fit?
■ Does it conform to the British or European Safety Standard?
■ A one-latch harness makes it easier to fasten your baby.
■ A head hugger gives extra comfort for young babies.
■ Large side wings offer protection from a side-on collision.

■ Adjustable seat positions give safety as your baby grows.
■ Are the covers removable for washing?

Baby car seat: Rear-facing only, portable and suitable until your baby weighs about 10 kg (nine months old) although some seats go up to13 kg (12–15 months).
Two-way seat: Either rear- or forward-facing although it shouldn't be used in a forward-facing position until your child reaches a weight of 10–13 kg. These are supposed to last until your baby is about four years old but your baby may outgrow it by two or three years of age.
Forward-facing seat: Suitable from when your child is over 9 kg and can sit unaided.

Baby carrier/sling

These allow you to carry your baby close to you when you go out, leaving your hands free. Babies enjoy being carried around next to you or your partner as they like the movement and can hear your heartbeat and your voice. Slings are suitable from birth to about nine or 12 months. From birth you can carry your baby on your front facing you, but once over three months you can carry your baby facing outwards.

What to look for when choosing
■ Ensure that the sling provides head and neck support for your baby and that it is comfortable for you.
■ Make sure that it is easy to put on and take off and that your baby is secure.
■ Choose one with wide padded shoulder straps so that it won't dig into your shoulders due to the weight of the baby.

Baby massage

This chapter was written with the help of Peter Walker, Britain's leading expert in baby massage. Touch is the most developed of the senses at birth and as such is regarded as the 'mother' sense. It is no surprise, therefore, that babies need and love to be held, cuddled and caressed; it makes them feel safe, cherished and secure. However, massage is not just a way of showing your love for your child but provides a whole host of benefits for your baby (see box, right).

Babies can be massaged from newborn to the time when they are able to sit up and move around. The sooner you massage your baby the better as touch is very important to a newborn baby and young babies are generally very responsive to massage. At first your newborn baby may enjoy being massaged for just a few minutes but you can lengthen the sessions as she gets older. Once a baby learns to crawl, she is unlikely to lie still for long enough to be massaged.

When to massage

Choose a time of day when you are relaxed and not in a hurry and your baby is calm but alert, perhaps in the morning or evening. One of the best times is after your baby's bath. Maybe feed your baby a little from one breast, then massage her and finish the rest of the feed after the massage. After a full feed you should wait at least one hour before massaging your baby.

If your baby has a pattern of crying at a certain time during the day, it might be a good idea to massage your baby about an hour before this niggly period to see if that might help.

How to massage

To begin, have everything ready – massage oil, a soft towel, a clean nappy and some clean clothes – and find

The benefits of baby massage
- Enhances a loving relationship between you and your child, bringing pleasure to both the giver and receiver.
- Promotes growth and development – during massage there is an increase in growth hormones flowing from the pituitary gland. Research shows that premature babies who are massaged gain weight more quickly.
- Improves the texture of your baby's skin.
- Massaging the abdomen can help digestive problems: abdominal pain, colic, constipation and wind.
- Massaging your baby is a good way to improve your confidence in handling her.
- It can help boost your baby's immune system by stimulating the circulation of blood and lymph fluid.
- It helps develop body awareness and strengthens your baby's muscles and joints.
- Massage can help, calm or relax an irritable baby.
- It can help your baby to sleep better.

a warm quiet place where you will not be disturbed. A good place to massage your baby is to lay her on a towel on the floor. You can kneel or sit facing her but make sure that you are comfortable and that you are not straining your back. If you have a hard floor, put your baby's changing mat on the floor and drape a towel over it.

Remove any jewellery and ensure that your hands are clean and your nails are trimmed so that you don't scratch your baby. Undress your baby, lay her on her back and kneel or sit facing her. Put plenty of oil on your hands – if you don't use enough oil, your hands won't glide easily over your baby's skin. Rub your palms together to make sure your hands are warm.

> **Q How do I know if I am massaging my baby the right way?**
> **A** A parent's touch is intuitive so don't worry that you might harm your baby. When you massage him use a gentle pressure, but if your touch is too light, he will not get the true benefit of the massage. Your baby will soon let you know if you are pressing too hard or making him feel uncomfortable.

As you work through the routine given overleaf, watch your baby's reactions to find out her likes and dislikes. If your baby cries, stop and rest the palm of one hand on her chest and the palm of the other on her abdomen; this can have a calming effect.

You don't always need to give a full massage if you don't have much time. Just do your baby's favourite bits or simply massage your baby through her clothes. It is important to make sure that your baby is always kept warm. When it is cold you can massage your baby through her clothes without oil.

What type of oil?

Choose an organic/pure oil such as grapeseed, sweet almond, sunflower or virgin olive oil. These are safe and gentle to the skin and are edible in case your baby puts an oily hand in her mouth. Sweet almond oil is made from the flower, not the almond itself. Nut oils should never be used on a baby in case of allergies.

After three months you can add some essential oil but always do a skin test on your baby first. Mix 5 drops of the essential oil with 100 ml (3½ fl oz) of the base oil. Apply a small amount on your baby's forearm and leave it for 30 minutes to see if there is any adverse reaction.

Aromatherapy oils designed for adults are not suitable for babies under 12 weeks as a young baby's liver is not equipped to deal with essential oils.

Up to eight weeks

For the first few days after your baby is born you can massage her through her clothes. Lie on your side facing your baby or sit holding her in your arms, rub her back, stroke her head and get the feel of her limbs by stroking them. You can also lie on your back with your baby on your chest, preferably skin to skin, and stroke her hand over hand down both sides of her spine.

For the first six to eight weeks you probably won't launch into a full massage routine but it is really good if you can rub oil into your baby's skin every day. Lay your baby on a warm soft towel and gently massage the oil all over her body except for her face and head. After eight weeks you could move on to the routine given overleaf.

When not to massage

- If your baby has a temperature or is unwell.
- If your baby has any skin disorders like eczema.
- Avoid massage for the first 48 hours after immunisation and avoid massaging the injection site for about a week.
- Don't massage over the soft spot of your baby's head.
- Don't massage any bruised or swollen areas.
- Don't massage any stiff or painful limbs or joints.

Good essential oils to use

- **Camomile:** This has a calming effect, aids digestion and helps induce sleep.
- **Frankincense:** This is good for relaxing and helps deepen and improve breathing rhythm.
- **Lavender:** Good for when your baby has a cold as it can help unblock congestion.
- **Rose:** This is good for dry skin and smells good.

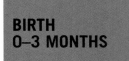

The art of baby massage

It is important to make this a fun time for your baby and it is also great for communicatication so keep eye contact and talk or sing. She will love it if you blow on her neck and kiss her legs, arms or chest – do whatever comes naturally. It is also very soothing to play music while you massage your baby: piano music is ideal. Babies often fall asleep during or just after a massage.

When you turn your baby over on to her tummy, bring her elbows forwards. If she can't keep them in position or if you find she isn't comfortable, put a rolled up towel across the front of her chest and under her arms so she can rest her weight on her elbows. This also helps to lift her face off the towel so she can see what is going on. Babies don't like lying down with their face flat on the floor.

Repeat each of the following movements several times and make sure your hands are well oiled throughout the massage.

Gentle massage

1 Lie your baby on her back and stroke down her whole body from shoulders to feet with warm, relaxed, well-oiled hands.

> It is good for babies to spend time on their tummies as this will help strengthen their neck, back and shoulder muscles.

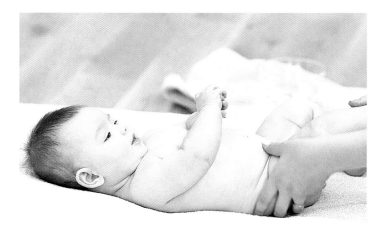

2 Take one leg and give it a gentle shake. Gently pull the leg hand over hand through your palms from thigh to foot. Repeat several times, then do the same with the other leg. Having massaged both legs, hold your baby by the ankles and gently bicycle them.

3 Hold the soles of your baby's feet together and push them down onto her belly. Hold her feet with your left hand, place your right hand on her lower spine and massage around the base of the spine for about 20 seconds. Gently shake her legs. Bend and straighten them and stroke down the front of her legs to the feet using the weight of your relaxed hands.

4 Rest your hand on your baby's tummy and, using just the weight of your hand, massage in a clockwise direction. This is a sensitive area and if your baby is anxious she may resist you, but persevere; the benefits are great. Place your palms over the centre of her chest and massage upwards and out-wards over her shoulders, always returning to the centre.

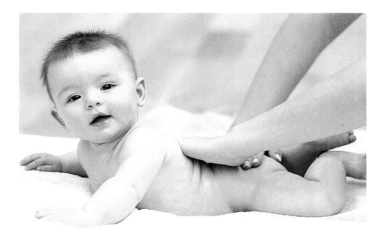

5 Place your hands together, palms over the centre of your baby's chest, and massage upwards and outwards over the shoulders, gently pulling her arms down by her sides. Glide your hands back to the top of her chest and massage upwards and outwards over her shoulders and gently pull her arms out horizontally in line with her shoulders. Repeat several times. Give the arms a little shake. Stroke down the whole body again from shoulders to feet, then pick up your baby, give her a cuddle and turn her onto her tummy.

6 Massage hand over hand down your baby's back with the palms of your hands on either side of the spine. Cup your hands and pat gently with alternate hands from the shoulders to the spine's base. Repeat several times. Massage clockwise around the base of the spine and buttocks. Then massage her legs, pulling them hand over hand through your palms. Stroke from your baby's shoulders down to her toes. To finish, wrap your baby in a warm towel and cuddle her. She will probably be ready for milk and a good sleep.

What you may be feeling

During this time you may be feeling very sensitive, the third day blues may come in (see page 89) and in some cases your breasts may become unbearably sensitive and tender, yet your baby still has to feed (see page 126). To add insult to injury your tummy will be soft and wobbly. Post-natal exercises should begin as soon as possible after the birth, normally the next day. Women who have Caesarean sections will be given special exercises in hospital like pelvic tilts, which they should continue when they go home, but they will generally need to wait six weeks before doing any other form of exercise. Their tummies remain larger because the muscle has been cut and they cannot exercise. This does not mean that the tummy will not return to normal, but it will need to be worked on daily.

Some women find passing urine painful after the birth for a few days. This may be caused by stitches or grazes and relaxing in the bath or shower can help. You could keep a clean water bottle by the toilet and fill it with warm water and then pour it over your vulva while peeing, which can help reduce the stinging. Drink lots of water. Cranberry juice and barley water are also good. A sore perineum plus stitches may make you feel nervous about opening your bowels after the birth; you may feel better if you support your vulva with a pad of tissues when you bear down.

When the placenta separates from the uterus it leaves a wound and, as this heals, it creates a discharge of blood and mucus called the lochia. Blood loss after the birth is heavy and you should expect it to last three to six weeks – use sanitary pads, but not tampons. Passing small clots in the first couple of days is quite normal. Unless the discharge increases, contains lots of fresh blood or clots or smells unpleasant, there should be no need to worry.

In general, this is what happens:
- Heavy red blood appear in the first two days.
- This is followed by less heavy brown blood.
- Then it becomes pink and scanty.

Some women bleed for six weeks after the birth.
To help yourself:
- Rest.
- Eat well – particularly iron-rich foods.
- Take a post-natal vitamin and mineral supplement as it can take quite a long time to recover good nutritional status after giving birth.
- Drink lots of water.

You must tell your GP if:
- You pass large clots.
- The bleeding becomes bright red after the first week.
- The vaginal loss or sanitary pad smells offensive.
- You have lower abdominal pain.
- You have a temperature.

This may mean that a small part of the placenta has been left behind or that you have a uterine infection.

Stitches
Your perineum may feel sore, achy or very painful after the birth and in some cases painkillers may be needed. Otherwise take two baths a day filled with just enough water to cover your bottom to allow you to soak. Tea

> **Pelvic floor exercises increase blood supply to the area and can help ease perineal pain as well as aid healing and getting muscles back in shape.**

tree oil can be helpful: add 4–6 drops to the bath as the water is running. Stitches may also make walking difficult especially when going up and down stairs, getting up and down in a chair and sitting to feed your baby. If this applies to you, you might want to use an inflatable swimming ring to sit on when feeding. In general, most mothers are over the physical pains and discomfort of birth within two to six weeks, so if you are feeling discomfort now, know that it will go away soon.

Weight loss

For most women about half to three-quarters of the gained weight is lost just after the birth. Remember that it has taken nine months to put the weight on, and therefore it might be a good idea to set a target of between six and nine months to get your body shape back and lose the weight.

It takes weeks for your womb to return to its usual size and often quite a lot longer for your tummy to get back to normal. Once you feel strong enough start doing some gentle abdominal exercises. It's important to do pelvic floor exercises as your muscles will have become slack and repeatedly tightening them will help prevent incontinence. Breastfeeding helps the uterus contract so will help you regain your figure.

Fathers after the birth

Many fathers immediately after the birth are simply relieved that the labour is over and that their partner and baby are safe. They then often feel quite alone, wishing that they could have stayed with their new family rather than going back home.

Babies need as much love as they can get from both their parents. If your partner is breastfeeding, then obviously she is the only one who can feed your baby,

---

Restoring your body shape
■ Watch what you eat – don't consume too much chocolate and biscuits.
■ Take some exercise each day – a short walk is enough.
■ Yoga and pilates are good post-natal exercises as they stretch the body so gently and yet effectively.
■ Remember to do your post-natal and pelvic floor exercises daily.
■ Once vaginal bleeding has stopped, swimming is a good all-over body exercise.
■ Watch your posture when sitting and standing as pregnancy may have altered this for a while and poor posture, particularly when feeding and changing your baby, may contribute to a bad back.

---

but at other times your baby will love to be held and cuddled by you. It's important that your baby learns to feel secure with both of you and if you are involved as much as possible, you will bond much better with your newborn baby.

Many fathers are reluctant to get involved in the day-to-day care of their newborn baby because they feel clumsy or think they lack the skills needed, but it's really important to share in the care of your baby. If your partner is breastfeeding, you can share in the experience by winding your baby and settling her afterwards or play with her, massage and bath her. By participating in this way you get to know your baby better and your partner can have some time for herself.

Ensure you have frequent skin-to-skin contact with your baby so you can quickly develop a close bond. Maybe share a big bath together.

Bonding with your baby

Bonding is really just a fancy name for love. Some parents are in love with their baby during their pregnancy, others from birth and don't want to let their baby out of their sight. Others may take weeks or months to bond with their baby. Don't worry, this is all perfectly normal. We all fall in love in different ways and sometimes falling in love takes time. Try to relax and let it happen at its own pace. Certain issues may interrupt the bonding process, however. These are:

◼ Premature labours.
◼ A sick baby.
◼ Unplanned pregnancy.
◼ Financial problems.
◼ Work issues.
◼ Family and relationship problems.
◼ Ante- or post-natal depression.
◼ Long, difficult, slow labour.
◼ Caesarean section.
◼ Post-traumatic birth syndrome (mother experienced a difficult birth).
◼ The baby is the 'wrong sex'.

Seek help from your health visitor or GP if you feel you need support. You could also try some of these ideas:

◼ Skin-to-skin contact is the perfect way to bond. Undress your baby down to her nappy, take off your top and lie under the bedclothes together. Let your baby gaze up at you and make eye contact and chat or sing to her.
◼ Give your baby lots of cuddles. She will love to be held close to you, either in your arms or over your shoulder.
◼ Massage will soothe your baby and is a great way to bond with her.
◼ Limit visitors in the first few days so that you and your partner can spend time alone with your baby.

Coping with a demanding baby

◼ All babies are demanding; they have to be to get what they need, when they need it. Some babies are much more demanding than others. The way in which newborns are demanding is by crying whenever they are put down. The reason for this is simple, the baby has been with you for the whole nine months of the pregnancy and in the early weeks and months may find it difficult to be away from you. The warmth, smell and softness of your body, the sound of your heart beating and your voice will help your baby to feel loved and secure. This is all very well from the baby's point of view but can sometimes make life feel unbearable for the mother.

It's important to remember that the baby is not being naughty. Little babies cannot be naughty. This is a passing phase, but no one can say for sure when this will happen. Some babies find the transition from the womb into the world more difficult than others.

Ways to help your baby:
◼ **Swaddling her can be helpful.**
◼ **Sleep on the blanket that you swaddle the baby in so that it becomes impregnated with your smell, as this will help your baby to feel close to you.**
◼ **Play soft music or even a tape of womb sounds helpful.**
◼ **Rocking her in your arms or a cradle, or pushing her in her pram may soothe her.**
◼ **Snuggling into Daddy's strong arms, listening to his deep voice, may relax her.**
◼ **Sometimes, and quite often, only a cuddle with Mummy will do.**

Post-natal depression

With all the medical science around us, we still don't understand the cause of post-natal depression, yet one in ten women are said to suffer from it. There are varying levels of post-natal depression:

There is a great fear of being seen not to cope but if a mother understands that it's normal to feel low after the birth and that it is only temporary, this may help.

The blues

Sometimes known as post-natal blues or 'baby blues', these are mood swings caused by the huge surge of hormones that your body produces in labour and immediately after the birth. You may feel euphoric one moment and depressed the next and it affects at least half of all mothers. Lack of sleep, the exertion of childbirth, worries about your altered figure and the realisation that life will never be the same can all contribute. It is the most common form of post-natal distress and tends to come a few days after the birth, typically between day three and ten when the milk comes in. You may feel tearful for no apparent reason and completely unable to cope. Don't worry – let the tears flow. Even though you may cry, it doesn't necessarily mean that you are unhappy. The blues will probably stop as suddenly as they began as your hormones begin to settle down. This period may last for about a week after the birth. If it goes on longer, seek advice.

Post-natal blues don't need any treatment other than lots of support, understanding and love. It is a biological and normal response to the hormonal after-effects of having a baby.

■ Try to talk to your partner about how you feel.
■ Accept offers of help from friends and relatives.
■ You will probably be exhausted from labour and lack of sleep, so try to rest.

Post-natal depression

True post-natal depression can come on after birth at any time in the first year, the most common time being between four to six months, although a quarter of cases start in the first month. The common signs are lack of energy or enthusiasm, mother not caring for herself, not sleeping when she has the opportunity to do so or being unable to sleep. She may be tearful and forgetful, have mood swings and no appetite. With this degree of depression, the mother generally cares well for the baby in a practical way but without enthusiasm or joy. The mother may be very upset or cranky with her partner and may feel lonely and unsupported by her partner, family and friends.

Often the mother is aware of how much she is struggling but is frightened to say in case the baby may be taken away from her. She may worry that she may be perceived to be an inadequate mother, not coping like other mothers and not capable in a way that she sees other mothers or society expects mothers to be.

Post-natal depression often goes unnoticed by everyone except the woman herself and most often her partner. It can be so well covered that some men are completely unaware of how their partner is feeling and all too often post-natal depression is only diagnosed retrospectively.

The best therapy for helping to overcome post-natal depression is 'talk' therapy, and as little as six 30-minute sessions can turn the situation around. Events that may trigger post-natal depression include:
■ Relationship problems.
■ Depressive illness in the woman or her family in the past.
■ Difficult pregnancy.
■ Premature labour or a very difficult birth.
■ A baby that is difficult to feed or cries excessively.
■ A sick baby.
■ Single mother.
■ Difficult living conditions and no support network.

■ Divorce.
■ Death in the family.
■ Financial worries.
■ Concern about being absent from work.
■ Use of drugs or alcohol.

Most health visitors are trained to recognise the symptoms of post-natal depression. They can get to know a mother and her circumstances and can give a lot of support. If necessary they can refer her for medical help. Your GP will also be able to help. If you think you are suffering from post-natal depression, you can possibly help yourself to cope better by:

■ Telling your family and friends how you are feeling.
■ Asking them to help by taking over some of the daily routines or childcare that you find particularly difficult.
■ Talking to your health visitor or GP.
■ There may be local groups you can attend; get in touch with the National Childbirth Trust or join a post-natal exercise class (see Useful addresses, page 268).
■ Take vitamins and minerals daily; zinc supplements are often beneficial.
■ Eat well every three hours.
■ Take exercise; even just a walk in the park will be helpful.

Fathers may also suffer from depression after the birth. They have extra responsibilities and may feel that all the attention is now turned towards mother and the baby. Be aware that your partner might be struggling to come to terms with sudden changes in lifestyle, talk things over and try to arrange things so that you can still spend time together as a couple.

Partners and friends can also help a mother to overcome this disabling problem:
■ Make sure she isn't left alone too much.
■ Give her lots of tender, loving care.
■ Talk and listen to her; you will be a huge help if you make an effort to understand how she feels.
■ Remember that this is a major lifestyle change, especially if she worked before and now is at home all day. She needs help re-establishing self-esteem and identity.
■ Don't assume that she will snap out of it if you reason with her – this is unlikely to happen.
■ Try to get her to rest and eat and drink properly.
■ Spend time together with her and the baby so that she can work out how the baby best can fit in with her life.

Post-natal anxiety

This is far more common than post-natal depression but hardly ever spoken about. Anxiety is a natural part of life. Some people are more anxious than others, some less. Some have already worked out coping mechanisms; others find it difficult to cope when anxious. We know that anxiety levels rise at difficult, stressful times of life, that tiredness can lead to anxiety and often increase anxiety levels. So we should not be surprised when new mothers become anxious.

New mothers have to recover from pregnancy and birth and learn how to be a good mother because there is no handbook which comes with newborn babies. A mother's body will feel weaker, she may be in pain from stitches, piles, breastfeeding and Caesarean section scars. She will be tired, but the biggest overriding factor is worrying about the baby. It is a 24-hour, 7-days-a-week responsibility that lasts for years. In addition, many decisions have to be made very quickly after the birth about vaccinations, keeping your baby safe

The importance of rest

■ To care for your baby, you and your partner have to look after yourselves. This is not selfishness but a priority. While the baby is very young the mother has the lion's share of caring for her baby. You will both have sleepless nights and busy days with which to cope. You may find that the days and nights are worked in shifts to begin with, leaving little time for you as a couple. Having meals together often proves to be difficult as the baby has an uncanny way of waking up as soon as hot food reaches the table.

When we get tired, we all become very irritable, rows become easier and feelings fly high. This period should be one of the happiest times of your life and it's a shame to spoil it by becoming over-tired and irritable. Here are some practical ideas that might help:

■ Ask visitors to bring food not flowers.

■ Have as much help around the house as possible; this can be a lifesaver.

■ Where possible, use family and friends to help in whatever ways they can.

■ If family and friends are unable to help because of geographical obstacles, think about employing a mother's help or cleaner. This is expensive but for your health it may be the greatest treat you can give yourself. As little as four weeks can really help change things around.

■ Try to catch up on sleep when your baby naps during the day or at least find the time to relax with your feet up. It's often useful to turn off the phone to ensure uninterrupted rest.

■ Go to bed as early as possible.

■ Eat well during the day and try to take a walk each day or do some yoga.

■ Let your partner take over, even if it is just for one night per week (he can use expressed breast milk) to allow you a good night's sleep.

and well, trying to look after yourself and your relationship, keeping the house clean and presentable and having food to eat at meal times.

It makes me feel dizzy just thinking about it. In a working environment, skill juggling is a recognised achievement that brings promotion, financial reward, admiration of others. The multi-tasking skills that are needed by mothers are not often recognised and rarely appreciated. They are taken for granted, but wrongly.

As time goes by, the anxieties do reduce, life returns to a more normal pace, sleep returns. In the meantime, help is at hand. You are not alone. Talk about how you are feeling, join groups, even if you are not a 'group' person. Post-natal groups are different from therapy groups as all the mothers are in the same boat, which brings you closer together. You will meet mothers with older babies and you can see that improvements lie ahead. These mothers will share their tested, successful (for them) ways in which they coped. Also:

■ Rest when you can.

■ Eat well every three hours.

■ Avoid sugar as this can give you immediate highs and plunging lows, increasing anxiety.

■ Avoid alcoholic and caffeinated drinks.

■ Take extra vitamins and minerals.

■ Have early nights when possible.

■ Buy in food through Internet shopping or get someone to do your food shopping for you.

If your anxieties are increasing rather than decreasing, talk to your health visitor or GP, as they may be able to help you or refer you to a specialist who may help you discover the root of your anxieties. Highly anxious mothers can produce highly anxious babies. Help is needed to prevent this happening.

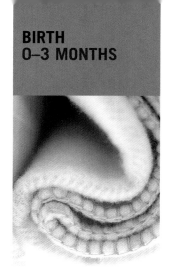

SLEEPING

One of the biggest challenges of being a parent is adjusting to a disturbed sleep pattern. Whoever coined the phrase 'sleeping like a baby' could never have had children of his own. Nothing you can do will make a newborn baby sleep more or less than she wants to; even the sleepiest newborn will tend to sleep for only three-hour stretches before waking up hungry or in need of the comfort and reassurance of your presence. Many babies take two naps each day, one in the morning and one in the afternoon, while other babies prefer to cat nap rather than sleep for longer stretches during the day.

Sleeping patterns

Newborn babies sleep on average about 16–17 hours a day. Unfortunately you will need to fit in with your baby's sleep pattern and rest when you can as your baby is unlikely to have a predictable sleeping pattern until around eight weeks when she is able to sleep for longer stretches.

Most babies will not manage to sleep through the night until they are three or four months old as up until this point they are physically too immature and their stomachs are too small to hold enough milk to keep them going through the night. At first this sleep is most probably evenly spaced around the clock with eight hours' sleep during the day and eight hours at night. Night feeds are inevitable. Your baby's tiny tummy means that she can't go much longer than two to four hours without waking for milk. Your baby will probably drop off to sleep after most feeds.

Newborns up to the age of six months have shorter sleeping patterns and therefore wake up more easily than older babies. Babies also double their birth weight in the first three to six months and consequently require frequent feeds during the night.

How much sleep does your baby need?

This is only a rough guideline so don't worry if your baby's sleep pattern isn't exactly the same. How much your baby sleeps will depend on how busy her day has been, how much she has eaten and how well she is feeling.

Age of your baby	Total sleep needed	Daytime sleep	Night-time sleep
Newborn	17 hours	8 hours	9 hours
Two months	15–16 hours	3–4 hours	12 hours
Four months	14–15 hours	2–3 hours	12 hours
Six months	14 hours	2–3 hours	12 hours
Nine months	14 hours	2–3 hours	12 hours
One year	13 hours	2 hours	11 hours

Reducing the risk of Sudden Infant Death Syndrome

Sudden Infant Death Syndrome (SIDS), which used to be known as cot death, is the sudden and unexpected death of a baby for no obvious reasons. In 2000, 333 babies died from SIDS in England and Wales, 80% of these occurred among babies under six months. Since 1991 the number of babies dying has reduced by over 70% after parents started following the advice below.

■ Studies have shown that there is less risk of SIDS if babies are put down to sleep on their backs. Should your baby vomit, she is not more likely to choke in this position. If your baby has rolled onto her tummy, turn her onto her back again and tuck her in, but don't feel you have to keep watch. At about five months it is normal for babies to roll over and that is fine; this is the age at which the risk of cot death falls rapidly, but still put your baby on her back to sleep.

■ Place your baby with her feet at the foot of the cot to prevent her from wriggling down under the covers. Do not put her to sleep on her side because she can easily roll onto her front from this position.

■ It is a good idea to keep your baby's cot in the room with you at night for the first six months. However, although it is lovely to have your baby in bed with you and the link between SIDS and having your baby in bed with you is unclear, the recommendations from the Department of Health err on the side of caution. So while your baby is tiny, let her sleep in her own cot as much as possible.

■ If your baby is under a year, do not use soft bedding like duvets, quilts or pillows as they incur an increased risk of SIDS. Instead, use one or more layers of lightweight blankets with air holes in them. Babies who are unwell with an increased temperature need fewer not more bedclothes.

■ There is an increased risk of SIDS if your baby gets too hot; the ideal temperature for her room is between 16 and 20°C. To keep an eye on the temperature, use a room thermometer – ideally a thermostatically controlled heater that will switch off if the room gets too warm. Don't position your cot near a radiator or heater. If your baby is sweating or her tummy feels hot to the touch, take off some of the bedding. Don't worry if her hands, face or feet feel cool; this is normal.

■ Keep your baby's head uncovered and remove cot bumpers as soon as she can sit or wriggle around. Babies lose heat through their head so if it is buried in a bumper heat loss will be reduced, increasing the risk of SIDS.

■ Sleep your baby on a new, firm, clean, dry mattress. Make sure that it doesn't sag or show signs of deterioration. Ventilated mattresses (with holes) are not necessary.

■ Do not sleep on a sofa with your baby.

■ A mother who smokes in pregnancy increases the risk of SIDS. Don't let anyone smoke in the same room as your baby. The risk is doubled for babies of parents who smoke and it increases further with the number of cigarettes smoked.

Equipment planner: bedtime

Moses basket

This is ideal for your baby to sleep in during the day as it is easy to move around the house so that you can keep your baby close to you. At night you can put it next to your own bed. The disadvantage is that your baby will probably outgrow this by the age of six months. Moses baskets are light to carry as they are made from wicker or palm-leaves and you can buy separate wooden stands to put them on.

Carrycot

A carrycot that fits on a frame with wheels gives you a cot and pram in one. However, carrycots are generally heavier to carry than a Moses basket. Your baby will outgrow a carrycot quite quickly so it's not worth buying a really expensive one – perhaps you could borrow one from a friend.

Crib

This looks very attractive and being slightly larger than a Moses basket, will last longer. But it is not so practical as it is not portable.

Cot

Although at first your baby may seem rather lost in a full-sized cot, she will soon grow into it and it will last until she is about two years old. You can also buy a bedside cot that has adjustable heights and is on casters so you can line it up to the height of your own bed and sleep with your baby next to you. The side drops down and is removeable to stow under the cot.

What to look for when choosing

■ Make sure the drop side is easy for you to lower (even with one hand) but not easy enough for your baby to operate.
■ Check that the cot has a multi-position base, which can be adjusted as your baby grows.
■ Ensure the cot is sturdy enough for an active toddler who might start wanting to climb out.

Cot bed

This is suitable from birth to around five years. It is larger than a standard cot and converts to a toddler-sized bed.

Mattress

Buy a firm, flat, well-fitting mattress that is easy to clean and conforms to British or European Safety Standards.

It is recommended that you buy a new mattress for every child because used mattresses are thought to increase the risk of SIDS (see page 93).

Baby monitor

You can choose a plug-in or a portable monitor but I would advise that you choose the latter because it allows you to move around your home while monitoring your baby.

Baby monitors should not be used as a substitute for checking on your baby in person. Indeed, if you have a small flat or house, you may not need to get a monitor at all as you may easily hear your baby cry wherever you are in your home.

What to look for when choosing
- A sound-activated light display that allows you to turn down the volume but you can still see whether your baby is crying or not.
- Two channels, allowing you to switch channels to avoid interference.
- A parent unit that warns that batteries are low or if you are out of range.
- A rechargeable model, which is initially more expensive but it will save you money in the long run.
- A talk-back feature, which allows parents to respond to their babies.

Baby sleeping bags

These are now becoming very popular, they tend to be cosier than sheets and blankets and your baby can't kick them off so she won't wake up cold and crying. Also she can't wriggle under a sleeping bag and get overheated.

There are two different weights of sleeping bag. For the winter you will want 2–3 tog (equivalent to an adult 13-tog duvet) and for summer you will want 0.5–1 tog (the equivalent of two sheets). Choose one with deep armholes to allow air to circulate. When in the sleeping bag your baby only needs to wear a cotton sleepsuit in the winter or a cotton vest or T-shirt in summer.

Make sure the sleeping bag is a good fit so that your baby's arms cannot slip out, which might result in your baby slipping down in the bag and her face and head becoming covered.

Q Is it OK for me to bring my baby to sleep with me in my bed?

A It's lovely to have your baby in bed with you for a cuddle or a feed and some parents find it easier to bring their baby into bed to sleep with them, especially if there are other people in the house who they don't want to disturb. It also makes it easier for night feeds.

However, parents shouldn't share a bed with their baby if they are smokers, obese, unwell or have been drinking alcohol, taking drugs or medication that makes them drowsy or if they are excessively tired.

If you plan to sleep with your baby, don't let her head get covered and don't use a duvet either on top or under your baby, or pillows, because of the danger of suffocation. Use lightweight blankets – overheating is thought to be one of the causes of SIDS and your baby will have to cope with the body heat from you and your partner. Also take care to place your baby in a position where she won't fall out of bed and be careful not to put her close to the wall if there is any chance she could slip between the mattress and wall.

Alternatively keep your baby close by, placing her Moses basket next to your bed, or remove one side from a cot and position it so it is level with your bed and the cot sides are touching it. Ensure there is no danger that your baby could accidentally slip between the two mattresses.

Bedtime routine

It is hard to offer advice about a daily routine to start with as babies are all so different. As a result, some of the 'expert' advice available from childcare manuals can result in enormous anxiety for parents. The most important thing is to develop a routine that suits you and your baby. The routines in the following chapters should be used flexibly and only as a guide.

As your baby grows, becomes more active, sleeps less during the day and eats more, she may well sleep through the night of her own accord but many babies cannot achieve this on their own. It is up to you to steer your baby away from around-the-clock habits and encourage a consistent bedtime routine, which will signal to your baby that it is time to sleep. Don't start too soon before your baby's bedtime. For example, if your baby goes to bed at 7pm, start your bedtime routine at 6.15–6.30pm.

■ Bath your baby. Some parents massage their baby as well (see page 82).

■ Take your baby to a quiet, dark bedroom to feed.

■ Put your baby down in her cot/crib when she is still just awake, allowing her to settle down to sleep herself. She may cry. Stay close and firmly rest a hand on her 'comfort' spot, e.g. her tummy or head. Then sit by your baby's cot, stroking and soothing her as necessary, maybe singing some lullabies. Over several nights gradually move your chair further away until your baby falls asleep with you outside the door.

Some babies find a bath stimulating rather than relaxing. If this applies to your baby, bathe her during the day and leave out of the bedtime routine.

Three-month routine

■ Don't worry about getting your baby into a set routine in the early weeks; she is too young to respond. By three or four months, however, most babies are more settled and your baby may naturally begin to sleep longer at night as she is able to go longer without the need for food. It can be a good idea to wake your baby for a late night feed at your bedtime in the hope that she will then be able to go for six or seven hours without a feed. A typical routine may be like the one set out below, but use this as a guide only as every baby is different.

Possible routine	
6–7am	Wakes up and has milk feed, play, nappy change.
8–9am	Back to sleep.
10am	Wakes up and has milk feed, wash, change into daytime clothes, play.
11am	Out in pram or sling – may sleep.
12 noon–1pm	Midday milk feed, play, nappy change.
2–4pm	Sleep.
4–6pm	Wake, nappy change, play, milk feed.
6–7pm	Bath, massage, night clothes, play.
7.30–8pm	Milk feed in bedroom, bed.
11pm–12 midnight	Milk feed (if you choose to wake your baby before you go to sleep).
2–3am	Possible milk feed.

Many babies will be going through the night at this age but may still wake up early at around 5 or 6am. Your baby should sleep for no more than about three hours during the day.

■ Try not to pick up your baby when settling her as this teaches her to cry and then wait to be picked up. Older babies learn very quickly to cry for rewards: the reward of being picked up, for instance. The more they are rewarded, the more difficult they become to settle.

■ If your baby cries and does not settle, leave her for a few minutes, then go back in, stroke her and speak soothingly. Leave the room again returning after five minutes if she is still awake, repeating the soothing. Gradually increase the time you are gone.

Learning how to get to sleep

When your baby was in your womb, your walking lulled her to sleep. Newborn babies enjoy being rocked or fed to sleep but, for your own sanity, start good habits now by letting your baby fall asleep on her own.

The nature of our sleep cycles means that we all wake briefly at intervals during the night. The difference between a baby who 'sleeps' all night and one who wakes her parents frequently is that the 'good' sleeper sends herself back to sleep whereas the 'bad' sleeper needs her parents to re-settle her. One of the greatest gifts you can give your baby is to teach her how to fall asleep by herself.

■ From birth, gently wake your baby if she falls asleep at the breast or bottle before putting her down so that she is aware of where she is and that feeding is over.

■ If your baby drops off during a feed, hold her against your shoulder and gently rub her back to help her wake up a little and then put her down in her Moses basket when she's drowsy but still awake.

■ Newborns enjoy being rocked to sleep and it might be the only solution for some small babies who seem to find motion soothing. But spend less and less time rocking your baby until she can settle by herself.

■ Try adding a couple of drops of lavender oil or camomile to your baby's bath as they are calming. You could also massage your baby with a tablespoon of olive oil mixed with 1–2 drops of lavender or camomile.

■ If your baby doesn't seem to want to go to sleep, she may need more stimulation during the day (see pages 110-17 for ideas).

Staying asleep

In the first three months, all babies will wake for feeds. It is very rare for them to sleep all night. It would be unkind to leave a baby hungry, so if she cries, go to her and feed her as soon as possible. However, it is important not to help your baby develop bad habits so:

■ Make night-time as boring as possible so don't talk or play with her.

■ Keep lights dim.

■ Don't change your baby's nappy unless necessary.

■ Wait for your baby to wake up. Lots of babies make noise and sucking movements in their sleep. When left

> During the first few weeks of life get your baby used to noises such as television, music, the washing machine and dog so they sleep through undisturbed. If you are too quiet, your baby will wake at every noise.

to their own devices they may drift off to sleep again. Jumping up too soon will encourage your baby to wake more often. At night it is the one time when it is better to wait for your baby to cry a little rather than respond to early feed cues. But do not allow your baby to become distressed or you may have difficulty feeding her.

■ If you are bottle feeding, make night-time feeds easier by having a bottle of milk ready in the fridge and a thermos flask filled with hot water ready to warm your baby's milk. Do not keep milk warm during the night.

■ Babies can't control their own body temperature and they can't kick off the bedclothes when they are too hot. Your baby may cry when she feels uncomfortable but this can easily be misinterpreted as a cry for hunger.

If your baby wakes frequently during the night and is not really hungry, check whether there are any other reasons for her waking up. Is she too hot or cold? Is her clothing too tight? Is she wet or dirty? Is she unwell?

Keeping a safe temperature

Each baby has her own ideal temperature and soon you will work out what suits your baby. It is important that babies are not overheated as this is a contributory factor to SIDS (see page 93).

■ In summer, if it is very warm, your baby may not need any bedclothes other than a sheet.

■ Babies lose excess heat from their heads so make sure your baby's head is not covered with bedclothes.

■ If your baby is unwell and develops a fever, remove some bedclothes and, if necessary, clothing so she can cool down. Young babies cannot regulate their own body temperature.

■ Babies should never sleep with a hot-water bottle or electric blanket, next to a radiator, heater or fire, or in direct sunshine.

To check your baby's body temperature, touch the nape of the neck, or slide a finger inside her babygro to feel the breastbone. You would expect these areas to feel warm but if they feel hot or wet, take off one of the covers or a layer of clothing. If it feels cold, wrap up the baby more.

Swaddling

Many babies feel more secure and sleep better if they are swaddled – use a lightweight material like a brushed cotton sheet. Your baby should wear a vest or babygro before being swaddled, but don't overheat her by then adding a blanket. Some babies like to be swaddled with both their arms wrapped up but some prefer to keep a hand free to suck on. After about eight weeks it is best not to wrap up your baby as she will probably want more freedom of movement. You can half swaddle, leaving arms free, or try using a baby sleeping bag.

There is no evidence to suggest that swaddling is unsafe. The baby with brisk reflexes that wake her up will enjoy it but those that like to suck their thumbs or fingers will hate it. Try it to see what happens.

How to swaddle

1 Spread a cotton blanket on a flat surface with one corner folded down about 15 cm (6 in). If it is large, double it over first. Place you baby on the blanket diagonally with her head above the folded corner.

2 Take the corner near your baby's left arm and pull it across her body. Lift the right arm and tuck it under her back. At first, your baby will probably lie with her arms bent and hands by her shoulders.

3 Pull the other side across your baby's right arm (elbow flexed) and tuck it snugly under her back on the left side, again leaving her hand free.

4 Lift your baby a little and tuck the end of the blanket under your baby's feet and body. If your baby prefers, you can wrap her below the arms, leaving her arms free to move around.

CRYING

Babies need to be able to communicate with their mums and dads. Unlike adults, who communicate consciously with language and subconsciously with their bodies, babies combine the use of their bodies and crying to inform their parents of what they need. Learning to understand your baby's use of body language is very important in developing your relationship. It is worth spending time simply watching and enjoying how your baby is communicating with you: look at her facial expressions, hand movements and eye-to-eye contact.

Why your baby cries

All babies cry, some for long stints, two or three times per day, others little and often. Crying is always distressing for the parents as we view the baby's crying in an adult way – something is wrong – and forget that it's a small baby's only way to communicate. In many ways, it's reassuring to know that your baby will cry when she needs something. As a parent our primitive instincts are to protect our baby and we search frantically for reasons for the crying so we can try and stop it. If you can accept there are times when your baby needs to cry to express her emotions and can relax about it that will help her to calm down.

All mothers hear their babies crying more loudly than anyone else's. A mother has a hormonal release that makes her want to care for her own baby instantly. No other person will have the unique bonding with this child. Crying can be extraordinarily difficult to listen to and may cause a great deal of concern for parents, but remember that crying is your baby's way of communicating and that they often have a lot to say. Sometimes your baby may just be bored and be seeking stimulation.

Your baby has many cries that will all sound the same in the first few days but, as time passes, you will learn to recognise your baby's mood by the different types of crying that she has. Your baby will also use facial expressions or body movements to help you understand her needs.

As babies grow they find other ways to communicate and change to smiling or cooing and it is reassuring to know that by the time they are four months old they are likely to cry much less.

Dummies

Many babies are perfectly content without dummies; however, other babies have an emotional need to suck and it would be cruel not to allow this to happen. You will probably see your baby sucking her hands or fingers on the scan and the best source of comfort sucking is your baby's own hands as they are always available and more hygienic than anything else. If your baby cries a lot, doesn't want to suck on her own hands and seems miserable, a dummy may help her to settle, but use it sparingly – try not to pop it into her mouth if she is not crying. The more you limit the use of a dummy, the easier it will be to break the habit later.

There are pros and cons with dummies and you have to see what works for you and your baby (see below). However, if a dummy makes the difference between a crying baby or a peaceful evening, I know which I would choose.

Dummies and finger sucking are only a problem if made into one. Otherwise they each work well in their own way. However, if you do choose to use a dummy, it is important that they are only used in the short term. Babies can remain attached to certain things for many years – whether a cloth, a favourite toy or a dummy, which they will want to keep with them all the time – and so it may be wise to remove the dummy at about six months old or restrict its use to bedtime only.

If you are going to use a dummy, purchase a few to give you a supply of sterile dummies should the dummy in use be dropped. You can also leave a spare dummy next to your baby in her cot should she need to find it in the middle of the night.

Sterilise a dummy every time it falls on the floor. Replace dummies as soon as they get worn as split teats can cause choking.

> ### Q Should I leave my baby to cry?
>
> A I don't believe in leaving very young babies to cry as this is a form of rejection. It also takes much longer to calm a tiny baby who has been crying for 15 minutes than a baby who has only been crying for a couple of minutes.
>
> Before three months crying has nothing to do with being naughty and you will not spoil your baby by giving him the love and affection that he craves. On the contrary, responding to your baby will make him feel secure and create a loving bond. Besides, if you don't attend to your baby, he will probably just cry for longer until he eventually gets what he needs and you feel stressed out.
>
> It is better to respond to your baby when he starts crying and see if you can soothe him. However, once you have tried everything and he is still crying, it may be better to leave him for a while. The exception to this rule is bedtime when babies need to learn that once they have been put down for the night it is time to sleep and the party is over (see page 158).

The advantages and disadvantages of using a dummy

Adavantages	Disadvantages
■ It can help a baby to settle herself. ■ It allows a baby who needs to suck for comfort the opportunity to do this. ■ A newborn baby does not have the ability to get her hands and fingers into her mouth without help. ■ If a baby is content to suck on a dummy, it gives parents more time for themselves. ■ It can help a baby who cries excessively to calm down. ■ It leads to fewer problems with teeth. Sucking on a finger may cause rounding of the upper jaw, leading to wiggly teeth at some stage. This may require orthodontic treatment.	■ If your baby relies on a dummy to fall asleep, what is going to happen in the middle of the night when she can't find it and put it back in her mouth? ■ When a dummy falls out, an adult needs to put it back. ■ Dummies need to be sterilised. ■ Using a dummy frequently in the daytime may limit your baby's experimentation with new sounds. ■ Babies can come to rely on dummies and will not settle without one.

When your baby cries

Adding body language to a baby's cry can help parents determine the plan of action. Your baby may be hungry, uncomfortable, too hot or cold or have a dirty nappy. She may want the reassurance of a cuddle or she may just be fed up or tired and whingey. All these different cries will be heard at various times, some more often than others. As a parent you will learn all the main types of crying very quickly.

Some babies are just unsettled for no apparent reason and they cry a lot. Often when they develop the ability to play and express themselves in other ways, the crying reduces.

The problem	The signs	What to do
Hunger If your baby has been asleep for a few hours and cries insistently it may be that she needs some food. Tiny tummies can't store much milk. Bathing or changing your baby when she is hungry can cause crying as it will delay your baby's feed and irritate her.	A hungry cry is usually a fretful cry, which becomes louder and more urgent each second, coupled with head movements and sucking/rooting action. It is better to learn quickly body language cues such as fist sucking or tongue flicking or back arching while looking for breast or bottle rather than wait for your baby to be very hungry.	If your baby is hungry then nothing else will comfort her. If she isn't getting enough milk from the breast she'll continue to cry, so make sure she latches on properly in order to stimulate the let-down reflex (see page 119). Also make sure you get adequate rest to keep up a good milk supply. If you are bottle feeding, check the teat hole size to ensure the flow is OK. There will be times when your baby goes through a growth spurt and needs to be fed more frequently.
Discomfort Some babies feel very uncomfortable if they have a wet or dirty nappy and some even cry when they are doing a poo. Your baby may continue to cry when you are changing her but will generally calm down once in a dry nappy and dressed.	Other than being hungry, this is another possible reason for crying and waking in the middle of the night or too soon after being put down to sleep. Your baby may squirm, moving her bottom from side to side, if she has a dirty nappy.	Check to see if your baby's nappy needs changing and to see if there is any sign of nappy rash. Also check to see if her clothing or bedding is causing her discomfort.
Tiredness When babies become over-tired they often cry. You know what you are like when you are tired – ratty and irritable – and babies are no different. Lack of sleep can make your baby miserable and although she may be tired, she will need help to relax.	This will be a moaning type of cry. Often the eyes are shut or closing, or slowly close and spring open several times. There may be eye rubbing, yawning or head movement from side to side.	It's best to keep to some sort of sleep routine so your baby doesn't get over-tired, and arrange visitors or outings around these times (see page 63). Sometimes babies settle better if you swaddle them in a soft cotton sheet (see page 99). Keep to a regular bedtime routine (see page 96).

The problem	The signs	What to do
Loneliness, boredom Babies often cry because they want company or want to be held. Sometimes it's comforting enough just to know that you are in the room.	This will be eyes wide open staring straight at you and it can vary from quiet whimpering to major sobs depending on how frustrated she is. Hands may be held up to you as if saying 'pick me up'. She will probably cry intermittently, pausing to see if you are coming to her.	Young babies get frustrated because they are not able to do much for themselves. Being tucked up in a crib all day isn't very exciting but your baby will love being a part of your everyday life (see pages 110–17 for ideas). Take your baby out but don't restrict her to the pram; sometimes hold her in your arms or put her in a forward-facing sling so she can look around
The need to suck Some babies need to 'comfort suck' and will cry if they can't find anything to suck on – hence a dummy can be useful. But some babies are happy to suck on their own fingers or thumb.	Your baby cries and opens her mouth to suck but if you give her a bottle or breast she just comfort sucks without taking much milk.	Comfort sucking on a dummy can make your baby less keen to latch on to the breast and suck hard enough to stimulate the 'let-down' reflex. However, for some babies it may be the only way to stop them crying (see the previous page). By the age of four weeks, many babies find it comforting to suck their thumb.
Too hot or cold Babies sometimes cry if they feel too hot or too cold.	Your baby's cry will vary according to the level of discomfort and the length of time she has been feeling this way. She may feel clammy if hot and her hands and feet may have a bluish tinge if cold.	Feel your baby to see whether she feels hot or cold. If she is too hot, adjust her clothing as necessary (see page 98). If she's cold, her skin will feel cold and lips may look a little blue and she could be trembling. You can warm her with a cuddle, clothing or extra blankets.
Anger Babies can become angry if no one attends to them when they cry.	This will be a sharp cry. Her eyes may be open or closed and her chest may be pushed at you. Your baby may avoid eye contact with you.	Babies this young forget why they are crying after ten minutes so you may be able to distract yours. After you have tried everything to pacify your baby, put her down so she learns you are not always going to pick her up the moment she cries.
Your baby is unwell Your baby may have earache, abdominal pain, a blocked nose, fever, etc.	Babies can cry in a quiet, pitiful way if they are unwell. If they are in pain, the cry is often high-pitched, urgent and continuous (see page 162). If she has wind or abdominal pain, your baby's legs may be pulled up to her chest.	Check to see if there are any signs of stomach upset or fever, if your baby is lethargic, her skin looks different or she has rapid or shallow breathing. Rocking your baby in your arms may soothe her and sucking may offer a distraction if she is in pain. If you are worried, call a doctor. Young babies can quickly become seriously ill.
For no apparent reason The cry that is most difficult to cope with – it might just be that your baby has become over-tired as the day has gone on but the cause may be colic (see page 104).	It can very difficult dealing with a baby who cries for no apparent reason because it frequently coincides with the time when a mother is at her most tired. It generally comes on at about 4pm and may go on for many hours.	Sometimes your baby wants the reassurance that you are there for her and she will stop crying if you give her a cuddle. If this does not work, try: walking around the room, taking her for a walk or a drive, lying her on your chest and stroking her firmly and rhythmically, or massaging her half an hour before her usual crying time.

Colic

Despite over 40 years of research, it still remains unclear what causes colic. Some people think it is just the extreme of normal crying at a time when both parent and baby are tired, but the most widely held view is that colic is a spasm in the gut. The gut becomes hard, the baby screams either with knees bent and a red face or becomes pale and arches her back. It tends to occur most commonly between 4pm and midnight. The period of crying can be the same every day, lasting three to four hours and, in some cases, five. It is often confused with hunger – the mother offers food, little is taken and then the crying begins again. It suddenly stops when the spasm passes.

Is it really colic?

Colic generally starts at two months and has usually settled by six months. Typical symptoms are:

- Long periods of crying, which are usually worse in the evening and your usual efforts at comforting fail.
- Your baby doesn't just cry but screams and draws her knees up to her belly in pain.
- Your baby's abdomen feels rigid and hard.
- Your baby goes red in the face and may clench her fists.
- Her tummy may be distended and feel taut and she may pass wind.
- A similar pattern is repeated daily at about the same time.

The colic may be due to trapped wind, which causes pain in your baby's tummy. Sometimes a cow's milk allergy or an intolerance to lactose (the natural sugar found in milk) can cause discomfort and can be mistaken for colic. If you are breastfeeding, you may need to cut dairy products or other foods out of your own diet.

Whatever the cause, having a colicky baby in the house can make life miserable for everyone concerned.

But don't despair: try some of these suggestions to soothe your baby and bring some comfort to you.

- Sometimes your baby can be soothed by laying her on her tummy on your lap or up on your shoulder and swaying her from side to side while you rub her back.
- Try rocking her in your arms, carrying her in a sling, taking her out in her pram or popping her in a car seat and taking her for a drive.
- Some people believe that feeding your baby in a more upright position may help to prevent the build-up of wind that might be the cause of colic.
- Massage and/or a warm bath taken just before her crying period may help.
- If you are bottle feeding, you may want to try using a teat that slows down the milk flow to prevent your baby from gulping in air. You could also try using a different style of bottle.
- Perhaps seek advice about whether an alternative to cow's milk formula may be appropriate for your baby.
- Try infusing a few fennel and mint leaves in boiling water for a few minutes. Strain, leave until lukewarm and give in a bottle. Make this up fresh each time.
- Try colic drops like Infacol or gripe water. You can also buy drops that break down the lactose in formula milk, making it easier to digest.
- Give the baby a dummy or finger to suck on.
- Cranial osteopathy may alleviate colic (see box opposite).

Reflux

Reflux is not colic, it is a condition that needs, in its most severe state, to be treated with conventional medicine. The picture may be similar to colic, with lots of crying and difficulties in feeding, but over time the situation worsens. More information is given on page 120.

Coping with crying

A baby's constant crying can wear anyone down, but a tired mum recovering from a long labour or Caesarean with engorged breasts, a flabby tummy and lack of sleep, can feel truly drained. If you feel at the end of your tether and angry with your baby, try to remember that this won't last forever and your baby will grow out of it. You may feel that your baby's constant crying will push you over the edge and worry that you might harm your own baby. These are all normal feelings so try not feel guilty. Put your baby safely in her cot or pram and calm yourself. Many women find a crying baby very frustrating and hard work. It's not about you and it doesn't mean you are a bad mother. It is simply something that your baby goes through.

Try to organise support for yourself during these daily bouts. Go to your mother's/mother-in-law's house, ask a friend around, see if your partner can come home early during this time to help you.

If your partner is at home, it may help to look after your baby on a rota basis; say, 30 minutes on and 30 minutes off.

If possible, put your baby in another room for a while and put on some music or listen to the television.

Get help, talk to someone, a friend, your midwife or a GP, as they may be able to help.Or talk to someone at Serene (see Useful addresses, page 268).

Reschedule family routine so that the minimum has to be achieved during this time.

Most babies respond better to vertical rather than horizontal holding, especially if being held on the left side. This may be because they can hear the heartbeat of the person cradling them and they find it soothing.

Paediatric/cranial osteopathy

The aim of paediatric osteopathy is to correct imbalances in a baby's body structure that may have occurred within the womb or during birth, which may be responsible for an unsettled or unhappy baby. For example, it can help to realign the malleable bones of the skull, which mould themselves to fit through the mother's birth canal during delivery. A paediatric osteopath uses his hands to locate and release areas of abnormal tension and compression. It is particularly effective on young babies because of the pace of development and the flexibility of their bodies, and can help with many problems including colic and sleeping disorders. Make sure you choose a qualified osteopath who has a diploma in paediatric osteopathy (DPO).

Try to find a mother and baby group where you can discover how other mums cope.

Sometimes you just have to accept that your nights are going to be disturbed and the only way to catch up on much needed sleep is to take naps during the day when your baby is sleeping.

You may feel that you have lost your sense of identity and all you do is care for your baby and home. How you feel has a lot to do with the way you look so take time to look after yourself. Let your baby sit and watch you while you put on a video and do your post-natal exercises or yoga. Many health clubs have crèche facilities so take advantage of these or treat yourself to a trip to the hairdresser.

It's also important to make sure that you continue to eat a good diet as you will need all your strength at this time. Eat plenty of iron-rich foods (see page 17).

DEVELOPING

In the first year a baby develops faster than at any other time in her life. She changes from a tiny infant who sleeps and feeds most of the time to a child who is beginning to walk and talk. Throughout this book there are planners charting the average development of a baby from her first week through to her first birthday. But every child develops at her own rate so use these charts only as a guide – let your baby take things at her own pace.

How babies develop

The first part of the body that your baby learns to control is her head, then her shoulders, arms, hands and fingers, followed by her back, until at eight or nine months she is beginning to sit unsupported.

Learning through play is important to babies and young children and you will be your baby's favourite playmate so try to make time to have fun together. Your baby learns by example, but she also needs love and encouragement to give her the confidence to reach her full potential. The most important influence on your baby will be her relationship with you.

Play is an important way for babies to practise new skills; they explore their world by testing and experi-menting. Fine motor skills develop very slowly because they involve the intricate timing and interaction of dozens of small muscle groups. A baby learns fine motor skills through play. You may think they are just banging an object against a wall, but they are actually finding out all sorts of things like how to pick it up and move it, how heavy it is and what kind of noise it makes when it is dropped!

You may wonder why babies put everything in their mouth. They do this because they generally develop from head to toe, and to begin with, babies can discrim-inate texture and shape much better with their mouth than with their hands so they prefer to explore objects with their tongue and lips rather than their fingers.

Young babies need frequent unrestricted movement, whether it's lying under a baby gym or rolling around on a mat. They need to grow, learn and move at what-ever rate they find comfortable, and entirely at their own pace. You should let your baby play regularly throughout the day for at least 15 minutes at a time. They must have the freedom to learn from experience.

A baby's head seems large in proportion to her body due to the rate of growth of a baby's brain in the first year. The brain grows dramatically between birth and

You will need to find a suitable safe play area for your baby. A special playroom in some tucked-away part of the house is no good. Your baby will want to be near you and the centre of activity. The ideal scenario would be a dining room off the kitchen that could perhaps be made into a playroom. A baby is much more likely to occupy herself and play happily if you are close by, and can check on her.

three years and most of the growth takes place in the first year. Although learning never stops, the growth and activity slows down so that once your baby is three her head and body should be more in proportion.

A baby's brain doubles in weight in the first year because of the growth in the number of connections between brain cells. These connections only begin to form when a baby has to think about something. Stimulating your baby's senses with new sights, sounds and textures helps these connections form. The connections that are used most frequently are strenthened and the connections that aren't stimulated are lost.

Premature babies

If a baby is premature, her development will be behind that of a full-term baby by the number of weeks early that she was born. In 80–90% of cases, premature babies catch up, but it is important that parents of premature babies get regular developmental checks and if they have any worries they should seek help.

Growth in the first year

A newborn baby may weigh anything from 2.5 to 4.5 kg (5½ to 10 lb). Generally, a baby loses about 10% of her birth weight in the first few days of life, which is usually regained after about ten days. The average weight gain per week for the first weeks of life is 100–175 g (4–6 oz). In the next six months she gains weight rapidly, probably at a rate of about 1 kg (2 lb 4 oz) a month. From seven to 12 months her weight gain slows down to about 500 g (1 lb 2 oz) a month.

It's best to weigh your baby before a feed and when she is naked. There is no need to weigh her more than once or twice a month. You can get your baby weighed and measured at your local health clinic. If you take her to be weighed every week, you will probably find that sometimes she gains quite a lot of weight while at others she gains none at all. Babies don't grow at a constant rate. Some remain around the same weight for a while and then have a growth spurt, so don't worry if your baby doesn't gain weight each week. If your baby seems happy and lively, then the chances are she is getting all the nourishment she needs.

Over a period of a few weeks your baby should show a pretty steady growth line roughly parallel to the middle line of her weight chart (see page 264). However, if there is a sudden drop or increase in measurements, it might be due to feeding difficulties or illness and your health visitor or GP will be able to help.

Girls and boys

In the first year (and through to puberty), the development of girls is often in advance of boys. Research shows there are differences in the way a baby girl's brain processes information about faces, which suggests girls are developmentally in advance of boys. Girls tend to learn to walk earlier than boys – partly because they are usually lighter. They can have a more acute sense of hearing and their language skills often develop more quickly. This is because the left side of the brain develops earlier in girls so their fine motor skills and speech develops earlier too.

Boys are more prone to language disorders like dyspraxia and dyslexia as well as hyperactivity and attention deficit disorder. Dyspraxia and dyslexia affect about three boys to every girl. However, boys have better spacial skills and they are more active. This is because the right side of the brain tends to develop earlier, and this controls physical activity. As a result, boys are more restive and fidgety.

Equipment planner:
chairs and rockers

Somewhere for your baby to sit during the day soon becomes a necessity. She will not be content with lying in her Moses basket or crib all day and will be far happier sitting up so she can survey her world.

Bouncing chair

This is a lightweight chair with a steel frame covered in fabric and it is designed to bounce as the chair moves. These chairs are suitable for your baby from a few weeks until she reaches 9 kg (20 lb) or until she can sit up unaided. Babies love to sit in them as they are able to look around and they can create their own movement. Bouncing chairs are also good for putting your baby in when you are feeding her solids.

Do not leave your baby for too long in a bouncing chair as they do not support a baby's back very well. Furthermore, as the chair props your baby at an angle, she won't then try to lift her head to look around. Also, always ensure that your baby is safely strapped into the chair, never leave the chair with her in it unattended and never put it on a raised surface or she may fall.

What to look for when choosing
■ A sturdy chair with a strong safety strap.
■ A chair with an easily removable washable cover.
■ A removable head hugger is good for small babies.
■ You can buy bouncing chairs with a two-speed, battery-operated vibration unit to soothe and entertain your baby.

Rocker chair

These have the advantage of lying flat as well as propped up so that you can let your baby stay in them longer. They are suitable from birth to 9 kg (20 lb) or until your baby can sit up unaided. Choose one that is well padded. Some models have a removable toy bar, a musical feature or can vibrate to soothe your baby.

Swing

Babies love the gentle rocking action of battery-operated swinging chairs. These are suitable from birth to 11 kg (24 lb), have seats that recline in different positions and can swing at different speeds.

High chair

Once your baby can sit unsupported, she is ready for a high chair. Choose one that will suit your baby's needs from 6 to 18 months. Some come with a padded booster seat to be removed once your baby is bigger. Many have more than one height setting and some convert to a low table and chair. For travelling, buy a baby chair that clips onto a table or a portable booster seat.

What to look for when choosing
■ Check that your baby is at the right height for her to eat. The tray should be level with her tummy, not her chest.
■ Ensure the harness is easy to do up. Your baby should be secured at all times with the harness and should never be left alone in the high chair.

Your baby at 1 week

Most mammals are on their feet within days, but human beings are much more vulnerable in the first 18 months and nowhere near as capable of looking after themselves. Getting used to the world outside is a momentous change – your baby must breathe for herself, suck for her milk and excrete by herself. Suddenly there is air on her skin, the light is brighter, she feels hunger and she is able to cry. There will be so many new things to look at and listen to. There is much to learn: she does not even know that the hands she moves in front of her face belong to her. However, she is programmed to survive, with some basic reflexes.

Newborn reflexes	Hand-to-eye coordination	Language	Learning	What your baby enjoys	Stimulating play
■ A newborn baby's movements are generally uncontrolled. She is born with certain reflexes that are key to her survival. ■ Rooting reflex (to four months): If you brush your baby's cheek with your nipple or a teat she turns towards it, ready to feed. ■ Stepping or walking reflex (to 11 weeks): If you hold your baby upright under her arms and lower her onto a flat	■ A newborn baby is only able to focus on objects 20–25 cm (8–10 in) away. She doesn't see you clearly unless you're very close. However, your baby looks intently at your face when you hold her. Newborn babies prefer to look at faces with eyes looking directly at them. ■ Your baby recognises you more by smell and sound than by vision. She may recognise your face shape and the	■ Newborn babies look, listen and learn. ■ Your baby tries to look at you when you speak. ■ Your baby knows your voice and turns her head to find you. ■ She prefers high, sing-song sounds and will respond best when you look directly at her. ■ The first three years are the most important time for	■ Your baby can recognise you and your partner. ■ Your baby has a good sense of smell and by about five days is able to recognise you by smell and use her sense of smell to find your nipple. ■ Within three or four days she knows the sound of your voice. ■ Your baby learns that by crying her needs will be met.	■ Skin-to skin-cuddles; babies love to lie on your chest and feel the rhythm of your breathing. ■ Baby massage – touch is the most developed sense at birth and your baby will love being stroked and caressed by you. ■ Being in your company. ■ Being fed. ■ Being stroked with a soft brush or feath-	■ Try this to see how your baby communicates with you. During the first days of life if you hold her about 30 cm (12 in) away from your face and poke your tongue out, she may try and mimic you. ■ Talk and sing to her. ■ Let her grasp your finger with her hand. ■ Tie lengths of brightly coloured ribbon onto a wooden spoon handle and

Newborn reflexes	Hand-to-eye coordination	Language	Learning	What your baby enjoys	Stimulating play
surface, she moves as it to walk. If you hold your baby upright near a step, she lifts her foot to 'step up'. ■ Grasp reflex (to five months): When you put your finger or an object in your baby's hand, she grasps it tightly. ■ The Moro or startle reflex (to 16 weeks): If startled, your baby arches her back, throws her arms and legs in a star shape with her fingers outstretched and opens her eyes. ■ Sucking reflex: Your baby sucks when a soft object is placed in her mouth. You may also find she sucks on her fingers or on yours. Babies practise in the womb. ■ Babinski's reflex (until able to walk): If you stroke the sole of your baby's foot from heel to toe, her big toe bends backwards and her other toes spread out.	style of your hair but if you change the way you wear your hair she may not recognise you until you come up close. ■ Any mobiles you hang above her cot are visible but blurred so choose one with plenty of contrast such as black and white. ■ One area of action that a newborn is at least quite good at is eye movement, which is 'reflexive' at this age. There is still much development to go. ■ Your baby was attached to you in your womb for nine months and now she has no concept that she is separate from you. It will be a while before your baby realises that her hands are a part of her or that she has any control over them. ■ She often holds her hand in a fist.	language development. If two or more languages are spoken regularly in your home, your baby will learn to speak them both. ■ Mothers naturally adopt a special 'sing-song' way of talking to their baby: they tend to raise the pitch of their voice, speak slowly, accentuate their vowels and elongate words. This helps babies to receive clear signals that will help her to interpret your language and this method of talking will aid her speech development.	■ She enjoys company and responds to your voice. ■ She moves her arms and legs when excited. ■ Get some white paper plates and add black patterns to them with a thick marker pen. Place these in the side of the pram or crib. When your baby is awake encourage her into a side lying position with a rolled up towel against her back to support her position letting her focus on one pattern at a time (do not allow your baby to sleep in this position).	er or you gently blowing on her skin or face. ■ Being talked to. ■ Being held over your shoulder as you rock from side to side. ■ Being carried in a sling or taken for a walk in the pram. ■ Being gently patted or rubbed on her back, either over your shoulder or when lying across your lap on her tummy. ■ Listening to calm music, especially the music you played most often when you were pregnant.	gently wave the ribbon from side to side in front of your baby. This will help develop her visual tracking and as she gets older she will try to catch the ribbons. ■ From birth your baby can see strongly contrasting images like black and white stripes or spirals or bright contrasting colours like red, yellow and blue, so show her pictures and colourful toys like these. ■ Try lying your baby on different materials when she is awake, e.g. silk or sheepskin. ■ Lie your baby on her tummy some of the time when awake.

Your baby at 1 month

A one-month-old gains more control of her body and loses some of the jerky movements of a newborn baby. She has increased head control but you still need to cradle her head in your arm for support. At this age a baby still has no sense of being separate from you. There is a striking but perfectly normal phenomenon that occurs in about half of babies at around four to six weeks. This is called 'sticky fixation' in which a baby appears to be staring with her eyes locked on some point in the distance (maybe at the wall or the floor) for a long time, sometimes even for several minutes.

Movement	Hand-to-eye coordination	Language	Learning	What your baby enjoys	Stimulating play
■ Your baby can lift her head briefly a couple of inches when lying on a flat surface on her stomach. ■ She responds to your voice by turning her head and moving her eyes. ■ She kicks her arms and legs in the air – this helps to both lengthen and strengthen her muscles. ■ She begins to smile, although this	■ Your baby focuses better at any distance. ■ She follows with her eyes an object that is moved from side to side quite close to her face. ■ She moves her hands, which are usually clenched in a fist without much control but she can put her fist in her mouth. ■ If you open her fingers she is able to grasp an object for a	■ She has demanding cries and maybe makes some grunting and cooing sounds. ■ At around six weeks she can probably make 'oo' and 'aa' sounds. ■ She screams and cries to let you know if she is hungry, uncomfortable or unhappy. ■ You soon learn to recognise what your baby needs from the different types of	■ She cries for comfort or feeding. ■ She recognises her parents' voices. ■ Your baby probably responds to familiar tunes (e.g. 'soap' themes) more or less from birth if she has been exposed to them regularly in the womb. ■ Babies like to look at mobiles with bold black and white faces or patterns, or simple primary-	■ Being fed when hungry. ■ Sucking on objects, e.g. a dummy or a finger. ■ Cuddles, skin-to-skin contact. ■ Movement, e.g. being held over your shoulder as you rock from side to side, being carried in your arms or in a sling or taken for a walk in a pram. ■ Hearing her parents' voices.	■ Your baby loves to gaze at your face more than any toy or object so introduce her to some facial expressions. Stick out your tongue, purse your lips, wiggle your nose. Babies are great mimics and you may find that she imitates you. ■ Hang a black and white or colourful mobile over her cot or put black and white pictures in her cot.

Movement	Hand-to-eye coordination	Language	Learning	What your baby enjoys	Stimulating play
is a muscular response rather than a social smile. The corners of her mouth turn up but the smile is not yet reflected in her eyes. You will need to wait until your baby is about six weeks old for her first proper smile where her whole face lights up.

■ At around six weeks you can put your baby into a bouncing chair (see page 109) so that she is in a more upright position and can see what is going on around her. (A little baby needs to be placed high in the bouncing chair so that her back is straight. Sometimes babies can end up scrunched up at the bottom of the chair.) | couple of seconds before dropping it. | cries that she makes (see page 102).

■ She makes contented sounds when happy. | colour shapes. Musical mobiles that go round and round help develop your baby's tracking skills. You may find it best to hang the mobile to the right or left of your baby as newborn babies tend not to look straight ahead. | ■ The feeling of having something soft placed in her hand.

■ Eye-to-eye contact and staring at your face.

■ Sounds with a deep, regular beat, which remind her of her mother's heart-beat.

■ Sitting up in a bouncing chair. | ■ Help her track objects by moving a brightly coloured squeaking toy or rattle across her line of vision from side to side. Take care not to move it too fast or too far away. When she stops looking hold the object still encouraging her to focus again before you continue.

■ Put a baby-safe mirror in her cot so your baby can enjoy looking at herself although at this age she won't know that the reflection she sees is her face.

■ Lie your baby on her back and gently move her legs in a bicycle movement while singing a song like 'The Wheels on the Bus Go Round and Round'.

■ Put your baby on her tummy, hold a bright toy in front of her face, call her name and see if she is able to lift her head just a little. |

Your baby at 2 months

Your baby now spends more time awake and wants to exercise her limbs, punching out with her arms and kicking with her legs. Your baby's ability to suck improves and she sucks on almost anything – a blanket, a dummy, her hand. However, she knows the difference between sucking for food or comfort. She will suck contentedly on a dummy when she is not hungry but when she is hungry she will spit it out and cry for her milk.

Movement	Hand-to-eye coordination	Language	Learning	What your baby enjoys	Stimulating play
■ At around six weeks your baby will smile properly for the first time. Her eyes will light up as she smiles and if you smile back, she will respond with a big smile.	■ A baby's sight is still nowhere as good as an adult's – distant objects and people will still be quite blurry. This is why babies prefer to look at bold, contrasting patterns.	■ Coos, squeals and gurgles. ■ Your baby begins to connect the shape you make with your mouth to the sound, so will anticipate an 'oo' sound if you make a circle with your lips. So exaggerate movements and let her see your mouth when you speak.	■ Your baby becomes excited in anticipation of feeding or bath time. ■ She protests if unhappy. ■ She might smile in response to your smile.	■ Attention. ■ Being held in your arms or worn in a sling. ■ Lying in a rocking chair. Lie your baby on her back on a small blanket. With your partner, lift the blanket at opposite ends to form a hammock and swing your baby gently from side to side.	■ Lie your baby on her tummy and dangle a toy a little off the floor in front of her or lie on the floor opposite her. This encourages her to lift her head, which will help to strengthen her neck muscles.
■ Your baby's neck muscles will have gained strength and she is able to hold up her head for short periods. ■ Her muscles are continuously getting stronger and she now stretches out and uncurls from the foetal position.	■ Your baby tries to reach for an object but the ability to judge the distance between her hand and an object is quite poor. ■ She likes to move her head and eyes around to follow you and can track a slowly moving object	■ You may feel that talking to your baby is pointless because she doesn't understand what you are saying, but she's soaking up all	■ She begins to amuse herself when left alone by looking around, or tries to swipe at nearby objects. ■ This is the age when a baby recognises her parents' faces as opposed to	■ Looking at mobiles, especially black and white patterns. ■ Baby exercises.	■ Place a rolled-up towel under your baby's arms when she is on her tummy, encouraging the arms forwards and giving her more chance of success in lifting her head. ■ Wave a colourful

Movement	Hand-to-eye coordination	Language	Learning	What your baby enjoys	Stimulating play
■ Your baby's movements become less automatic and jerky and more controlled. She may try to swipe at a toy. ■ Her sucking ability improves. ■ Early reflexes, such as the Moro and grasp (see page 111), are fading. ■ It is important that during the day your baby spends plenty of time on her tummy. This helps her to develop head control, and lifting her head from this position gives her a new perspective on the world.	from about six weeks. ■ Hand control begins. She closes her fingers around a small object like a rattle placed in her palm and moves it to her face. ■ You can encourage the development of head control by giving your baby's hands plenty of freedom so it's best not to keep her arms swaddled. ■ She can vaguely mimic facial gestures. ■ Likes to peer at her fingers and toes, which are now more flexible.	speech ready for when she can talk herself. ■ Cries when put down.	their hairstyle/general face shape, etc. If you dye your hair a different colour or style it in a different way before your baby is two months old, she may not recognise you. After two months, she will. ■ Babies learn to grasp before learning how to release a toy. Slowly take a toy from your baby, giving it straight back to her again. This will encourage her to work out grasping and releasing. ■ Your baby has an acute sense of smell. Introduce her to new smells like flowers, freshly baked cakes, fresh basil.	Lie your baby on her back and, holding her hands, gently raise and lower each of her arms alternately; holding her feet, gently cycle her legs. ■ Music, so play music or sing nursery rhymes to her. Lots of babies seem to love the low sound of a vacuum cleaner or washing machine; it seems to remind them of the noises in the womb. ■ Sucking on anything she can, including her thumb or fingers, which she may have located. ■ Splashing in the bath. ■ Lying under a baby gym or cradle gym and playing with it. Your baby enjoys bright colours and objects that move and make a sound. She'll enjoy it if you make the toys move and play with her. ■ Baby massage.	scarf or handkerchief about 30 cm (12 in) above your baby's head. Bring it close and then move it further away. As your baby gets older she will try to grab it. ■ Give her toys that fit small hands, like rattles. A two-handed rattle or toy is good at this age. ■ Attach an assortment of objects at the bottom of your baby's crib for her to kick. Especially good would be a little toy that makes a noise when your baby kicks it. ■ Try stroking your baby's skin with different textures like a feather, velvet, fur so that she gets to know how they feel. ■ Lie in the dark with a torch, slowly moving the beam around the room for your baby to track. ■ Play peek-a-boo behind your hands or a blanket.

Your baby at 3 months

At around this time your baby starts practising rocking by bringing both legs together and rolling onto one side or by twisting her body. To roll from her back onto her tummy she needs to thrust her hips forward, bring one arm and leg over her body and push herself over. Gently move her left knee over her right knee when she is turning to her right and vice versa. This will help her to complete the roll. A few babies roll over as early as eight weeks old although most don't do this until six months of age. Nevertheless, never leave your baby lying on a bed, sofa or other raised surface, just in case.

Movement	Hand-to-eye coordination	Language	Learning	What your baby enjoys	Stimulating play
■ Your baby's head control is much better whether she is lying on her tummy or on her back and she may be able to raise her head to 45 degrees, giving her a better view of her surroundings. ■ Increased back strength allows your baby to start sitting upright on your lap, although she can't do this without support. ■ Leg movements become quite vigorous and she is just beginning to control	■ Your baby can stretch out her hand to a nearby object but generally misjudges the distance. ■ She may also reach out to try and brush your face with her fist or fingers. ■ She is beginning to open her clenched fist and starts to use touch to explore things. ■ Your baby can see objects further away much better. ■ She can follow you with her eyes as	■ Your baby uses a wider range of cries and you can distinguish between the cries of hunger, boredom, tiredness, etc. ■ Sounds become louder and your baby is able to make some vowel sounds like 'aah', 'ooh' and 'eeh' and may also include consonant sounds like 'm', 'b', 'g' and 'p'. ■ Improved listening skills means that she looks to see where the source of the sound comes from.	■ Your baby discovers a link between her hand movements and the reaction of the object that she holds, e.g. shaking a rattle, swiping a dangling object. ■ Before three months, babies turn their eyes in an automatic way towards a loud sound but after three months they turn towards a sound because they choose to. ■ Your baby stares at pictures in a book	■ Being held in a standing position with her feet on your lap and bouncing up and down – this will help her muscles develop. ■ Leaning on your chest and looking over your shoulder. ■ Moving her arms and legs vigorously when lying on her back. ■ Activity gyms where she can reach up and swipe at the toys. Choose a gym with toys that make a noise as your baby	■ Respond to the first sounds your baby makes, even though they are not real words. Have a little conversation repeating some of the sounds she makes and trying out some new ones for her. ■ Smile and encourage her to talk more. Leave gaps of silence for your baby to talk back to you. ■ Stretch some pram toys across your baby's pram for her to watch and play with.

Movement	Hand-to-eye coordination	Language	Learning	What your baby enjoys	Stimulating play
her hands and feet. She may also start reaching for her toes. ■ She can roll onto her side. ■ Your baby's legs are much stronger and if you hold her standing up supported under her arms, she can bear most of her weight for a few moments. ■ She sucks her fingers and fists.	you move around the room. ■ She can grasp a toy like a rattle and shake it, but she can't yet pick it up by herself. ■ She stares at nearby objects and tries to explore them by putting them in her mouth. ■ She may start to swipe at things but in an uncoordinated way. Your baby won't be able to reach accurately for things until about six to seven months.	■ Some babies start to initiate simple sounds made to them such as repetitive clicks.	and tries to touch them. ■ Your baby's memory is more developed. For example, when she gets undressed at the end of the day, she becomes excited as she remembers that it is bath time. ■ She imitates exaggerated facial expressions. ■ She tends to cry less as she finds other ways to express herself. ■ At three to four months, your baby starts to enjoy 'anticipation' – predicting the next event in a sequence. Games like 'Incey Wincey Spider' and 'This Little Piggy' come into their own.	will like making them squeak or rattle. ■ Pram rattles, grab rings and shaker toys. ■ Playing peek-a-boo. ■ Watching herself in a mirror. ■ You singing to her, and listening to nursery rhymes. ■ When you blow raspberries on her tummy, base of her feet, etc. ■ Rhyming games like 'This Little Piggy' or 'Round and Round the Garden' where you play with her and tickle her.	■ Ring a bell or hold a squeaky toy where your baby can see it. Move away just out of the range of your child's vision, sound the bell again and see if your baby turns her head to locate it. ■ Activity gyms are great for encouraging your baby to reach out and grab or kick her legs. She will love to try and grab and kick the dangling toys. Make sure the toys can be dangled from the right height for your baby to reach up to. ■ Playmats are great with different textures to explore and sounds to amuse your baby. They will encourage her to use her neck muscles. ■ Colourful toys that make sounds or music and encourage your baby to interact are good.

FEEDING

Whether breastfeeding or bottle feeding, you will be spending many hours nursing your baby. You will know great satisfaction as she fills out; there will also be times when you feel exhausted and wonder just how many more sleepless nights you will suffer. Try to go with it – all too soon your baby will be feeding herself, wreaking havoc with your clean kitchen floor. This chapter looks first at breastfeeding. On page 138, I look at combining breastfeeding with bottle feeding and then on page 142 I write about bottle feeding in its own right.

Breastfeeding

Breast milk is the most natural food for your baby. It contains all the vital nutrients that she needs. The vitamins, minerals, protein and fat content are ideally balanced for her and are in a form that she can easily digest and absorb. Breastfeeding also creates a special bond between mother and baby.

By breastfeeding your baby you pass on your antibodies, which help strengthen your baby's immune system and promote resistance to stomach upsets, coughs, colds and other infections. With breastfed babies, there is a 40% lower incidence of gastro-intestinal illnesses and 30% lower incidence of respiratory illnesses in babies who are breastfed for at least four months. If she is breastfed, your baby is also less likely to get ear and urinary tract infections and is less likely to develop diabetes.

> If you had pethidine towards the end of your labour or your baby has jaundice, she may be sleepy and unwilling to feed for the first day or so and may need encouragement. Ask your midwife to help you with this.

Benefits of breastfeeding

■ Breast milk is rich in omega-3 essential fatty acids, which are important for brain and nervous system development.

■ Breast milk is convenient, it is at the right temperature, sterile, needs no preparation, there are no bottles to wash and it's free!

■ Breastfeeding has been shown to delay the onset and reduce the severity of allergies in children from families with a history of asthma, hayfever, eczema and food allergy. Also, if there is a history of food allergy in your family, you should breastfeed your baby for at least six months before you start introducing solids.

■ Breastfed babies tend not to be constipated as breast milk is more easily digested. Breastfed newborns tend to have lots of stools a day but later on, just before they are three months old, they pass fewer stools than bottle-fed babies. For this reason breastfed babies also tend to suffer less nappy rash than bottle-fed babies.

■ Breastmilk composition changes to meet all your baby's individual requirements from feed to feed and during a feed.

■ It is especially important for premature babies as it heightens their immune system.

As a mother, the benefits of breastfeeding include a lower risk of pre-menopausal breast cancer, a lower risk of ovarian cancer and breast cancer and a lower risk of osteoporotic hip fracture later in life. Furthermore, a baby's sucking at the breast causes the uterus to contract. Although these contractions initially increase bleeding during the feed itself, this is normal. In the long term, the uterus will return to its normal size much faster (see also box at bottom of page 120).

Breastfeeding is a skill that needs to be learned and although it is natural, it is not necessarily instinctive. It is useful to find out as much as you can about breastfeeding while you are pregnant. If you have the opportunity, try to attend a breastfeeding class or support session before you have your baby. Your midwife and health visitor will be able to give you support, or contact your local National Childbirth Trust or La Leche League facilitator (see Useful Addresses on page 168), who will give you details of your nearest breast-feeding counsellor.

Breastfeeding is more likely to be successful if feeding starts early after birth and it is best if you first try to initiate breastfeeding during your baby's alert period after birth, which occurs within the first two hours. As soon after birth as possible ask for skin-to-skin contact between you and your baby. Skin-to-skin contact helps to establish breastfeeding and increases long-term breastfeeding success. Uninterrupted skin-to-skin contact also allows your baby to show signs of wanting to feed, such as sucking and rooting, and can help make her more content and cry less. Babies are born with a natural sucking reflex and if you hold your baby to your breast, she may suckle within 30 minutes of being born. Ask your midwife to help you find a comfortable position (see also page 122).

> **Q Are breastfed babies less likely to be overweight adults?**
>
> **A** Recent research suggests that breastfed babies are less likely to grow into obese children. Infancy is the critical period for fat cell development. Human milk is known to contain growth hormones that help prevent fat cells from growing whereas in formula milk fat cells are not constrained in the same way. It is also thought that mothers using formula milk may overestimate the amount their baby needs, laying down a pattern for over-eating later in life. The research showed that the first six to eight weeks after the baby has been born is the most important time for the benefits from breast-feeding to be felt but that six months or more of breastfeeding is preferable.

The let-down reflex

The sucking action of your baby sends messages to your brain to release the hormone oxytocin into your bloodstream, which causes the muscle cells around your milk glands to contract and squeeze out breast milk. This is called the 'let-down' reflex and you may feel it as a warm tingling censation under your breasts and armpits.

Colostrum

It is worth breastfeeding your baby even for a week as your breasts produce colostrum for the first three or four days. This thick, yellow fluid is high in proteins, mostly in the form of antibodies, which help protect your baby against infection before her immune system can start functioning properly. You may not produce very much colostrum but it is very high quality and is just what your baby needs. The more your baby feeds, the more colostrum you will produce. Colostrum also acts as a laxative to help your baby pass meconium, the first sticky, tar-like bowel movements.

Letting your baby suck frequently in the first few days after birth ensures she gets the valuable colostrum that you produce and also stimulates the production of your milk. After two to four days of feeding, milk production is established and colostrum becomes more milky and gradually changes into mature milk. This period is commonly known as when the milk 'comes in'.

Mature milk

Mature milk generally 'comes in' on the third or fourth day. Unlike formula milk, the type of milk that you produce changes during a feed. The early part of the feed consists of 'foremilk', which looks thin and white or bluey-white and is a thirst-quenching drink, high in lactose (sugar) and some proteins but low in fat. The later part of the feed consists of 'hindmilk', which is thicker and creamier in colour and contains two or three times the fat and one-and-a-half times as much protein.

> **Particularly with second and subsequent babies, you may find that at the beginning of a feed you feel a mild contraction similar to a period pain; this is caused by the uterus contracting as a result of your baby sucking. It is good as it is helping your uterus contract to its normal size. This pain should start to wear off within a week or so. However, if it gives you a lot of discomfort, you could try taking a paracetamol about 20 minutes before a feed.**

Reflux

■ Reflux, or (in full) gastro oesophageal reflux, occurs when the muscle at the lower end of the oesophagus is too weak to keep the milk in the baby's stomach and it comes back up again together with acid from the stomach causing a painful burning sensation – heartburn. All babies reflux – it is part of the process causing babies to posset – but some suffer more than others.

■ Babies with reflux are often very difficult to feed and tend to bring up a lot of their milk. It helps to keep your baby in a fairly upright position during and especially after feeding when it's best not to lie your baby down for about an hour after she has been fed. Also, don't give too much milk at each feed and make sure that your baby is winded if bottle-fed. The majority of babies outgrow this condition either when they begin to eat solids or when they spend more time upright.

■ If your baby suffers from reflux, elevate the head end of the cot by placing something under the mattress so that there is an incline of about 20 degrees. This may well help to alleviate the symptoms. Whereas current advice is to put your baby to sleep on her back, it may be better for babies who suffer from reflux to sleep on their side. Seek advice from your health visitor before altering a baby's sleeping position in this way.

■ A very few babies with reflux fail to gain weight and your doctor may advise giving antacid or anti-reflex drugs or Carobel (a tasteless thickener derived from the carob tree), which you can add to your baby's formula milk. Reflux can be a symptom of an allergy to cow's milk.

Due to the changing composition of milk, it is best to allow your baby to empty one breast before offering the other one. It is the hindmilk, rich in fats and calories, that really satisfies a hungry baby.

Equipment planner: breastfeeding

Nursing bras

When breastfeeding you should always wear a supportive nursing bra, which should be firm enough to prevent your breasts from sagging. It should be made from cotton and have wide straps and front opening flaps that allow you to undo one side at a time, preferably using just one hand. It is important that the bra is not too tight as not only will this be uncomfortable but it can also lead to an infection like mastitis. It is also best to avoid underwires as these can also cause a blocked duct under the breast.

Only buy one or two bras initially. It's best to wait until you are about 37 weeks pregnant before you get yourself measured. Once your milk is established you can then buy another bra which might be a better fit.

Breast pads

You can buy packs of disposable breast pads, which fit inside your bra and protect your clothes from leaks of milk. Breast pads that are contoured to the shape of the breast are the most comfortable.

You can also buy washable reuseable breast pads. Plastic-backed pads are not recommended as they can stop air getting to the nipple, which can cause sore or cracked nipples.

Do not allow your breasts to be exposed to soggy breast pads for a prolonged period of time because it can contribute to soreness and be a means of infection. Change your pads regularly, not just when feeding is necessary.

Breast shells

Some mothers find that when feeding from one breast the other breast leaks a lot of milk. If this happens to you, you can buy breast shells that will collect the milk, which can then be stored for a later feed. These fit over your nipples and are held in place by your bra. Only wear the shells when feeding. Ventilated shells, which protect sore or cracked nipples as the holes allow air to circulate, are also available.

Nursing pillow

This is a horseshoe- or V-shaped cushion, which is ideal for resting your baby on for a comfortable breastfeeding position. You could use an ordinary firm pillow instead.

Reusable thermal gel packs

These can be used warm or cool to soothe discomfort. They help provide fast relief from pain caused by blocked ducts, mastitis or engorgement.

Q Are there clothes that make it easier for me to breastfeed when I'm out?

A As well as using the nursing bras described above choose clothes that provide quick access to your breasts, like shirts that button down the front. Some mothers are confident to breastfeed in public but you may prefer to use the special mother and baby rooms offered in shops and supermarkets.

The art of breastfeeding

Successful milk production depends on nipple stimulation to trigger release of the milk-producing hormone prolactin and the milk-releasing hormone oxytocin (also known as the 'let-down reflex') together with the actual removal of milk from the breast either by your baby feeding or by you expressing. Your baby feeding at the breast is the most effective mechanism to stimulate and maintain your milk supply. It is a true supply-and-demand mechanism. The more your baby feeds, the more milk you will produce (see page 130).

Latching on

Hold your baby so that her back is straight, her chin is stretched upwards against your breast and her nose is level with your nipple. As soon as your baby smells your milk, she should open her mouth to suck. If she is not already rooting for your breast, you could touch her lips with your nipple and wait for her to open her

Keeping a finger against the breast tissue to 'allow' your baby to breathe can be positively harmful as it can lead to blocked ducts and mastitis developing.

mouth wide. Your baby should take the nipple and a good proportion of the areola into her mouth in order to stimulate the breast to produce milk.

Don't push your baby's head towards your breast. Instead, let her head tip back a little and rest on your fingers. There should be more of your breast in your baby's mouth below your nipple than above it – if you see any of the areola while she is feeding, this should be above, not below your nipple. If your baby sucks only on the nipple she will get frustrated because she will not be able to get enough milk. As a result she will probably try to suck harder and you will get sore and possibly cracked nipples (see page 126).

Signs that your baby is correctly attached

■ Your baby's cheeks are rounded and not being pulled in when sucking.

■ Her top and bottom lip are turned outwards at the breast.

■ Her nose and chin touch your breast. Don't worry about this suffocating your baby – her top lip creates an air channel, which allows the baby to breathe.

■ Your baby feeds rhythmically: first quick, short sucks, followed by longer sucks where the jaw drops down and swallowing can often be heard. Your baby will then rest and start again. This rhythmical sucking is a sign that your baby is feeding well.

■ Your baby is content at the breast and relaxed (you can often see her toes relaxing and splaying apart).

Incorrect attachment

Incorrect attachment will make your nipples sore. You can recognise this because an incorrectly attached baby will latch on and then pull off after a while and cry furiously as she cannot get the milk. Another sign of incorrect attachment is that the baby wants to feed

Feeding in the bath

■ This is an excellent place to feed your baby if she is fretful and you are experiencing problems attaching her to the breast. The water relaxes you and your baby and some people believe that it mimics the womb environment and helps your baby to re-learn breastfeeding and overcome any problems that may have developed. To breastfeed in the bath, have someone else with you initially to pass your baby to you once you are settled in the water and to help position your baby. The water should be comfortably warm and not overly hot. Fill the bath so that it reaches just below your breasts when you are sitting upright. Initially just allow yourself and your baby to enjoy the warmth, closeness and skin contact together with no pressure to feed.

■ Once both of you are relaxed, you often find your baby will start to lick at the nipple. Once this happens you can position your baby so that her chest is against your chest, nose level with your nipple, and as she opens her mouth, bring her to your breast. Ensure that the baby is submerged in the water enough to keep warm and relaxed but sufficiently above the water level to be able to breathe and feed easily. Women with epilepsy should never bath with their baby.

Unlatching your baby

■ When your baby sucks she creates a strong vacuum so don't pull your nipple out of her mouth or your nipple could become sore. To break the suction, gently insert your little finger in your baby's mouth, between your breast and the corner of her mouth.

Breastfeeding problems

Sometimes breastfeeding isn't all that straightforward. To help you, there is a chart on page 126 for the most common complaints. Here are a few extra tips to start you off:

■ Sometimes if you make a baby wait too long when she is hungry, she can exhaust herself by crying. You should cuddle and soothe her as there is no point in trying to feed her until she is calm.

■ If your baby is not keen to take the breast, express a few drops of breast milk onto her lips so that she can smell and taste it. Alternatively, express some onto a sterile spoon and allow your baby to lap it up; this usually stimulates a feed.

■ If your breast is engorged, it can be difficult for your baby to latch on so it is a good idea to express a little milk – just enough to soften the areola before putting your baby to the breast.

very frequently (every hour) because she is unable to get the milk as efficiently when incorrectly attached. If you recognise these signs, ask someone who understands breastfeeding to watch you feed your baby as this can often help to resolve this problem very quickly.

You may feel a fleeting pain at the start of the feed in the first few days but if the pain persists, your baby has probably not latched on properly. Remove your baby from your breast (see box, above), re-position her and try again. It may take many attempts before you get a good latch but it is important to persist to ensure satisfactory feeds for your baby and comfort for you.

Q When can I expect my baby to sleep through the night?

A All babies are different and some may sleep through from four months. However, from around six months onwards, all children are physiologically capable of sleeping through the night. The average time spent sleeping at this age is 14½ hours, with about 11 hours of sleep during the night.

Positions for breastfeeding

If your breasts are very large, it might help to support the breast that your baby is feeding from with your hand. Place a flat hand against your ribs with the side of your index finger on your breast. Maintaining support can lead to problems, however, as it can block milk flow and cause blocked ducts and mastitis. So ensure that you move your hand around in an undulating movement so that no particular area gets blocked all the time.

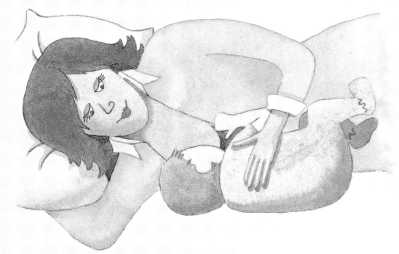

1 Sitting You will need a chair with arms that supports you sitting upright – you may feel more comfortable with a cushion behind your back. Do not to lean backwards because this will change the shape of your breast and make it difficult to attach your baby properly. Your feet should reach the floor so that your knees and lap are level; you may want to rest your feet on a thick phone book. Bring your baby to your breast rather than leaning over; you might find it easier if you raise your baby up to breast height by putting a pillow over your knees for your baby to lie on. Lay your baby across your lap with her body facing your chest and her head supported on your forearm, with it acting as a 'shelf' to support her head. Her nose needs to be level with and facing your nipple. Support your arm using an extra cushion.

2 Lying down This is a useful position for night feeds or if you have had a Caesarean section. Both you and your baby lie on your side, facing each other with your baby tucked in to your tummy and her nose level with your nipple. Rest your head, arm and shoulder on some pillows. With your other arm cuddle your baby, guiding her to your breast. For the second breast, add extra pillows under her to raise her up. However, if you are uncomfortable, you may want to turn over for the second breast.

3 **Underarm** This is particularly useful position for feeding after a Caesarean as it avoids pressure on the scar. You will need to be supported well forward on a chair with cushions at your side to give your baby room to stretch out her legs. Support her body with your arm and cradle her head with your hand so her nose is opposite your nipple and her chest is facing yours and she is in a slightly sitting-up position.

Cradle either side of your baby's head with your thumb and third finger – take care to position your hand so that she can tilt back her head at will. Using your other hand, support your breast and tease your nipple on the baby's lips and wait for her mouth to gape widely. Then quickly but gently bring your baby to the breast. Once the baby is attached, support the arm holding the baby with a pillow.

4 **Feeding twins** The best position in which to feed your twin babies is the 'double football hold'. For this you will need a two pillows or a V-shaped cushion (made especially for breast-feeding mothers). Place the pillows (or cushion) on your lap. Tuck one baby under each arm with their legs stretching out behind you and resting on the pillow. Cradle their heads in your hands so they are opposite your nipples. Of course, to do this successfully you will need to be able to scoop up each baby with one hand.

Try to learn to position your babies yourself but in the early stages it is useful to have someone to lend a hand until you get the hang of it. If necessary, add extra pillows to sup-port your babies so that you can use your hands if you need to reposition one of them.

Breastfeeding problems

The problem	How to help
Engorgement This is when your breasts overfill with milk and are hot, swollen, heavy and hard. The veins on your breast are often very prominent as well. It is normal for your breasts to feel very full when your milk 'comes in' around the third or fourth day.	■ Feed your baby frequently to avoid fullness. ■ Use warm flannels on your breasts before a feed to improve milk flow or take a warm bath or shower before a feed or use reuseable thermal packs (see page 121). ■ A good old-fashioned remedy is to put chilled cabbage leaves (use hard, dark green cabbage) inside your bra for 10–20 minutes every four hours – they have anti-inflammatory properties. First, crush the stems of the cabbage with something like the back of a fork to release the enzyme that helps to break down inflammation. ■ Put cold flannels or a compress like a bag of frozen peas on your breasts between feeds.
Sore nipples Sore nipples are caused by your baby not latching on properly, taking in most of the areola (see page 122). If you experience pain, ask your midwife, health visitor or breastfeeding counsellor to watch you feed as sometimes the smallest amount of adjustment can resolve the problem and prevent you getting very cracked and sore nipples. Some women will experience discomfort at the beginning of a feed in the first few days of breastfeeding. This type of discomfort often stops when the 'let-down' reflex is triggered as then the milk starts to flow more freely. Nipple soreness can be extremely painful in the first week or so but as you continue and become more expert at positioning and attachment and the nipple becomes more used to the sensations of feeding, the milk supply comes in more easily and the pain will disappear.	■ Make sure your baby latches on properly (see page 122). ■ Keep your nipples as dry as possible between feeds. Nipples can become soggy and are more likely to crack if left inside a moist bra, so change breast pads frequently. Also leave your bra off sometimes and expose your nipples to the air for about 20 minutes a couple of times a day. ■ Wash your nipples with water, but do not use soap as this is drying. ■ Express some milk after a feed and rub it onto your nipples and let it dry. Breast milk contains substances that promote healing and help prevent infection. ■ If only one nipple is sore always start feeding your baby on the other breast until the situation improves but not forgetting to feed from the affected breast to prevent engorgement. ■ Take care not to pull your baby off the breast at the end of a feed. Instead, slip your little finger into the corner of your baby's mouth to break the suction. ■ If your breasts are engorged, express milk to soften the areola before feeding, otherwise it is very difficult for your baby to latch on and she may end up chewing on the nipple. ■ If your nipple looks red and shiny it could be a sign of thrush. Your baby may also have white spots in her mouth. This can occur if you or your baby has a course of antibiotics. You should both be treated with anti-fungal medication. ■ If you are finding the area particularly sensitive, apply an ice cube to your nipple area before you feed your baby. This can numb the area and make it more comfortable for you. ■ For cracked nipples, use Jelonet, a gauze soaked in paraffin, which you can buy in a chemist. However, only use creams on the advice of a health professional; it is better to use natural remedies first.
Cracked nipples If sore nipples are not treated, they can become cracked and you may feel a shooting pain as your baby sucks. If you don't moisturise them they can get worse and can be a route for infection.	■ Massage the nipple area gently for a few minutes after a feed using a natural oil like almond oil and then expose your nipples to the air for a few minutes. ■ An unusual but effective treatment is to put grated carrots onto breast pads for 20 minutes after each feed and apply them to your breasts. The vitamin A and moisture from the carrots helps healing. ■ Use white paraffin or Calendula cream on the nipple and surrounding area.

The problem	How to help
Cracked nipples (continued)	■ Sometimes expressed milk rubbed around the nipple area after a feed and left uncovered to dry for a few minutes can help. ■ You may need to stop feeding from the affected breast until it has healed but it is important, even if you are too sore to feed your baby, that you express your breasts regularly or you can become engorged and then be prone to mastitis.
Blocked duct A blocked duct is a small tender lump on your breast caused by something that has stopped milk from flowing freely, like a tight bra or engorgement.	■ Massage your breast towards the nipple when you are feeding or expressing. ■ Use reuseable shaped thermal packs to soothe painful breasts (see page 121). ■ Offer the affected breast first as your baby's stronger suck may clear the blockage. ■ Feed more frequently and, if your breast still feels full and lumpy, express after a feed. ■ If the lump is persistent, place your baby on a bed with her head towards your waistline. Lean over and guide your nipple into your baby's mouth. You will be feeding her 'upside down'. The bottom jaw is most effective at removing the milk and so will help ease the blocked duct. Be careful if you suffer from back problems.
Mastitis As milk flows to your nipples it passes through ducts, which sometimes become blocked. This can occur if your baby is not latching on properly or not sucking efficiently enough to drain your breast. **Reactive mastitis** is when the body produces a red, inflamed area on the breast or there is a hot spot, a lump or a hard area on a heavy-feeling breast. You may also have a slight rise in temperature. **Infective mastitis:** only half of mastitis cases are described this way. If bacteria from your skin enters the blocked duct, the milk it contains may become infected and in severe cases your breasts will be very red and painful. You may also have a slight rise in temperature, possible flu-like symptoms, loss of appetite and lethargy.	■ Because mastitis can be prevented and is also treated by clearing the milk ducts, it is important to carry on feeding if you possibly can. ■ Feed more often if possible. If it is very painful, you could ask your health visitor to recommend a painkiller. Put warm flannels on your breasts before a feed to help the milk flow as this will help to unblock milk ducts and clear any infection. Alternatively, take a warm bath or shower before you feed. ■ Gently massage your breast towards the nipple using a natural oil like almond or grapeseed before a feed. You can also gently massage the breast towards the nipple while your baby is feeding. ■ If feeding is painful, change positions but not breasts often so that your baby puts pressure on different areas of the breast. ■ Soothe the area between feeds with a cold compress; a small bag of frozen peas wrapped in muslin is ideal or you can buy reuseable cooled thermal packs to place on the breast. ■ Sponge your breasts with warm water to help ease discomfort, or hold a hot compress against the affected area. ■ If you don't feel better after a few hours, contact your doctor, who may prescribe antibiotics. An untreated blocked duct or mastitis can result in a breast abscess (see left column). ■ Use cold cabbage leaves as a compress (see page 126). ■ You can take paracetamol to help reduce your temperature. ■ If your mastitis is reactive rather than infective, Ibuprofen, available from chemists, reduces inflammation.
Breast abscess An untreated blocked duct or mastitis can cause a breast abscess. You may feel unwell with a fever and flu-like symptoms and there will be a very red and painful large lump on your breast.	■ Your doctor will probably prescribe antibiotics or you may need surgery to drain the abscess.

Feeding patterns

Once your milk supply is well established and you have mastered the art of breastfeeding, you can start getting your baby into a routine. However, to begin with it is more important that your baby should gain weight at the right rate than stick to a rigid schedule. In the first couple of weeks it may seem that you are feeding a lot but you will benefit as your baby will grow quickly, her stomach will grow to accommodate more milk and she will become more efficient and quicker at feeding.

> **Q Sometimes my baby is much hungrier than normal. Why is this?**
>
> **A** Babies have 'growth' spurts as they develop and may spend longer at the breast during these phases. Growth spurts tend to occur between ten and 14 days and approximately at three and six weeks and they generally last 24–48 hours. You may feel that you do not have enough milk but it is important not to restrict your breastfeeding or give your baby formula feeds at this time. As with frequent feeding, your breast milk supply will rapidly compensate and your baby will become more content and then return to feed less frequently again. This is why it is vital that you are not overly reliant on set feed times or restricting your baby's access to the breast.

In the first week you will need to feed your baby frequently and she will probably take only quite small amounts (about 50 ml/1–2 fl oz) as her stomach is only about the size of a walnut. However, by two weeks, lots of babies need to feed from both breasts although some continue on one. Feeding about ten times in 24 hours is average for a very young baby (newborn to one month). This usually settles down to about one to four hours between feeds. At around three months your baby may be taking about 175 ml (6 fl oz) milk at each feed and you may begin to see a pattern emerge. You can now gradually manipulate the timing of feeds into a more regular routine by postponing feeds or letting them go on for longer. Try not to allow your baby to go longer than six hours between feeds, except at night. If concerned, ask your midwife for support.

Start feeds on alternate breasts since babies generally get more milk from the first breast. A lot of mothers 'weigh up' the breast by cupping it in their hand to make sure they are starting on the correct breast or it may feel obviously fuller. If you have difficulty remembering which breast to start from, you could put a small piece of coloured ribbon into your bra to remind you each time. Once feeding is established, most women instinctively know which breast to feed from. If your breasts are very full you may need to express a little milk before offering your baby the breast to make it easier to latch on. Hand expression to drain off a little milk is often particularly good at this time.

All babies have their own personalities and likes and dislikes, which they sometimes find hard to communicate. Some babies take a full feed every few hours and then go off to sleep, others take a while to establish the feed because of feeling irritable or sleepy, but eventually latch on to the breast and feed well and go to sleep for a while. Others graze: they snack regularly

 All babies get hiccups and babies with full stomachs tend to hiccup more.

and you may feel that you are feeding all the time. All of these are normal. Breastfeeding gets easier with practice and as you learn about each other. It is said that breastfeeding is like learning to dance with a new partner: you both have to take time to learn each others movements and rhythm.

One breast or two?

A baby who is well latched on to the breast will stop feeding when she has had enough. You should aim to feed for at least 20 minutes on the first breast because many babies need at least this long to reach the hindmilk, which helps your baby go longer between feeds as the fat takes longer to digest. You should always offer your baby both breasts but she may not always want both and that is fine. You will know if your baby is getting enough milk if:

■ She is steadily putting on weight.
■ She is breastfeeding contentedly.
■ She has regularly wet nappies.
■ She has regular soft yellow stools.

You should call your GP if:
■ She is listless and uninterested in feeds.

When settling down to feed, have everything you need nearby like a glass of water (breastfeeding tends to make your thirsty) and a phone, because you may be sure that the moment you sit down , the phone will ring! This is a good time to catch up on any films that you've recorded and never had time to watch so you might want to have your remote control for the TV and video next to your chair.

● *Q Do I need to give my baby any other drinks?*
A Your baby may feed frequently during hot weather because breast milk is both drink and food to your baby. If your baby has free access to breast milk, even in the hottest weather, she will not need any other fluids. It should not be necessary to give your baby water and can reduce breastfeeding success and affect your baby's weight gain as it fills your baby's stomach and does not provide any calories or other nutrients. Worse still is to give your baby water with sugar as this provides empty calories and can lead to tooth decay.

■ Her fontanelle appears either sunken or bulging.
■ She has very few wet nappies and her urine is a dark colour and has a strong smell.
■ She is whiney and miserable and cries for long periods.

Newborn babies usually lose weight for the first few days, which is due mostly to passing meconium (see page 120 Most babies regain their weight within about ten days although by 21 days is acceptable.

Babies can spend from ten to 40 minutes sucking at the breast but most babies get 90% of their milk in the first 5–10 minutes of a feed. The remaining slower sucking gives your baby the hindmilk that she needs, which is three times fattier than the foremilk at the beginning of the feed. It is the hindmilk that helps your baby go longer between feeds as the fat takes longer to digest. If your baby is unsettled, try leaving her on one breast for longer.

Learn to look for early cues from your baby that indicate she needs feeding, such as:
■ Mouthing at her hands.
■ Flicking her tongue in and out.

Feeding on demand

To begin with you should allow your baby to decide when she needs to eat and when she has had enough. In the first week your baby will need to feed little and often as her stomach is very small. Only she is capable of deciding how much she really needs and if your baby is allowed to feed as often as she wants, she will in effect be telling your breasts how much milk to produce. The more often she feeds and the more milk she takes at each feed, the more you will supply. This is known as 'supply and demand' so it is best to avoid giving formula milk as a 'top up' as this will mean that she has less room for your milk and so your body reacts by producing less milk. Also, the formula milk given to your baby reduces some of the protective effects of breastfeeding, particularly in relation to allergy.

Until your milk supply is well established, usually at around six weeks, it is best for your baby to be fed on demand (i.e. whenever she is hungry) and for as long as she needs. Provided you do this and your baby is feeding correctly, there is no reason you shouldn't produce enough milk for her.

■ Avoid supplementing breastfeeding with a bottle of formula until your milk supply is fully established as your breasts may respond by producing less milk

■ It is sometimes useful to wake your baby and offer a feed if your breasts are feeling very heavy and full, particularly in the early days. You will immediately feel more comfortable and your baby will also benefit. Once feeding is established, the first feelings of engorgement and fullness will ease. Sometimes women perceive that as their breasts are smaller their milk supply has diminished. However, this is not the case.

■ In addition, the size of your breasts bears no relation to how much milk you can produce. A woman with

Q What do you do if my baby falls asleep at the breast after only a few minutes but is due for a proper feed ?
A Skin-to-skin contact is best as the close contact works very well at encouraging your baby to feed. Take all your baby's clothes off except the nappy. Undress your top half and place your baby directly on your skin close to your breasts. You can cover yourself and your baby with a blanket if necessary. Express a little milk from your breasts and drip it onto your baby's lips. The smell and taste of your milk will often encourage your baby to feed. If the baby is otherwise well and still does not wish to feed do not force her to the breast but merely maintain skin-to-skin contact for longer or try again in an hour or two.

small breasts can produce just as much milk as a woman with large breasts.

Comfort sucking

Some babies continue to suck at the breast long after they have finished taking their milk. This is fine provided you are happy and that your nipples don't become sore. It will help stimulate the milk supply because of the release of prolactin in response to the sucking.

Night feeds

You should teach your baby the difference between night and day right from the beginning. Give the last feed in a dimly lit, calm, quiet bedroom and when she wakes in the night, keep the room dark. This can be a lovely intimate time for you and your baby, but don't offer any distractions, talk as little as possible and keep it quite boring. If you find it easier you can feed your baby in your own bed in the middle of the night.

For more information on feeding and sleeping, see pages 96–8.

By four weeks, aim to get your baby to take most of her daily milk requirements between 7am and 11pm. In this way you may get a less interrupted night.

Feeding twins

Due to the advances of fertility treatment, there is an increase in the number of twins born and about 1 in 70 pregnancies in the UK is a twin birth. Establishing breastfeeding is rarely plain sailing for any mother, but when you have twins it is even more daunting. You will need all the support you can get so that you can concentrate on getting breastfeeding established.

Twins especially benefit from breast milk's protective properties as they may have been born prematurely. It is possible to feed twins simultaneously but it takes practice and it might be best to feed one at a time until you are confident and have found a comfortable position (your midwife will show you different positions). Eventually you will be much better off feeding the babies together (see page 125) or you will feel as though you never do anything else. As long as you don't limit the amount your babies feed, your body is capable of producing enough milk to feed twins or even triplets.

> If you are feeding twins you will find that different babies have different appetites, so one may finish first. You could wind this baby by lying her on her tummy across your knee as you finish feeding the other one. Eventually you will find that you can lift one to your shoulder to wind her while the other finishes her feed.

Q My baby is in the habit of falling asleep at the breast and then ends up wanting to feed again in an hour or two – what should I do ?
A First of all, take your baby from the breast. Change her nappy to wake her up and then put her back to the breast. Some babies might be better taking half the feed, then having a stretch and a kick for a few minutes and then be happy to take the rest. Keep a playmat near you when breast-feeding. Other things you can do to encourage your baby to stay awake are:
■ Make sure she is not too warm. Open or remove outer clothes and don't cover your baby while you are feeding. Alternatively, sit by an open window to allow cool air to stimulate your baby.
■ If possible, feed her with skin-to-skin contact (see box opposite).
■ Stroke her face. Tap her hands and feet. Blow on her face.
If all else fails – put your baby down, she may not be hungry – and wait until she wakes up again before trying to feed her. If your baby continues to be too sleepy to feed or difficult to wake, she may be unwell. Speak to your GP or health visitor.

Possible problems
■ Twins are often smaller than single babies and they may find it difficult to latch on properly and suck efficiently. They may also tire more easily and will probably feed little and often.
■ It is more difficult to feed twin babies when you are out and about and it may be easier in these circumstances to feed one at a time.
■ You may have had a Caesarean delivery, which might make holding two babies difficult. You may find that the underarm position is the most comfortable or you could feed one baby at a time lying down.

Eating and breastfeeding

The key to successful breastfeeding and a good milk supply is to make sure that you eat well and drink plenty of fluids and rest when you can. Well-nourished women are more likely to be successful at feeding their babies. You actually need to eat and drink more than when you were pregnant – drink enough to satisfy your thirst and eat about 500 extra calories a day. Continue to follow the rules for a healthy diet outlined on pages 10–19 but make sure you also:

■ Include sufficient iron-rich foods in your diet when breastfeeding and, to improve absorption of iron from food, consume vitamin C-rich foods and juices. Many mothers are deficient in iron after the birth of their child and this could lead to anaemia, which will leave you feeling very run down and more prone to infection.
■ Drink enough fluid to avoid becoming thirsty. Water is especially good for your body and contains no hidden calories or artificial sweeteners.

The suggestions for good snacks containing 200 calories given on page 11 are just as valid as energy boosters when breastfeeding.

Dieting and breastfeeding

For most women successful breastfeeding with a good milk supply can be maintained during a moderate weight-reducing diet. However, although you are naturally keen to regain your figure as soon as possible, your growing baby is totally dependent on you for all her nutritional needs. Water-soluble vitamins (vitamins B and C) cannot be stored in the body so you need a daily intake of foods containing these vitamins to keep up the levels in your milk. If you choose to restrict your diet in order to lose weight when breastfeeding, it is important that you eat a well-balanced diet with plenty of fresh fruit and vegetables. As well as adopting a healthy eating plan, you will probably lose weight naturally while breastfeeding because the extra stores of fat put on during pregnancy are used up in the production of breast milk. Women have a higher metabolic rate when breastfeeding and also breastfeeding causes the uterus to contract and return to its normal size so you should get a flatter stomach faster.

What to avoid

There are no absolute rules about which foods are forbidden to breastfeeding mothers. Food is digested in the stomach, turning it to liquid, which passes into the bowel where essential nutrients are absorbed in the bloodstream. The nutrients are then taken up when your breasts are producing milk and transferred to your baby during feeding. There is no direct link from your bowel to the milk supply so it is illogical that fibrous elements can be passed into your baby's digestive system and cause wind. However, some women may notice that certain foods like dairy products adversely affect their baby and may choose to avoid them.

> **It takes a while for the body to recover from the birth of your baby so take a good quality post-natal mineral and vitamin supplement. However this is not a substitute for a good diet. Vitamin and mineral supplements can never hope to replace all the nutrients contained in food.**

Alcohol: This is transmitted to your baby via breast milk so drink only small amounts.

Caffeine: Foods containing caffeine, e.g. coffee, tea and some soft drinks, can affect your baby and act as a stimulant as well as causing colic.

Spicy foods: These can alter the taste of your breast milk and some mothers notice an increase in their baby's bowel movements. This may seem as if your baby has an upset tummy but it is merely a natural reaction.

Peanuts: If you or your partner or any other children in the family suffer from eczema, asthma, hay fever or other allergies, it is best to avoid eating peanuts or peanut products whilst breastfeeding.

Wheat and dairy products: These are both foods that can cause an allergic response so if your baby seems to get a reaction when you eat these foods, seek advice.

The Pill: Avoid using the combined oestrogen and progesterone pill as this reduces the quality and quantity of milk that you produce. The progesterone-only pill, however, is fine. Also, increased oestrogen has been linked to deep vein thrombosis and, immediately after the birth of a baby, women are particularly at risk of deep vein thrombosis because of their blood viscosity.

Medicines and drugs: These can pass into your milk so it is important to advise your doctor that you are breastfeeding.

Smoking: Nicotine from smoking passes to your breast milk. If you must smoke, try to leave the longest time possible between the last cigarette and breastfeeding your baby. This allows a chance for the nicotine level to fall. Nicotine will stay in breast milk for approximately one-and-a-half hours. Mothers who smoke heavily are also less likely to have a good breast milk supply and

Healthy snacks

Looking after a newborn baby is very demanding and so healthy snacks are important during the day to keep up your energy levels. The energy boost from sugary foods is short-lived and it is much better to have something like a baked potato or a sandwich.

■ Sunflower or pumpkin seeds. These are especially good if you spread them out on a baking tray, sprinkle with a little soy sauce and then grill for a couple of minutes, turning the seeds occasionally to prevent burning.
■ Fresh or dried fruit.
■ Pitta pockets, sandwiches or tortilla wraps with tuna, vegetables, chicken.
■ Baked beans on toast.
■ Raw vegetables and a dip, e.g. hummus.
■ Tuna salad.
■ Scrambled eggs.
■ Cheese on toast.
■ Natural yoghurt with honey or maple syrup.
■ A bowl of cereal, e.g. Bran Flakes.
■ Fruit smoothie.

risk inducing respiratory illness in their children. However, the overall protective benefits of breastfeeding outweigh this risk.

Expressing milk

There are times when you may want to express breast milk for example:

■ If you want someone else to feed your baby during the night so that you can sleep.

■ If you are going out for the evening.

■ If you are returning to work you may breastfeed your baby in the morning and evening, but express milk at lunchtime. Employers in the UK are required by law to provide women time off and facilities to express milk.

■ If your baby is in special care.

■ If your breasts are very full, you may want to express some milk to make it easier for your baby to latch on.

Most women find that first thing in the morning is the best time to express milk as this is when their breasts are very full. If your baby is generally satisfied with the first breast, you may wish to feed from one breast while expressing from the other or you may prefer to express once your baby has finished feeding. Another good time to express is if your baby has her last feed at around 8.30pm and you go to bed at 10.30pm. You could express some milk just before you go to bed. You could also feed your baby from one breast and express milk from the other if you find that your baby is generally satisfied with the first breast. Alternatively, you could express a little following every feed and allow it to accumulate through the day before you store it or provide the feed for the baby.

> If you are breastfeeding but are getting really tired because of all the sleepless nights, you could express milk in the morning and let your partner do the 10–11pm feed so that you can get some uninterrupted sleep.

Don't feel that you have to express milk – some mothers breastfeed very successfully without ever expressing. Many women find that mixed feeding can make a good compromise if they are going back to work, for example with breastfeeds morning and night and formula bottle feeds during the day.

Getting started

Many women find expressing milk very difficult and spend a long time doing it at first without being able to produce much milk. Don't get too disheartened, a baby is much more efficient at extracting milk than any breast pump. It is not an indication of how good your milk supply is, only how well your breasts allow milk to be expressed. Do not doubt your milk supply because you cannot express milk. Here are some tips to help:

■ Warm flannels placed on the breasts can help the milk to flow, especially when the breasts are very full on the third and fourth days after birth. Gently stroke the warm flannel towards the nipple to encourage the milk flow.

■ Breast massage towards the nipple will help to empty your breasts.

■ The more relaxed you are, the easier it will be to express. Sometimes a warm bath or shower can help you to relax. You may even find it easier to express milk while sitting in the bath. Start by submerging your breasts in the water and gently massage each breast using a rocking motion with your hand. Alternatively, sit down and put your feet up for a few minutes before beginning to express your milk. Relax your arms and back and take several deep breaths. Concentrate on letting the tension leave your body.

■ Having your baby near or thinking about your baby may help stimulate you to produce milk.

Expressing by hand

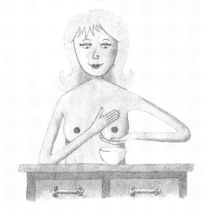  

1 Make sure your hands are clean. Hold your breast with one hand and massage around it with the other (you may be able to do this with one hand if you have small breasts). Use the flat of your hand and work from the outer edge of the breast towards the areola. Do not pull or stretch the skin and do not handle yourself roughly as this may cause tissue damage.

2 Cup your breast in both hands with your fingers underneath and your thumbs above. Locate the milk ducts, which are positioned near the end of the areola. They will feel like a ring of small beads or peas. Press on the area of the areola, backwards towards your ribcage and then press together firmly with your fingers and thumb, moving around the breast.

3 Press and release gently and rhythmically into a wide-mouthed sterile container placed at a convenient height so that you don't have to bend over. Work around the breast releasing milk from all the reservoirs. Continue until the milk flow stops and then move on to the other breast.

Expressing by pump

For more information on the different types of breast pump that are available, see equipment planner, overleaf. First place the 'shield' of the pump over your breast, making sure that your nipple is in the centre. By squeezing and releasing the handle, you create suction to draw out the milk. Generally the container for the milk doubles as a feeding bottle or you can express directly into pre-sterilised bottle bags, which come with clips for sealing, date stickers and bag holders. The milk can then be stored in the fridge or freezer.

When operating an electric breast pump, always use as little suction as necessary to remove your milk. It is best to avoid long periods of pumping. Try to have a few one-minute pauses during the session and massage both of your breasts during this rest period to help the milk flow.

> **If you are going to express milk at work, you will need access to a quiet, private room, preferably with a lock on the door. You will also need access to a fridge and you will need a cool bag and ice packs to keep the milk cold until you travel back home.**

Storing milk

Many women feel that expressing and storing milk is too much like hard work but with some planning and organisation it isn't too difficult to achieve. If you are expecting to return to work and don't feel comfortable with the idea of mixed feeds (breastfeeding first and last thing each day with formula feeds in between), it is worth getting into the habit of expressing and storing your milk so that your baby can continue to receive the goodness of your milk even though you aren't there.

Expressing for neonatal babies

■ If your baby is in an incubator, all the emotional cues that stimulate the let-down reflex for breastfeeding, like holding your baby in your arms as she sucks, are missing. Don't give up in your attempts to breastfeed, though; these early days are a vulnerable time for your baby and your expressed milk will help build up your baby's immunity to infection.

■ Ask the nurses and midwives looking after your baby to help you. Once your baby is able to breastfeed, it will be much easier for you both.

■ As milk is produced on a supply and demand basis, it is best to express regularly about every three hours during the day and every six hours at night.

■ Try to express as soon as you get up from a night's sleep as this is a time when you should have plenty of milk.

■ It can be very helpful to express by your baby's cot or incubator.

■ Don't worry if there is only a little milk in the first few days; this is normal.

● Q Should I express milk in the first few weeks?

A Expressing milk is probably best avoided for the first six weeks after your baby is born so that you can first establish a good milk supply. However, if your midwife or health visitor thinks that your milk supply may be low, it might be beneficial to express a little after each feed to try to stimulate the breasts to produce more milk. Also, if your baby is not good at sucking, you may need to express milk after a feed.

If a baby is slow to gain weight, it might be helpful occasionally to express milk and put it in a bottle for extra feeds to top up your normal breast-feeding. Some babies may find it easier to suck from a bottle.

Here are some tips for getting the most from your hard-won expressed milk:

■ Expressed milk should be stored in the fridge for only 24 hours.

■ Newly expressed breast milk can be added to expressed milk that is already stored in the fridge – it is safe to combine up to two or three sets of separate expressions.

■ If the milk is needed after 24 hours, then you can freeze it. Expressed milk will keep for up to two months in a freezer.

■ To freeze the milk, transfer to sterilised ice-cube trays (each cube is about 30 ml/1 fl oz), cover and freeze. Once frozen, turn out the frozen cubes into a freezer bag. Always label and date each quantity of milk.

■ To defrost expressed milk, take out whatever quantity you need, allow it to defrost, pop it into a sterilised bottle and then warm it in a jug of hot water.

Equipment planner: expressing

Electric breast pumps

Some mothers find that the best type of pump in terms of effectiveness is the large heavy electric pump, the type used in hospitals. Their rhythmical suction simulates the sucking of your baby, encouraging milk flow, and they work on variable suction levels. Hospital pumps are dual pumps, expressing both breasts at the same time. This can save a lot of time and research has 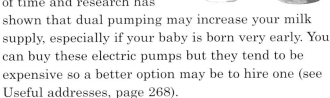 shown that dual pumping may increase your milk supply, especially if your baby is born very early. You can buy these electric pumps but they tend to be expensive so a better option may be to hire one (see Useful addresses, page 268).

There are also mini electric pumps available, some of which can work on batteries or have an adaptor available for use in the car. You can also buy cool bags, which hold all the equipment that you need for the mini electric pumps and also have the facility to keep four bottles of milk cool for 10–12 hours.

Manual breast pumps

These are cheaper and more portable than electric pumps. It's a good idea to take one with you when you are out and about. The Isis breast pump is the most efficient and comfortable and works in a different way to other manual pumps, all of which work on a piston action. The Isis pump mimics the compressive action a baby makes when suckling at the breast. It can express the same amount of milk in the same time as an electric pump. The pump has a silicone diaphragm and soft cushion 'petals', which fit over the breast. The diaphragm stretches and relaxes to create a vacuum to guide the milk gently away and, unlike other breast pumps, once you have pulled the handle to generate a little bit of vacuum, you can sustain the vacuum and the milk will flow without your having to pull the handle again. There are also soft 'petals' on the cushion in the funnel that fits over the breast, which work on the area around the areola in a manner similar to the way a baby's lip sucks on the breast to stimulate a natural let-down reflex.

Storing expressed milk

Some breast pumps come with freezer bags but you will need more. You can also buy breast milk storage kits, which contain pre-sterilised bottle bags, bag holders, clips and date labels. Express the milk into the bags, which can then be frozen and secured with a sealing clip. A bag can be put back into one of the bag holders for feeding once the milk has defrosted.

Travel kit

To make it easier for you to express milk when you are travelling or at work, you can buy an insulated travel bag complete with a breast pump and some storage bottles, breast pads and gel packs. The packs can be frozen and will keep milk cool in the insulated bag for up to six hours.

From breast to formula

You can breastfeed your baby for as long as you want. Most mothers, however, stop breastfeeding between four and six months. Some mothers continue to breastfeed for the morning and evening feeds and give formula milk (or expressed milk, see page 134) in between when they are at work .

If you choose to combine breastfeeding with bottle feeding, you will need to give your baby infant formula milk up until the age of one year. Cow's milk is not suitable as your baby's main drink before one year as it does not contain enough iron and other nutrients for proper growth.

You can either stop breastfeeding all at one or choose to drop feeds slowly. Each approach has its advantages and disadvantages. Read the following and decide which is more likely to work for you.

Cold turkey

To stop breastfeeding all at one:
■ Do not put the baby to the breast at all.
■ Don't express and don't massage.
■ Avoid getting hot water on your breasts when you bath or shower and wear a tight bra. It might help to wrap a towel tightly around your chest as this can help to reduce discomfort as the pressure inhibits milk production, and you can take pain relief tablets as their effects will no longer be passed on to the baby in the milk.

You might find that it is easier for someone else to give your baby a bottle or cup as your baby will smell your milk and be frustrated that she can't breastfeed.

Hot and cold compresses can reduce engorgement, as can cabbage leaves or grated carrots (see also page 126).

If you choose to stop breastfeeding completely and suddenly, your breasts will become very full and engorged. There will be no stimulation to the nipple to encourage milk production so the hormonal signal that milk needs to be produced will be lost.

The advantages:
■ Breastfeeding is over and done with within a week. Mother and baby know where they are – no more breastfeeding.

The disadvantages:
■ Some babies find this transition too abrupt and get very upset. Suddenly there is no breast and they have to use a bottle or cup.
■ For the mother, the milk will still be made and she may well go back to the same engorged feeling of the first few days of breastfeeding.
■ Once breastfeeding is established, stopping feeding in this manner can be very painful and can sometimes lead to complications such as mastitis.

Dropping feeds

If you have the luxury of time this is probably the easiest if slightly longer way of stopping breastfeeding once breastfeeding is established. Simply reduce your breastfeeding schedule by one feed every one to two days until the baby is no longer being breastfed. This will limit the stimulation for more milk and slowly milk production will reduce and eventually stop. For women going back to work this is probably the most convenient method and they will have the option of which feed to reduce to suit the needs of themselves and their babies. Many women choose to drop the day feeds because they have busy work commitments but like to keep the intimacy of the night feed, so this is usually the last feed to go.

The advantages:

■ It gives the baby more time to adjust to a bottle or cup.

■ This gradual approach gives the mother's breasts time to settle down.

The disadvantages:

■ This method takes time and some babies become confused which is breast time and which is bottle time. Many mothers become bored by the slowness of this approach and after dropping a couple of feeds go 'cold turkey' from that point.

Moving to a bottle/cup

All babies are different and encouraging your baby to make the transition to other means of feeding can be very challenging. Sometimes when babies are first introduced to a bottle after breastfeeding they tend to 'gag' on the teat. You may need to experiment with dif-

---

Cup feeding

■ If a young baby is unable to hold a cup, wrap the baby so that her arms and hands cannot knock the cup away.

■ Sit the baby upright whatever age she is. Excess fluid can make the baby cough and splutter or choke.

■ Never pour milk into a young baby's mouth. Place the cup so that the milk touches her lips. Newborn babies will lap up the milk.

■ As your baby learns to drink from the cup, be prepared for spillage (use bibs or cloths to protect her – and your – clothes)

■ Have patience and take a step back to enjoy how your baby learn this new skill.

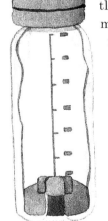

ferent-shaped teats (see page 147) or try cup feeding. Most mothers change to bottle feeding but for an older baby it might be best to go straight onto a cup in which case choose a spill-proof cup with a soft spout. It is sensible to try and introduce a cup or bottle in the two weeks prior to returning to work so that you are confident that your baby will feed happily. By six months many babies are able to drink from a cup so you may be able to avoid giving bottles altogether.

● **Q What do I do if my baby is not keen to feed from a bottle?**

A Try offering your baby milk from a small cup like an egg cup or spoon that has been sterilised. Experiment with different teats or soften the teat with a little boiled water that has been allowed to cool down a little. Try giving your baby milk from a trainer cup with a soft spout. Babies will smell your milk if you are the one feeding so get someone else to feed your baby

---

■ If your baby is reluctant to take a bottle, you could try softening the teat in boiled water and then allowing it to cool down.

Bottle feeding

Not all mothers want to breastfeed and, indeed, some women find that they just can't. Although bottle feeding isn't as good for your baby as breastfeeding, you can still give your baby a great start by enjoying all the advantages of skin-to-skin contact.

The advantages of bottle feeding are that:
■ You can see exactly how much milk your baby is getting at each feed.
■ Your partner can share in the pleasure of feeding his baby – and he gives you a break at the same time.
■ Formula milk is harder to digest than breast milk and stays in a baby's stomach longer and it also contains slightly more protein so babies will go longer between feeds.
■ You have more freedom as you are not the only person able to feed your baby, which also means that your partner can get up in the night sometimes, allowing you to get a good night's sleep!
■ You can eat and drink whatever you like.

The disadvantages are that:
■ Formula milk is made of modified cow's milk. However hard manufacturers try, they can never mimic human breast milk; it evolved to feed babies and cow's milk evolved to feed cows.
■ Formula milk doesn't contain antibodies like breast milk to fight infection.

> **Do not use softened water to make up your baby's feeds as it has a higher concentration of salt, which can harm your baby's kidneys. Generally there is always at least one tap that is not affected by a water softener and that delivers mains water.**

■ Formula milk can increase your baby's risk of contracting respiratory illnesses, gastroenteritis, ear infections or asthma.
■ If there is a history of allergy in the family, e.g. eczema or food allergy, it is best to breastfeed exclusively for the first six months.
■ Bottle-fed babies tend to suffer from wind more than breast-fed babies.
■ You have to be prepared to take feeds with you when you go out, which takes a little organisation. It is important that you keep these feeds cool and ask for them to be heated when you need them. If you keep them warm they will grow bacteria and make your baby unwell.

If you choose to bottle feed from birth, it will probably take a few days for your breasts to settle down and feel comfortable. Without the stimulation of sucking, milk production will gradually stop. Wear a good, supporting bra. If your breasts feel tight and heavy, they may have become engorged but there are ways to help you through this (see page 138).

Making up formula milk
The department of health has revised guidance on the preparation and storage of infant formula. Current advice is that bottles should be made up fresh for each feed. If you do need to prepare a feed for later, they suggest that water is kept in a sealed flask and fresh formula is made up when required. You should avoid making up enough feed for a whole day in advance or warming up bottles of formula milk which has been made from powder. This is because powdered infant formula milk is not sterile and there is a small risk of contamination from micro-organisms if made up.

Making up feeds with hot water just before feeding your baby is not really practical, so I suggest filling bottles with water in advance and then adding the formula just before you feed your baby. When out and about simply take the water in the bottle and the measured-out formula in a separate container.

■ Fill the sterilised bottle with water that has been boiled and left to cool. Don't use water that has been boiled more than once as this increases the sodium level.

■ You can make up 5 bottles of water in advance, seal them and then leave them at room temperature or store them in the main body of the fridge. Many babies are fine with their milk at room temperature. If you put the bottles in the fridge you will need to warm them in a jug of hot water before feeding your baby.

■ When you are ready to feed your baby add the correct amount of formula, put the cap on the bottle and shake it thoroughly to ensure that the powder has completely dissolved and doesn't clog up the teat.

■ If you keep the bottles of water in the fridge and reheat them, always test the temperature of the milk by shaking a little milk onto the inside of your wrist before feeding your baby.

■ Any left over milk from a feed should be discarded.

Positions for bottle feeding

■ Hold your baby close to you on your lap in a semi-upright position where she can make eye contact with you. If necessary, put a pillow on your lap to raise her up. Your baby will enjoy feeding more if you smile and chat to her as she takes her bottle.

■ Place the teat carefully in her mouth and gently stroke your baby's cheek to elicit the rooting reflex.

■ Always make sure you tilt the bottle so that the neck and teat are full of milk to avoid getting pockets of air, which could cause your baby to have wind.

> ● **Q How much milk does my baby need?**
> **A** To begin with your baby needs to feed little and often. Your baby may feed as frequently as every one to two hours and drink about 50 ml (1–2 fl oz). By two or three weeks your baby may settle into a pattern of three hours between feeds and may take about 100 ml (3½ fl oz). By the fourth week your baby may be taking 125 ml (4 fl oz). By 12 weeks your baby may be taking 200 ml (7 fl oz) but don't worry if she is taking less, provided she is gaining weight and thriving.
>
> A young baby's routine should be quite flexible as she will have growth spurts and may be very hungry and need extra feeds during these periods (see page 128).

■ If your baby seems unsettled during the feed, she may have wind and you could sit her up and try to get her to burp by rubbing her back (see different burping positions, overleaf).

■ When your baby has finished or you want to release the teat, carefully put your little finger into the corner of her mouth to break the suction.

■ Sit your baby on your knee with a clean tea towel or muslin square across your lap and rub her back gently so that you can dispel any trapped wind.

Pre-term babies

Pre-term babies have a greater need for certain nutrients like iron and zinc than babies who reach full term. This is because these minerals start to be stored in your baby's body in the last weeks of pregnancy. As a result, premature babies are usually given a special infant formula in hospital, which contains more calories, protein, vitamins and minerals than you find in standard formula milk.

Most babies are considered ready for standard formula by the time they are strong enough to go home although some pre-term babies may be sent home on a 'bridging' formula that is higher in certain nutrients than standard infant formula. If this is the case for your baby, you will be informed and advised by your hospital and health visitor as to which formulas are necessary for your baby.

Burping your baby

Some breastfed babies don't need to be burped, whereas bottle-fed babies do need burping. This is because breastfed babies tend not to take in as much air as bottle-fed babies. Sometimes, if a baby is not latched on properly, she may take in more air than necessary, which can cause wind.

If you put your baby down after a feed and she is content, then no burping is necessary. If, however, she squirms uncomfortably and is fretful, then a trapped air bubble is probably causing discomfort and she won't be happy until she manages to burp. There are three main ways of holding a baby to wind her and these are described opposite. They are:

- Sitting on your lap.
- Over your shouler.
- Lying on your lap.

All babies seem to regurgitate a small amount of milk mixed with saliva after a feed, so make sure that you protect your clothing when burping a baby. Never leave your baby to feed on her own by propping up a bottle because she could choke.

Making bottle feeding safer

- When you make up a bottle, make up about 30 ml (1 fl oz) more than your baby usually drinks. When she starts taking all the milk in the bottle, increase the amount of milk by a further 30 ml (1 fl oz). In the first few days your baby probably won't take more than 50 ml (1–2 fl oz) at a time.
- If you are warming milk by standing a bottle in a jug of hot water, it is very important to keep this well away from your baby. Many babies have been scalded by tipping the jug over themselves.
- It is not recommended to heat bottles in a microwave as the milk can be heated unevenly, leaving hot spots. If you do choose to use this method, shake the bottle thoroughly and always check the temperature before feeding your baby. You can also buy bottles with a heat sensor strip (see overleaf).
- If you are out and about, you can warm your baby's bottle by rotating it under a hot tap.
- If your baby does not finish her bottle or if you warm a bottle and she does not want it, never re-heat it. Always throw it away. Warm milk is the perfect breeding ground for bacteria. Clean and rinse bottles, covering and setting aside until you are ready to sterilise them.
- It is handy to have some ready-made cartons of formula to take with you when you are going out and know you won't be able to make up your own bottles.
- Although most parents warm their baby's bottles, it isn't absolutely necessary. Milk can be given at room temperature but it shouldn't be given straight from the fridge.

All babies posset but if you are worried that your baby brings up a lot of milk at each feed, this may be a symptom of reflux. This is most common in babies under one, and more information is given on page 120.

Different burping positions

Whichever way you hold your baby, the aim is to allow her to stretch her tummy so that any trapped air is released by a burp. Rub or gently pat her back until she burps.

1 Sit your baby on your lap with her weight forward and her head supported in one of your hands. With your other hand, rub and pat her back.

2 Hold your baby with her body resting against your chest and her head looking over your shoulder. Drape a muslin square over your shoulder so that any milk that your baby brings up doesn't land on your clothes.

3 Lay her face down on your lap, supporting her head with your hand. This is not advisable immediately after you have fed your baby.

Night feeds

■ Keep a thermos flask of hot water ready for when you want to heat your baby's bottle in the middle of the night.

■ Keep the lights low, trying to keep your baby in sleep mode, feeding and change her if necessary but bearing in mind that this is not a time for chatting or playing games. It is important for your baby to learn right from the start that night-time is for sleeping.

■ If your baby wakes you several times during the night and then drinks very little, it may be that she has got into the habit of 'grazing' during the day. It is best to extend the period between feeds during the day to break this pattern.

Away from home

■ Take cooled bottles of milk with you in a cooler bag or you can buy handy 225 g (8 oz) sachets of powdered formula. You simply empty one into a bottle containing 250 ml (8 fl oz) cooled, boiled water, which you can prepare in advance and take with you.

■ Alternatively you can use ready-made formula from a carton.

■ You can heat your baby's milk using a special bottle warmer or a jug of hot water but many babies are happy to take their milk at room temperature. If your baby isn't especially keen, it would be helpful to try to encourage her by slowly introducing cooler and cooler bottles.

Bottles

Bottles come in many shapes, sizes and design and you will need six to eight 300 ml (10 fl oz) bottles. Of course, bottles are the most important item when feeding your baby in this way but there are other pieces of equipment that you need to buy as well, which are described overleaf.

Standard bottles: These are the classic 250 ml (8 fl oz) cylindrical bottles that will fit a range of teats. They can be difficult to fill as unless you hold them they can easily fall over, and if you do hold them there is the danger that you can scald your hand with boiling water as you pour it into the narrow aperture.

Wide-neck bottles: Shorter, stubbier bottles pioneered by Avent. They are easier to fill and clean and usually take 260 ml (just over 8 fl oz) of milk. The Avent teat has an anti-vacuum skirt with a one-way air valve that opens and closes with a baby's natural sucking rhythm to let air flow into the bottle while she drinks but lets less air into her tummy, helping to prevent post-feeding discomfort related to colic. As your baby sucks, there is also a reassuring sound that lets you know your baby is taking milk. The more bulbous teat and longer nipple more closely resembles the natural shape of the breast and allows a baby to suckle using tongue and lips, similar to breastfeeding. Since babies use the same suckling motion on the teat as on the breast, transition between breast and bottle is made easier.

Shaped bottles: These bottles are designed to make it easier for babies to hold the bottle themselves – either

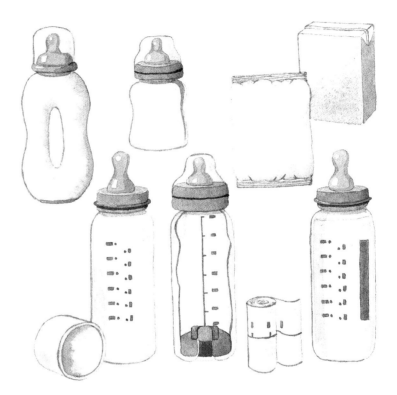

Top row (left to right): shaped bottle, wide-necked bottle, ready-mixed carton of formula milk. Bottom row (left to right): standard bottle, steri-bottle, heat-sensing bottle.

by the hole in the middle or because they are 'waisted'. However, it can be tricky to mix the formula thoroughly (it may be best to mix it in a jug first) and they can be

and formula milk

very difficult to clean. Also they may not fit some steriliser units.

Disposable bottles: In 1948 an American midwife invented the first disposable baby bottle: a plastic bag that contracted during feeding just like the breast. It was thought that babies fed using disposable bottles suffered less colic. This might have been true in the past but since the wide-neck bottle and teat was introduced in 1987, the design has improved with the result that babies take in much less air.

Using disposable bottles works out much more expensive but they are good for holidays as you don't need to sterilise the bottles; simply use the sterile disposable bags that fit into the bottle-shaped holder.

Steri-bottles: These bottles were the brainchild of someone who went on a picnic with a friend with a baby who had brought a carton of infant formula but had left her baby's bottle behind. Even though she had a pre-prepared carton of milk she couldn't just buy a bottle and use it because it would need to be sterilised first. The bottles come in packs of four in two sizes: 125 ml (4 fl oz) for newborn to three months, with a medium flow teat, and a bigger, 250 ml (8 fl oz) size with the choice of medium-flow teat for babies up to three months and fast-flow teat for babies over three months.

These are disposable, pre-sterilised, single-use feeding bottles which come complete with a special pre-sterilised teat which incorporates a valve that lets in just the right amount of air, allowing a baby to feed comfortably without accumulating excess wind.

Disposable steri-bottles make a good alternative when you are out and about, on a short holiday or just simply extra busy. The bottles are suitable for freezing and you can use them for storing and freezing expressed breast milk. The disadvantage is that they work out more expensive and for a long holiday a large supply of disposable bottles would probably be too bulky to take.

Heat-sensing bottles: These have a heat-sensitive strip, which changes colour if the milk is too hot.

Bottle coolers

Buy an insulated bag with thermal gel packs, which can be frozen to keep prepared bottles cool when you are on the move.

Bottle warmers

If you don't want to go to the trouble of boiling water in a kettle in the middle of the night, bottle warmers are a good idea. However, they are not essential; you can keep hot water in a thermos flask.

Formula milk

Most formula milks are based on cow's milk. However, if your baby has an adverse reaction to this, she may have an allergy or intolerance to cow's milk. If you are worried, consult your doctor who may advise you to give your baby a soya-based infant formula. But don't switch to a soya-based formula without seeking medical advice first as you might find that your baby is also allergic to soya proteins.

Equipment planner: sterilisers

Sterilisers

Most sterilising units hold four or six bottles and you should buy your bottles and steriliser at the same time as some have bottles included in the price and you don't want to buy more bottles than you need. Also, the steriliser must be compatible with your brand of bottles or you may not be able to fit all your bottles into it. Ideally it is best to buy a six-bottle steriliser as you will want to make up a supply of bottles for the day ahead in the morning.

Chemical steriliser: This is a lidded container that you fill with cold water to which you add a sterilising tablet or solution. It is important that all the feeding utensils are completely submerged in the sterilising fluid. Bottles are left to soak for 30 minutes and then need to be rinsed in recently boiled water.

This is a fiddly system and not to be recommended for constant use because of the chemicals, but it is good for travelling as all you need is access to clean water and a kettle. There is a special travel kit that you can buy which consists of sterilising tablets together with seven plastic bags, which hold the bottles in place of the rigid container.

Electric steam steriliser: Water is poured into a mains-powered container, which is then switched on. The sterilisation cycle takes eight to nine minutes and turns off automatically and you have clean, odour-free bottles without using any chemicals. Bottles and teats remain sterile in these units for up to three hours and it comes in a four- or six-bottle size.

For speed and convenience this is a good choice but it is quite bulky and expensive so it would be a good item to borrow if you know someone who has had a baby.

Microwave steriliser: You can sterilise your equipment in a microwave using a specially designed steam unit. You will need to check that the dimensions and wattage of your microwave are compatible with the specifications of the steriliser before you buy it. You also have to check that your feeding equipment is suitable for microwave use. The disadvantage is that the unit holds only four bottles. This method takes just four minutes plus cooling time. You can also buy microwave steriliser bags each of which holds two bottles plus their accessories and can be reused 20 times. Sterilisation takes just three minutes.

3-in-1 steriliser: This steriliser separates to create a chemical travel steriliser, electric steam steriliser and microwave steriliser.

What needs to be sterilised?

Bottle feeding: Bottles, teats, measuring spoons, caps and covers, soothers/dummies.

Breastfeeding: Breast pumps and any bottles or teats used for giving expressed milk.

Weaning: Spoons and beakers. Feeding bowls can be washed thoroughly in hot water or use a dishwasher. Dry bowls with a dry, clean cloth.

and teats

Sterilising bottles

■ Tummy upsets can make small babies very ill. Since milk creates an ideal breeding ground for the bacteria that cause serious tummy problems, it is vital to keep all feeding equipment scrupulously clean. Bottle-fed babies are much more likely to be hospitalised with diarrhoea and vomiting than breastfed ones. Bottles and teats should be washed in hot soapy water. Scrub the insides of the bottles with a bottle-brush and turn the teats inside out and squeeze them lightly to make sure that the hole is clear. Rinse bottles and teats thoroughly with cold water, then sterilise.

■ If using a microwave steriliser, a single bottle can be sterilised in two minutes and up to six bottles plus teats can be sterilised at a time. Use wide-necked bottles and then they can be sterilised by other methods, too, such as in a dishwasher. After cleaning your bottles and teats with a brush, run them through your dishwasher on a hot programme at a minimum temperature of 80°C. You will need to make up your feeds as soon as the washing programme is finished as, unlike a sterilising unit, there is no sterile container in which to store the bottles.

Teats

Teats come in two different kinds of material: the more durable silicone, which is transparent so it is easier to see if it is clean, and latex. Latex can be good for a young baby but it needs to be replaced every three weeks as it becomes sticky and hard to clean. There should be a reassuring 'zuzzing' sound, which lets you know that your baby is getting milk as she sucks.

There are also many different-shaped teats, such as orthodontic ones, which are more bulbous and are shaped to fit the contour of your baby's mouth. These can work well when you first switch your baby from breast to bottle.

You can also choose from slow-, medium- or fast-flow teats. A newborn baby generally needs a slow-flow teat, but an older, hungrier baby might need a fast-flow one. If your baby seems to take ages to finish a bottle or gives up in the middle, the hole may be too small and you may want to change to a medium-flow teat. If your baby is spluttering and choking as she feeds, the hole in the teat may be too big.

Choosing the right teat for your baby is simply trial and error. You may like to try variable-flow teats that fit wide-neck bottles and can give slow, medium or fast flow using just one teat. The valve built into the teat delivers more or less milk in response to the way your baby sucks. You can adjust the rate of milk by twisting the collar around the neck of the bottle. You may need to change your baby's teat to a faster one if:

■ You feel that your baby is taking too long over each of her feeds.

■ She gives up before taking the appropriate number of millilitres per feed.

■ Your baby's weight gain is too slow.

Regularly and carefully monitor your baby's teats to check that they are in good condition, especially if your baby sucks furiously on her bottle. If there is no zuzzing sound as she sucks, this means that there is no milk coming out.

CHAPTER THREE

SETTLING IN
4–6 months

PRACTICALITIES

By now you should be feeling more confident about handling your baby. At the age of six months he should be enjoying three meals a day and will probably have a more settled sleep pattern. During this stage you can gradually start getting your baby into some sort of routine. His curiosity know no bounds and his increasing ability to explore with his hands and mouth means you need to ensure your home is a safe environment. In addition, you may want to return to work soon, so you may need to start thinking about childcare.

Handling your baby

Now that your baby can support his head, you will discover that there are many different ways of picking up and holding him (see box, right). You can also have fun together, swinging him in the air or rocking him.

■ Swing him from side to side – hold him facing away from you with one hand between his legs, supporting his tummy, and the other hand under his arm, supporting his chest.

■ Hold your baby with both hands under his armpits, lift him up to your face and then swing him down between your legs. He will love flying through the air.

■ Lie on your back with your knees drawn up and balance your baby on his tummy on your shins and knees. Hold his hands and stretch his arms out to the side and rock him on your knees.

Moving to the big bath

At around six months your baby will be too big for the baby bath and will need to graduate to the big bath. To make the transition easy for your growing baby, it is a good idea for the first few nights to take a bath with him in the big bath. He'll love splashing you with water and playing with his bath toys, which will now have more room to float around.

Holding your baby

■ Lift your baby by putting your hands under his armpits. Then put one arm diagonally around his back and the other arm under his bottom.
■ Carry your baby on your hip with one arm supporting his bottom, leaving the other arm free, or you hold him with both arms, one around his back and the other supporting his bottom.
■ Carry your baby so that he faces forwards. Put one arm around his waist or chest so that he can look around and use your other hand to support him under her bottom.

We can tolerate hot water much more easily than a baby can, so make sure you don't make the bath water too hot. It's a good idea to test the temperature with your elbow before putting your baby in the bath. Wet babies are also very slippery so you should always put a non-slip mat in the big bath or use a specially designed baby bath seat. From six months you can use a swivel bath seat, which can be secured to the bottom of the bath with suction cups.

Your baby will not only enjoy playing with plastic toys but will also like playing with sponges, plastic cups, old shampoo bottles, etc. – basically, anything that he can fill and empty. Just make sure that all containers are well washed before letting him play with them and remove any small tops. There are also some great activity toys that operate by water being poured through them, which will fascinate your baby.

Don't pull the plug until your baby is out of the bath. The gurgling sound may frighten him and he may worry that he will go down the drain too.

Safety first

Every year over a million children are taken to hospital after being injured in the home. Over half of the casualties are under five years old and most will have been hurt as the result of a fall, banging into an object, choking on small objects, burning themselves or swallowing something poisonous. Many accidents are preventable and it is never too early to take precautions.

Changing

Most accidents at changing times happen when the baby falls off a changing unit or other high surface. Babies wriggle and kick and can even roll off a double bed if left unattended.

■ If you use a changing unit or any other high surface to change your baby, make sure that you can reach everything that you need before you start.

■ If you have to move away, take the baby with you. Never leave the baby alone on a raised surface.

Bathing

Never leave a baby alone in a bath even for a moment. A baby can drown in just a few centimetres of water.

■ Non-slip mats and bath rings can help you hold your baby in the bath but you should not rely on them – your baby still needs you there to support him.

■ Do not leave your baby alone in the bathroom with a toddler. The older child will not understand the risks and cannot be expected to take responsibility.

■ Always run cold water into the bath before hot and test the temperature with your elbow or inner wrist. Babies and toddlers have sensitive skin and need to be bathed at a lower temperature than an adult would find comfortable.

■ If you are bathing with your baby, place a towel on the floor and lift him out before you get out, to avoid slipping.

Smoke alarms

Having a working smoke alarm on each floor can give you vital extra seconds to get out of your house in a fire. Check your smoke alarm regularly and if it runs from a battery make sure you check it at least once a year. Make an escape plan and practise how you would get out of the house in an emergency.

Choosing childcare

Going back to work is always difficult. If you have taken maternity leave, you will know when you have to return to work. If you have stopped work or want a change in career, it can be quite difficult to make the decision to stay at home, to return to work or to work part time. I consciously made the decision to choose a career as a writer where I could spend quite a lot of time working from home yet still be with my children, which gives the best of both worlds.

Naturally you will want the best care for your baby and you will want to know that your child is safe and well cared for when you are not there, but working out what sort of childcare will suit you can be difficult. It is said that between a third to two-thirds of a mother's salary goes on childcare. Some mothers use their own mother or mother-in-law to help. This can work wonderfully well but sometimes different views and emotions can get in the way.

Ideally you should start your childcare a week or two before you return to work, depending on your budget. It will take your baby time to adjust and it is best to make a gradual transition, spending time with the carer to begin with to see that your baby settles in happily to the new routine.

Childminders

Childminders are self-employed carers based in their own homes. Often they are mothers themselves and will look after your children along with their own. A childminder must be registered with the Office for Standards in Education (OFSTED), which makes annual checks on a childminder and her home to ensure that they are safe.

How many children will there be with my childminder?

A childminder is allowed to look after up to six children under eight years of age, including children of her own – but only three of them should be aged under five years. Babies can go to a childminder from a few months old but at this age, a childminder is limited to just one or two babies at a time. Childminders who work with an assistant may look after larger groups of children.

Childminder advantages	Childminder disadvantages
■ Your child goes to a homely environment.	■ You have to take the baby to the childminder's home.
■ Because childminders look after only small numbers of children they can offer more individual attention than nurseries.	■ You may feel uncomfortable about your baby having to fit around your childminder's routine and the needs of children of different ages.
■ Flexibility to suit your needs, which is ideal if you have irregular working hours.	■ You may feel that your baby may not get enough one-to-one attention if there are five other children arounc.
■ Good if you have children of different ages and want them to be looked after together.	■ There is no back-up if your childminder is ill and she may need to cancel at short notice if there is a contagious illness in the house.
■ Continuity – childminders can care for children up to the age of eight and will often collect children from nursery school.	■ You can't take your baby if she is unwell.
■ A safe environment that is subject to regular checks.	
■ A childminder costs less than a nanny.	

Always check references thoroughly, even if you use an agency. Contact at least two previous employers and don't be afraid to quiz them about small details.

What sort of hours will childminders work?

Childminders are self-employed and so they decide on their working hours. Most childminders will provide you with childcare between the hours of 8am and 6pm. Some childminders will work early mornings, evenings and weekends as well. You will need to negotiate hours and terms and conditions with your childminder. Many childminders are happy to provide families with part-time places for children.

How to find a childminder

Your local Children's Information Service (CIS) can supply a list of childminders in your area. Contact them through ChildcareLink on 0800 0960 296 or visit www.childcarelink.gov.uk. Alternatively, contact the National Childminding Association on 0800 169 4486.

How much does a childminder cost?

Childminders are usually paid on an hourly basis and set their charges themselves as there is no national standard rate. Most childminders will charge between £60 and £120 per child per week for full-time care.

Some questions to ask when choosing a childminder

■ How many children does she look after? How old are they and how long have she been looking after them?
■ What is the childminder's routine? How often does she take the children out?
■ What kind of food does she provide?
■ What is her attitude on sleep, crying, potty training, watching television, etc.?
■ How does the childminder fit in household chores like shopping, cooking, and how will it affect your baby's day?
■ How long has she been childminding for and how long does she intend to continue for?
■ Can she give you the names and telephone numbers of other parents she works for? Ensure you follow these up.

Nannies

A nanny is someone you employ to look after your baby in your home. It is probably best to choose a qualified nanny to look after a very young baby although never underestimate the importance of experience. The Nursery Nurse Examining Board (NNEB) (a two-year full-time course) used to be the best-regarded qualification. The NNEB is now known as the CACHE Diploma in Childcare and Education (DCE), Level 3 (a two-year course). Other qualifications to look out for:
■ BTEC National Certificate or Diploma in Childhood Studies. The diploma is a two-year course, equivalent to the NNEB. The certificate is a lower level, usually a one-year course.
■ National Vocational Qualifications (NVQs), Levels 2 and 3 in Childcare and Education are popular with people already working with children. They allow for assessment while continuing to work. Level 2 is the most common, Level 3 is equivalent to the NNEB. A Level 2 qualification is fine for nannies working in a supervised role, but Level 3 is a better choice if you are looking for a nanny to take sole charge while you are at work.

What kind of hours would a nanny work?

There are no set hours for a nanny but they usually have weekends free and you can arrange babysitting in the evening. A nanny can 'live in' or come to your home for set days and hours. A nanny share with a friend who has a baby of a similar age and lives close by may be a good way to make this choice more affordable.

How to find a nanny
See box, right.

How much does a nanny cost?
You will have to pay anything from £150 to £400 plus tax and national insurance per week. You may also need to provide a car and petrol allowance. Nanny agencies charge anything between £500 and £1000 for introduction.

Some questions to ask when choosing a nanny
■ What qualifications and experience does she have?
■ Does she hold a first aid certificate?
■ How much experience does she have with children the age of your baby?
■ Why does she enjoy working with children and why does she want the job you are offering?
■ Why did she leave her last job?
■ How would she organise her day with your baby?

How to find a nany, au pair or maternity nurse
■ The *Lady* magazine, available at most newsagents, regularly carries adverts for nanny positions, au pairs, maternity nurses, etc. It also gives details of nanny agencies around the country.
■ Agencies may help you save time and guide you towards a suitable nanny but they are expensive and charge £500–£1000 to place a nanny. The National Childbirth Trust may have a nanny share register.
■ You can also place an advert yourself for a nanny or au pair in the magazine *Nursery World* (tel: 020 7782 3000) or *The Nursing Times* (tel: 020 7874 0400).
■ To find an au pair contact the Au Pair and Student Agency (freephone: 0500 823 666 or website: www.internationalaupair.com).
■ There is also a subscription-only magazine called *Simply Childcare,* which gives details of au pairs, nannies, childminders and babysitters. looking for jobs. If you take out a subscription you can advertise for free in the magazine. They also offer advice on childcare (tel: 020 7701 6111 or website: www.simplychildcare.com).

■ Discuss other duties like cooking for the baby, taking care of his room, shopping for food.
■ What hours is she prepared to work and how many

Nanny advantages
■ Convenience – you don't have to take your child anywhere. If you work from home, you can spend time with your baby during the day when you are not busy.
■ One-to-one care.
■ Regular babysitting can be written into the contract.
■ More control over your child's routine, what he does and what he eats.
■ Siblings can be cared for at no extra cost.

Nanny disadvantages
■ This is an expensive option. If a nanny lives in there are hidden costs, e.g. food, phone, and a nanny often expects there to be a car for her use.
■ You may not like someone else living in your house.
■ You have the responsibility of employing someone and sorting out contracts, holidays, sick pay, National Insurance, etc.
■ Nannies tend to want sole charge and you may feel worried that someone else will take over the care of your baby.

Au pair advantages	Au pair disadvantages
■ Inexpensive option. An au pair will often help with housework as well as look after your baby.	■ As an au pair is young and often has no training in childcare; she should not look after a young baby for any length of time unsupervised. ■ Command of the English language may be quite poor to begin with. ■ Often you don't meet the au pair you hire until she starts working for you as she may still be living abroad. However, if an au pair has left her previous job, you may get the chance to meet her first. ■ Six months is the average stay for an au pair so there is little stability. ■ An au pair only works part time. ■ She may become homesick or she may stay out late, having a whale of a time and a complicated love life!

nights babysitting duty?

■ What does she like to do in her time off?

■ Does she have a boyfriend?

■ Does she smoke?

■ What is her attitude towards sleep, food, crying, potty training, watching television, etc.?

■ How long she would be prepared to stay if the job worked out?

■ What about holidays?

■ Does she drive? Is the driving licence clean? Ask to see the licence so you can check it.

When you are satisfied you have found the right person set up a tight contract, which covers hours, duties, hand-over time, babysitting, holidays, etc. It's a good idea to organise a daily diary to be kept by nanny and parent(s).

Au pair

An au pair is usually aged between 17 and 27 years and works part time up to five hours a day, usually about 25 hours a week. Most au pairs stay between six and 12 months, many filling in a year between school and college. An au pair lives with you as part of the family and in return can do a mixture of childcare and light housework.

Au pairs come from non-English-speaking countries and they come to England to learn the language. Most au pairs go to college to study English for at least two hours once or twice a week and some study every day. A few come from EU countries but the majority come from Eastern European countries like the Czech Republic, Slovakia, Croatia, Hungary and also Turkey.

If you go to an agency to find an au pair, it is important to check that it has offices in the country where the girl comes from and that the staff there have interviewed her personally and checked her references. You should double-check these yourself.

Since an au pair's command of English is not usually that good and she is likely to be inexperienced in childcare, it is not advisable to leave her in charge of a baby full time. However, if a mother is at home with her baby and needs an extra pair of hands to help around the house, an au pair can be a godsend. Provided the au pair can speak some English and can easily phone you, she can also help with babysitting.

How much does an au pair cost?

An au pair will cost between £50 and £80 per week. Au pairs advertise their services in various publications (see box, opposite) but you can also go through an agency, although you will then need to pay an agency fee. Always check to see how long this covers you for; some agencies will find a replacement only if an au pair has left within two weeks.

As a rough guide, if you contract to hire an au pair for six months through an agency and wish to be covered for the entire period, it will cost around £195. If you wish to hire for one year with cover, it will cost between £200 and £300 and if you wish to hire for two years (this is the maximum period), it will cost between £400 and £500.

Maternity nurse

A maternity nurse is a qualified nanny specially trained to look after newborn babies. Quite a lot of maternity nurses are midwives or registered nurses. Maternity nurses aim to get your baby into a routine and sleeping well during the night. Your maternity nurse will be on duty 24 hours a day, six days a week.

How to find a maternity nurse
See box, page 154.

How much does a maternity nurse cost?
Maternity nurses can cost from £400 to £700 a week. You can also hire night nannies who will work a ten-hour shift. These are qualified or experienced nannies who not only care for your child but also offer advice on guiding babies to sleep through the night. Night nannies charge about £60 a night plus a £10 agency fee and a £150 joining fee.

Day nurseries/crèches

Day nurseries are for children under five years old where they play and learn and have fun in groups while their parents work. Some nurseries do not take under twos while others take babies as young as three months up to pre-school five-year-olds. Your baby will be cared for along with other babies and children by a team of professional staff trained in childcare.

There are many kinds of day nurseries/crèches – privately run, community, council and workplace – and they must all be registered and regularly inspected by OFSTED and have to comply with strict guidelines on staff/children ratios. In general these are:
- For under twos, one carer to three children.
- For two- to three-year-olds, one carer to four children.
- For three- to five-year olds, one carer for every eight children.

At least half of the staff in a nursery must be trained to work with young children. Some employers offer a crèche/nursery for their staff's children.

When are nurseries open?
Hours will tend to fit in with an average working day of 8.30am to 6pm and care is usually provided all year

Maternity nurse advantages
- They expect to work long hours.
- You can learn a lot about looking after your baby from a maternity nurse and she can help guide you to set up a routine for your baby.
- If you have had a difficult birth you will be able to get a lot of rest.
- You can breastfeed your baby in the night but will not have to spend time settling him afterwards.
- If you are bottle feeding, you can sleep through and the maternity nurse will feed your baby.
- Your will feel reassured that you are leaving your baby in safe hands.

Maternity nurse disadvantages
- Maternity nurses tend to be very expensive.
- You may not want to impose a routine on your baby at an early age.
- You may feel that the care of your child has been taken away from you.
- You may not like someone else living in your house.

Nursery/crèche advantages

- You feel reassured leaving your baby with a team of professional staff trained in childcare.
- If one member of staff is away ill, you can still rely on the nursery looking after your baby.
- You have continuity as your child could stay in the day nursery until he starts school.
- Nurseries are open most of the year.

Nursery/crèche disadvantages

- Your baby may not get one-to-one care.
- The hours are not flexible so will not suit irregular working hours.
- If your child is ill you will not be able to take him to the nursery.
- It may seem too busy an environment for your child.

round except for public holidays. Many nurseries are happy to offer you part-time places and often they organise these into morning and afternoon sessions.

How to find a day nursery

Contact the National Day Nursery Association (Tel: 01484 541 641, www.ndna.org.uk). Your local Children's Information Service (CIS) can also supply a list of day nurseries in your area. Contact them through Childcare Link on 0800 096 0296.

How much does a nursery cost?

Depending on where you live, a privately run day nursery costs anything from about £120 to £200 per week full-time. Community, local authority and workplace nurseries are often subsidised and cost less.

Some questions to ask when choosing a nursery

- Does the nursery operate a key carer system, which means your child will have one person who is responsible for him and with whom he can build a relationship? This is important for babies.
- What is the ratio of carers to children?
- What sort of staff turnover do they have?
- What will be your child's routine each day?
- What will your child eat? If you have specific feeding requirements, can these be met?
- How is information about your child's day conveyed to you?
- Is there an opportunity to talk to the staff at the

beginning and the end of the day?
- What is the nursery's settling in policy?
- Do they encourage parents to stay with their child until they feel totally safe and secure?

Helping your child settle in

- Introduce the new carer or nursery gradually. If possible, spend time with the carer or at the nursery with your baby for a few days so that you and he can get used to the new environment and form a relationship with the carer. Remain in the background if you can and even when you are around, let the carer take charge. Leave your baby for 30 minutes, then an hour and gradually increase the length of time that you are gone.
- Take something familiar from home, like a blanket or soft toy for your child to cuddle while you are away.
- Always say goodbye to your child even if he is upset and you feel bad about leaving him. Don't just disappear when he is distracted. If he looks up and finds you gone, how will he be able to settle confidently and concentrate on playing the next time? Tell him when you will be back.
- Talk to your child's carer and share information. For example, let her know the foods your baby particularly likes or dislikes or if your child has had a disrupted night or tummy upset. Make sure that you have enough time at the end of the day to ask about sleeps, eating, activities, your child's mood, etc.

SLEEPING

Now is the time to start laying down a routine and weaning your baby gradually away from the need for you to help him fall asleep. If your baby has an established sleep time during the day, it will help him to sleep at night. Babies find routines comforting; they also give the parents and baby a pattern to follow. Routines, however, are not set in stone: they must – and will – continue to change frequently.

Encouraging a routine

If the routine you set up for your baby is not working, try to stand back and ask yourself why. It may be that:
■ The timings are not right for your baby.
■ You are not following the routine often enough.
■ Your baby prefers to cat nap during the day rather take two longer naps.

Babies soon recognise that fathers going to and coming from work is a routine in itself. They begin to get very excited when Daddy comes home from work. For some babies, Daddy coming home at bedtime excites them so much that it is very difficult for them to settle. However, I think it's important that they spend time playing with their fathers, who can involve themselves in playtime, baby massage, feeding and bath time.

Sleeps during the day

An average four-month-old baby sleeps about 9–11 hours a night and will still need two to three naps during the day. You should find a time during the day when your baby generally gets tired and put him in his cot to sleep. If you keep your baby awake too long, he will get over-tired, cranky, may not eat and will be much more difficult to settle. This will make the day stressful for both of you.

Morning naps can usually be taken whenever it suits you and your baby. Afternoon naps, however, need to be watched because if you let your baby sleep for hours or late into the afternoon or early evening, you cannot expect him to go to bed at 7–8pm as he will need time to become tired again. Watch early-evening naps in the car, too. On the whole these are pretty unavoidable but they do make a difference to bedtime.

Some mothers stay at home for two of their babies' naps during the day. Try to fit in visitors and outings around nap times so as not to disrupt your baby's routine. When at home the baby would probably take his naps in his cot in the bedroom. Others have one nap at home (usually the morning nap) while the other is taken out and about either in the pushchair or car.

Follow your baby's natural patterns. You will soon recognise signs of sleepiness such as eye-rubbing or irritability.

Remember that if sleeping in his pushchair, your baby should be positioned on his back, lying flat.

There are other mothers that cannot bear to be stuck at home so their babies will nap when out and about in pushchairs or cars. There is nothing wrong with this; as long as the baby naps at least twice a day, a mother can suit herself.

Bedtime routine

From around three to four months, it will help if you establish a regular bedtime routine. This will help your baby to understand the difference between night and day and that night-time is for sleeping and daytime for playing. A typical routine might go something like this:
■ Start off by giving your baby a nice relaxing warm bath and maybe a massage (see page 82).
■ Dress him in his nightclothes, give him his last feed and a cuddle in a fairly dark, quiet room.
■ Lie him down while he is sleepy but still awake – playing some soothing music may help settle your baby.
■ Turn down the lights, say goodnight and leave him to settle. If he continues to cry after a little while, you can go and comfort him but don't pick him up.

You may want to wake your baby before you go to bed to feed him as this may help him to sleep right through the night. But when you feel the time is right, you can drop the late-night feed. If your baby takes very little milk at this feed, he probably isn't hungry and just enjoys a comfort suck so you could try letting him sleep through the night.

Falling asleep by himself

The difference between a baby who sleeps well at night and one who disturbs you several times is not the num-

Q *I know that I should put a baby to sleep on her back but my baby keeps on rolling over onto her tummy. What should I do ?*
A Once your baby starts wriggling don't drive yourself crazy by repositioning her on her back whenever she turns over. The advice on sleeping positions no longer applies.

ber of times your baby wakes during the night, but his ability to fall asleep again by himself. This is why it is so important that you don't let your baby fall asleep at the last feed or rock him to sleep before bedtime. In the short term it will be hard for you but you will reap the benefits in the future. If your baby wakes at night, consider the following:
■ If he sleeps for long periods during the day he may not be tired. Try to limit daytime naps to a maximum of five hours at four months and three–four hours at six months. Try not to let your baby sleep within three hours of bedtime.
■ If your baby has recently started eating solids, try to ensure that you don't feed him within an hour of bedtime and don't give any heavy or indigestible foods at night.
■ One of the most likely causes of waking during the night is hunger. Make sure that your baby is still getting enough milk. He should be getting about 600ml (20 fl oz) milk per day. If your baby eats plenty of dairy

If your baby is having difficulty sleeping because of a stuffy nose, you could use some saline drops to help clear his nose or sprinkle a muslin square with a decongestant capsule like Karvol, which contain a combination of aromatic oils – pine, cinnamon and menthol.

products like yoghurt or cheese then he can drink a lit-tle less milk.

■ He might also be thirsty. Although hot, humid nights are rare in the UK, if the weather is unusually hot, you may need to give your baby a drink of water.

■ Try to ensure that your baby takes some exercise (playgyms are good) and has some fresh air during the day and an active bath time.

■ Make sure that your baby is comfortable, check his nappy, see that his clothing isn't too tight and that he is not too hot or too cold. Put your finger under the clothing on his breastbone to feel if he is hot (you can also feel his tummy to see if he is too hot or too cold, but this might disturb him).

■ If your baby is unsettled, don't pick him up out of bed unless he needs his nappy changing. Go in to him and speak to him softly, leaving five minutes longer each time before returning.

■ Don't be too rigid: there are times when your baby may be going through a growth spurt and is therefore extra hungry and needs to be fed during the night.

Comforters

It's a good idea to let your baby select his own com-forter: it might be his thumb to suck on, a soft fabric square like a muslin cloth, a blanket or a soft toy like a teddy bear. A comforter is the one thing that will soothe

> The good news is that if your baby does wake in the middle of the night and you are breastfeeding, it is better if your partner goes to try and settle him. Your baby is more likely to settle if he can't smell your milk.

> *Q When can I expect my baby to sleep through the night?*
>
> **A** As your baby grows, becomes more active, eats more and sleeps less during the day so the chances of him sleeping through the night increase. All babies are different. By four months some babies are still feeding two or three times during the night, some feed just once and others can sleep through. If your baby is not yet on solids you may find that he begins to wake up more often because he is hungry. Once your baby is well into solid foods you will probably find that he begins to wake later and later for his night feed until he stops needing it altogether. By six months it is realistic to expect your baby to sleep for a long period dur-ing the night. Most babies are enjoying solid food so they do not need to be fed during the night to keep them going.

your baby when he gets distressed and will help him fall asleep when you are not there. Woe betide any par-ent who can't find their baby's comforter when it's time to go to bed. My three children all had security blan-kets, which they still wanted to sleep with when they were 18 months old even though these were all raggedy and torn. I learned too late that it's a good idea to buy two identical blankets and alternate them each week otherwise you may never get the chance to wash the comforter because your baby cries inconsolably and won't sleep without it.

Moving to a cot

If your baby has been sleeping in your room, you should really be thinking about putting him in his own room by the time he is six months old. This is not just for your own privacy but also because at this age your baby is likely to keep himself awake if he is disturbed and you might wake him when you come to bed or make a noise in the night.

Once your baby can sit up, kneel or is able to pull himself up into an upright position, he will need to be moved from a Moses basket or crib to a cot. Of course he may also simply outgrow his Moses basket. Cots need to have high sides so that once your baby can stand he is not able to climb out. Most cots have one side that drops down so that it is easier to reach your baby and most have two positions for the base and mattress so that the sides can be made higher for an older baby. Your baby may find a cot very big and open to begin with so it is a good idea to start to prepare your baby during the day for a cot.

■ Put the Moses basket into the cot so your baby gets a chance to wake up in the cot.

■ Put your baby down in the cot to play for short periods during the day.

Daily routine

Above right is a routine that you can work towards as a guideline, with milk feeds spaced approximately four hours apart – all babies are different so don't worry if your baby wakes and sleeps at different times. Also, babies go through growth spurts and during these times they will probably be more hungry and their routine may alter.

Play

Playtime becomes a very important routine at this age. Through play your baby will begin to learn sequence, expectation, reward, joy and fulfilment. See the development planners starting on page 166 to see what sort of activities you can do with your baby at this age. Babies cannot play for long periods – and neither can

Possible routine

6.30–7am	Wakes up.
7am	Has milk and solids (see Feeding, pages 174–83).
9–9.45/10am	Morning nap.
11/11.45am*	More milk and solids.
12/12.30–2/2.30pm	Afternoon nap.
2.30pm	Milk.
5.30pm	Supper.
6–6.15pm	Bath time, massage, etc.
6.30pm	Milk before bedtime.
7pm	Sleep.
11–11.30pm	Wakes for a feed (older babies may sleep through).

* When you start introducing solids, begin with just one meal at day at around 11am. Give half the milk feed first, then solids and then the remaining milk feeds. Eventually build up to three meals a day at around six months.

most parents – so short playing time several times a day gives mother, father and baby what they need.

Babysitters

Entrusting a young baby to someone else is a big responsibility so make sure you choose a babysitter who is reliable and experienced. Spend some time with your babysitter and your baby before leaving to go out. Always leave a contact number and an emergency number in case you can't be reached.

If anyone else puts your baby to bed, such as a relative or babysitter, make sure that they follow the same routine. Your baby may be more anxious in your absence so they may need to stay by your baby's bed to reassure him, but it's best not to pick him up.

 You may find that your baby still likes to be half swaddled (under the arms) when he goes to bed.

CRYING

All babies cry but at this age the crying generally reduces quite dramatically and it should become easier to distract your baby when he is crying. By four months you will probably have learned to understand some of the reasons why your baby cries and what he needs. The reasons for crying remain the same – hunger, he is wet or dirty, he is sleepy or bored, or he may be in pain or ill.

Understanding your baby's cry

Your baby will spend more hours awake now and expect you to play with him so he may cry if he's not getting enough of your attention. Keep your baby happy by giving him interesting things to look at, swipe at, touch and chew on and involve him in every-day activities. Prop him up in a bouncy chair or carry him in a sling so that he can feel a part of grown-up activities.

Your baby's short-term memory is not very long at this age so if he is crying because you have taken some-thing away from him, you should be able to distract him by giving him something else to play with. Once your baby starts on solid food, he may cry because he is hungry for food or because he is having trouble digest-ing his food and has a pain in his tummy.

Settling to sleep

No adult goes to bed in the evening without some kind of routine. A baby's routine will be less obvious, yet he does have one. Some babies scream when they are put into bed, then suddenly stop and go to sleep. Some babies talk to themselves and others thrash around. Most babies, however, cry and cry before they go to sleep. If this settling period is interrupted, then going

to sleep goes on and on. Watch your baby over a few nights to see if you can identify his settling routine. Sometimes if you simply allow it to run its course, your baby will sleep soundly sooner.

If your baby needs help to settle into a routine, be loving but firm. If you want the routine to work, it must be repeated every day for it to become a routine. Some babies of this age see the routine coming, which is good but it may be that your baby becomes upset because he knows soon it's time for bed or a nap. Reassure him, but don't change your routine if he cries. Gently comfort him while allowing him to settle and go to sleep.

At around four months you will want to start intro-ducing good sleeping habits and more of a routine. One of the most important skills that you can teach your baby is how to fall asleep by himself, and this is cov-ered on page 159.

Crying when ill

All babies cry when ill and their crying will then change, the sound differing according to the illness. The cry may become more prolonged than normal; the pitch may change, often becoming higher and uncom-

The problem	The signs	What to do
Earache	May clutch his ear, possible temperature.	Give infant paracetamol. Your GP may prescribe antibiotics.
Teething: This occurs from around six months to two years.	Gums may be sore, cheeks may be inflamed and red and your baby may dribble and be irritable. He may suffer from diarrhoea or an earache.	Rubbing an infant teething gel onto the gum may help – it contains a local anaesthetic. Or give infant paracetamol or a chilled gel-filled teething ring. Chilled raw vegetable sticks can help soothe sore gums.
Wind	Cries and wriggles during and after feeding	Lay your baby face down on your lap or hold him upright against your shoulder and rub or pat his back until he burps.
Constipation	Strains, cries and goes red in the face when doing a poo (it is rare for breastfed babies to be constipated).	See page 78.
Nappy rash	Ranges from mild reddening to inflammation with sores and broken skin.	See also page 74.

fortable. The baby may have tears running down his face. He may have red cheeks or a red face, or he may be banging or hitting his head or ears with his hands. This could mean a headache or earache. He may be pulling faces while crying and drawing up his lips. When ill, babies often cry and whimper in their sleep. They may look pale or seem to be working hard to breathe. You need to learn to tell when your baby is in pain and how to comfort him. Your baby may also be fretful, clingy and refuse food. The chart above will help you to identify a problem and show you what to do in times of need.

Remember that babies can become ill very quickly. So if you are concerned, see your GP and if you are still worried, take your baby to the accident and emergency department of your local hospital. Get help if your baby is floppy and listless, hasn't passed urine for more than four hours, has vomiting or diarrhoea for more than 12 hours, a fever over 37.5°C (99.5°F), or has blood in his poo or urine.

Feelings of anger

The 'baby blues' are mood swings caused by hormonal changes. You might feel ecstatically happy one minute and really low the next. This generally lasts only for about the first week or so after the birth and is a time when you will need lots of understanding and TLC.

You have high levels of progesterone and oestrogen during pregnancy but once you have had your baby, these levels drop and this can affect your emotions particularly as you are probably feeling very tired from labour and lack of sleep.

You may also find there are times when you lose your temper and have an urge to shake your baby. This is extremely dangerous. If you feel like this, put your baby down and try to calm yourself. Try to get someone to come round or phone a help group (see page 268) where you can be put you in touch with parents who have been in the same situation. Try to share the load and accept help from other people. It might be helpful for you to build up a network of new parents to talk to.

DEVELOPING

Parental-interaction is the best way to stimulate your baby, but there are some well-designed toys that will help your baby develop. In the first few weeks, your baby won't really need toys; you will be the focus of attention and he will want to be close to you. There are a few toys that he will have enjoyed playing with already, such as a playgym and baby mat, but now you can find more for him to do.

Helping your baby to develop

Rattles: Once your baby can grip, he will enjoy holding and shaking a rattle.

Activity boards: These help develop your baby's coordination and manual dexterity.

Pop-up toys: Press the button and a surprise toy bursts out.

Books: Those with sound buttons at the side and simple picture books are best (see also right).

Bath toys: Look for cups to fill and empty and toys that float.

Soft ball: Your baby will enjoy holding and squeezing it and watching it roll.

Squeaky toys: These and other toys that make a noise are just great for your baby – if not so good for you!

Glove and finger puppets: Your baby will love looking at the faces of finger puppets and you can bring them to life by moving your fingers and telling a story.

The easiest way to clean plastic toys is to put them in the dishwasher. Just make sure that the toys look sturdy enough to withstand the high temperature. Smaller pieces can be put inside a laundry mesh bag.

Important

Be very careful when choosing toys for your baby; be warned that everything he comes into contact with will go into his mouth, so anything with small parts is unsuitable.

Books

From around the age of four months, or as soon as your baby can focus properly, it's wonderful to look at books together, although to begin with your baby's attention span will be very short. Start with books that contain large, colourful, simple pictures like other babies, faces, animals and everyday objects. Choose sturdy books that will survive being chewed or thrown about and you can even get plastic books to read in the bath. Once your baby has better finger control, he will enjoy lift-the-flap books and books with buttons to press to make a sound. By the time your baby is a year old, he should be able to concentrate on a short story. Look for subjects that interest babies, like animals and their sounds, toys, nursery rhymes, babies and familiar experiences such as bath time.

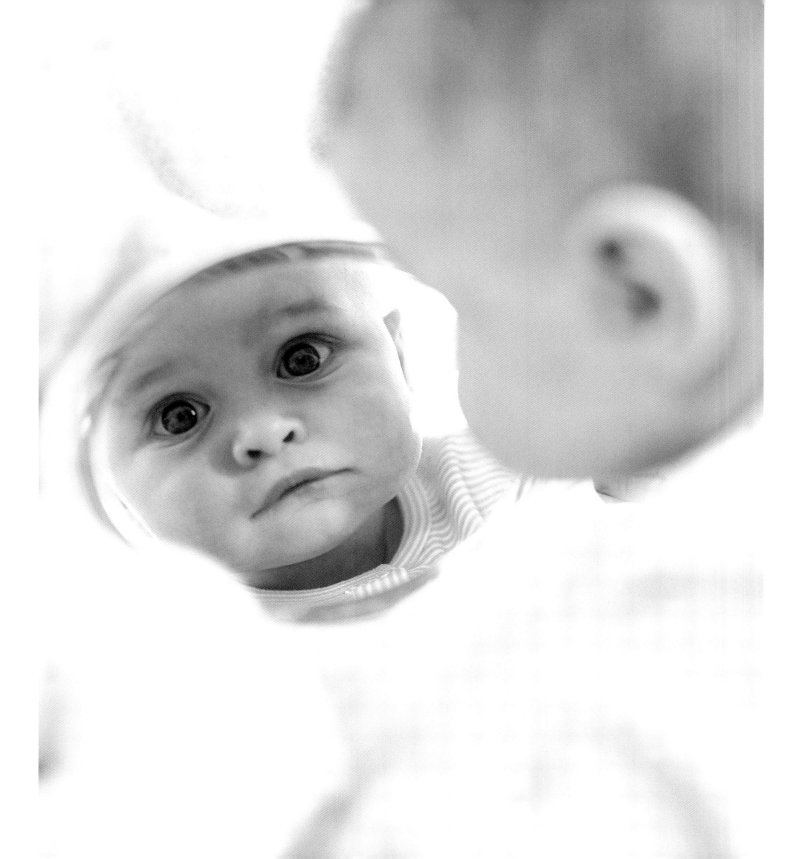

Your baby at 4 months

By now your baby takes two or three naps a day but he is likely to be alert for up to an hour at a time. Arm and leg movements are better controlled and he can move his hands and feet together and apart. He can also use his hands to explore his feet and by about five months he should be able to get his toes into his mouth. Your baby's concentration span has lengthened allowing him to enjoy examining his toys, usually putting them in his mouth – make sure there are no small objects within your baby's reach. At this time your baby begins to realise that his actions cause something to happen and so he will like to play with toys that make a noise.

Movement	Hand-to-eye coordination	Language	Learning	What your baby enjoys	Stimulating play
■ Your baby can sit in an upright position with support, but never prop your baby up and leave him as he can quickly roll over. ■ May start to roll over from front to back but he doesn't have sufficient strength yet to roll from his back to his stomach, which can be a source of endless frustration for him. ■ His head doesn't flop and he can now	■ Your baby now tries to grab objects within reach and likes to wave them around in his hand. ■ Sometimes he is able to grasp objects but his efforts are still quite clumsy. ■ He puts things into his mouth like toys, his blanket, his sleeve, his fist or even his feet. ■ Your baby's eyesight continues to improve and consequently he is better	■ He begins to laugh when he finds something funny or is tickled. ■ He starts making lots of new sounds like 'da', 'ba', 'ma', 'pa', 'ga'. ■ He reacts to tones of voice and will be upset by an angry voice. ■ Your baby can express himself with a wide range of facial expressions, like screwing up his face when he does-	■ He begins to realise that his actions cause something to happen. ■ Reacts to your tone of voice and senses if you are unhappy with his behaviour. ■ If he hears a sound, he looks around to find out where it is coming from. ■ Your baby's memory improves. If you give him a toy to play with and then	■ Exploring everything by putting it in his mouth. ■ Sitting on your lap and playing rocking games like 'Row the Boat'. ■ Listening to music, especially when you sing nursery rhymes with actions. ■ Being held and bounced in a standing position as he can bear his own weight when supported for a few	■ Tie a rattle to your baby's wrist or ankle and show him how to make it shake by moving his arm or leg. ■ Activity boards that require a wide range of hand movements to operate them like pushing, dialling, pulling, etc. are good, especially if your baby can see the result of his efforts. Your baby can only operate very simple knobs to begin with.

Movement	Hand-to-eye coordination	Language	Learning	What your baby enjoys	Stimulating play
hold his head upright. ■ He can turn and move his head in all directions. ■ May be able to pull himself around the cot.	at judging how far away an object is.	n't like the taste of something. ■ It's fun to make your baby aware of different parts of his body. Lay him on his back, touch his nose and say 'nose'. Then place his hands on his nose and say 'nose'. Do the same with eyes, ears, lips, tummy, etc. Take your baby's hand to your face with your hand so that he can feel your facial features too as you name them. ■ Books are a great way to help your child learn to talk. Snuggle up together and look at books with colourful pictures. Start by naming only one picture on each page. He likes hearing sounds for pictures as well as words, e.g. 'quack' instead of 'duck'. Turn to a page when your baby shows more response to one picture. Naming the objects helps your child build up a good vocabulary.	take it away from him for a few days, he will remember how to play with it when you give it back.	moments. Doing this helps strengthen his muscles, ready for crawling. ■ Exploring the pages and texture of a book. He will turn it over and over, put it in his mouth and gradually discover that it opens. He will probably explore the pages quite a bit before he notices the pictures inside.	■ Hiding games are great fun. Cover your head with a scarf or towel and let your baby pull it off to find you. Or hide a favourite toy under a scarf and see if your baby can find it. Show him the toy first then cover it in front of him. Out of sight will be out of mind and it will take jo, time to grasp the concept. ■ Play peek-a-boo together in front of a mirror. ■ Encourage your baby to splash his legs and arms in the bath. ■ Play give-and-take games with some objects or some of his toys. This will encourage him to open his fingers and grasp things.

Your baby at 5 months

By five months babies are usually able to hold small objects in the palm of their hand – they learn about objects by feeling them in the palm of their hand. Your baby will have more control over his movements so give him things to hold that make a noise and toys he can bash or kick. He may be able to sit up if supported but don't encourage this too early – a baby will sit when ready. He will explore anything he can reach with his hands and mouth and may become attached to a particular object and want to have it with him at night. Your baby is interested in his own hands and feet and he'll soon have enough coordination to reach for his feet and may pop one in his mouth.

Movement	Hand-to-eye coordination	Language	Learning	What your baby enjoys	Stimulating play
◼ Your baby can lift his chest off the floor by pushing up on his hands.	◼ Your baby can now reach for objects more accurately and has a firm grip.	◼ This is the month that you can expect to hear your baby's first laugh.	◼ Your baby starts to look for an object that he has dropped.	◼ Pushing himself up on his arms and looking around.	◼ Interest your baby in new noises like scrunching up paper or shaking coffee beans in a jar.
◼ He can hold up his head when supported in an upright position.	◼ He follows you with his eyes as you move around the room. He also now looks for and watches more distant objects.	◼ Chat to your baby as much as possible. Tell him what you are doing and talk about things that he can see. Name objects that you are using with your baby, such as: 'Teddy', 'Teddy in bed', 'More milk', 'Bath time', 'Bread.' A lot of his language learning will come from hearing you talk every day.	◼ He learns to imitate your facial expressions. ◼ He can accurately locate where a sound comes from.	◼ Exploring and touching any objects within reach. ◼ Pushing against the floor with his feet and bouncing up and down. Your baby will enjoy time in a baby bouncer.	◼ Place your baby on his tummy and encourage him to push up so that his arms are straight by holding a toy at eye level in front of him.
◼ He can support his weight on his legs when held in a standing position. ◼ Your baby's body language becomes more expressive. For example, he may raise his arms if he wants to picked up.	◼ He can hold a small toy in his hand and likes to shake objects. ◼ He likes to grab people's hair,			◼ Hitting and grabbing a string of toys hanging across his pushchair or pram. ◼ He may enjoy	◼ Babies can get dispirited if they are not able to grab objects that they want. Sometimes you can dangle a toy on a string in front of

Movement	Hand-to-eye coordination	Language	Learning	What your baby enjoys	Stimulating play
■ He can now sit up for a few minutes if supported by lots of cushions. ■ He is just beginning to move around by rolling and twisting his body. ■ He can also turn his head.	Daddy's tie, glasses, your necklace, etc. If you wear dangly earrings, now is the time to remove them!	■ Try and use key words repeatedly when talking with your baby. Use your baby's name often when you talk. ■ Talk in short sentences when you can, e.g. 'Daddy's going out.', ' 'Let's eat here.' ■ If you leave gaps when talking to your baby you may find that he, in turn, babbles back to you. ■ He listens intently and tries to mimic sounds that he hears. ■ He may vocalise to draw your attention if you are talking to someone else. ■ He can combine vowels and consonants, e.g. 'baba'.		sleeping cuddled up with a favourite soft toy or blanket. ■ Playing with people but can be shy with strangers. ■ A gentle tug of war. Give your baby a small toy to hold and playfully try to pull it away from him. But don't pull so hard that he loses his grip. ■ Action songs like 'Pat-a-Cake', 'Incey Wincey Spider' or 'The Wheels on the Bus Go Round and Round'. Hold your baby's hands and get him to do the movements too – he'll love it!	your baby, wait until he has reached out for it and then slowly lower it towards his outstretched hand so that he can grasp it easily. Success will encourage him. ■ Fix up a toy that your baby can swipe at as on a babygym – preferably one that makes a noise if he is successful at grabbing something. ■ When your baby is lying on his back encourage him to kick or push against your hands, a soft toy or a ball and give a little resistance; this will help to build up his strength. ■ Introduce your baby to the feel of lots of different textures.

Your baby at 6 months

Being able to sit up is an important milestone in your baby's development and he can most probably now be fed while sitting in a high chair (possibly supported by a small pillow), which makes it easier for him to join in with family meals. Many babies are also becoming more mobile by six months and are able to get around on their tummies, pushing with their legs and pulling with their arms. Some babies are beginning to crawl on their hands and knees with their tummy off the floor. Babies usually crawl backwards before mastering going forwards as they instinctively push rather than pull. Others master sitting up but are not quite ready to move around yet.

Movement	Hand-to-eye coordination	Language	Learning	What your baby enjoys	Stimulating play
■ Your baby is getting better at rolling from front to back and back to front.	■ Your baby can use both hands together and he is able to pass an object from one hand to the other.	■ Your baby may start to understand simple phrases like 'Mummy's taking you out.'	■ Your baby can play by himself for longer now that your baby can sit up – it's important that he learns how to amuse himself.	■ Standing up and bouncing up and down using his knees with you supporting him securely under his arms.	■ Lie your baby face down and encourage him to move by placing a favourite toy or object just beyond his reach – he will want to try and reach for it or crawl after it.
■ When lying on his tummy, he pushes his head, chest and shoulders off the floor.	■ He starts to feed himself and may try to grab hold of his bottle or to grab the spoon as you feed him.	■ He recognises names and simple words and will turn towards you when you say his name.	■ He knows his name.	■ Bringing his foot to his mouth to suck on his toes.	
■ It will take at least six months before your baby is able to sit up on his own and this will open up a new outlook on life and a whole new range of play activities. You can help your baby to sit up	■ Sitting frees up your baby's hands to explore things and he is now much more adept at reaching out and grasping an object.	■ He babbles and talks to himself.

■ If you talk to your baby and leave gaps, he may synchronise his speech to yours and you may find yourself | ■ He recognises himself in a photograph.

■ He looks for objects that he has dropped.

■ He can hold a toy in each hand with- | ■ Dropping toys, watching them fall and listening to the noise they make.

■ Banging on the table.

■ Playing alongside other children and | ■ Activity centres like push-button musical toys where you push and turn knobs to make a sound are good as they help your baby to learn about cause and effect.

■ Encourage your |

Movement	Hand-to-eye coordination	Language	Learning	What your baby enjoys	Stimulating play
by arranging some cushions behind his back or use a U-shaped cushion – you may have used one for breastfeeding him – or a purpose-made 'play ring'.

■ He rocks and kicks and is able to move around a little by himself.

■ He may show first signs of crawling by drawing one knee up to his tummy.

■ From about six months your baby will try to bend and straighten his legs in a jumping movement when he is held in a standing position. He enjoys the sensation of taking his own weight and this will help strengthen his legs in preparation for walking.

■ Your baby can now stay awake longer and will resist the urge to sleep if he is having fun. | Your baby starts to make an effort to reach out for objects that are placed out of his reach, so soft rolling toys or balls are a good idea. By bending and twisting at the waist, he is able to reach out further but if he stretches too far, he may find himself flat on his face. However, toppling over onto all fours isn't such a bad thing as your baby will probably be strong enough to start crawling.

■ Shaking things that make a noise will help develop coordination. You can make your own maracas for your baby by filling empty spice bottles or a baby's bottle with dried beans or small pasta shapes. As your baby gets older you can try and encourage him to shake these in a rhythm. | having a little conversation. Copy your baby's babble and sounds as much as possible waiting and leaving a space to see if he will repeat the sound again.

■ He produces more vowel and consonant sounds like 'ma-ma', 'da-da', 'ga-ga'.

■ He imitates some of your sounds and starts a conversation.

■ Try introducing new sounds by holding your baby so that he can see your face as you mouth the sound and he may imitate you. | out dropping them. May start to clap both toys together with his hands.

■ Your baby should now understand that his hands are connected to his arms and have pretty good control of his movements. He wants to explore his environment, stroking and grabbing at everything around him.

■ At six months your baby's upper body is quite well developed but his legs aren't strong enough yet to allow him to crawl. A little support from behind can encourage your baby to begin crawling. Lay your baby on his tummy and let him push against your hands or a rolled-up towel to move forwards. | watching what they do, even if he doesn't interact with them.

■ Seeing photographs of himself.

■ Holding on to a toy while you pretend to try and take it from him.

■ Exploring and putting everything in his mouth. But he gets frustrated when he can't do something.

■ Pop-up toys where different characters pop out of a hatch when a button is pressed.

■ Sitting on your lap as you read to him. Cardboard, cloth or plastic books are good as he loves to look at pictures and will particularly enjoy books with different textures, lift-the-flaps, pop-up sections, and buttons that make a noise when pressed. | baby to feed himself by giving finger foods that are easy to pick up, like sticks of cucumber or fingers of toast.

■ Lie your baby on his back and hold a toy in front of him to encourage him to lift his head and reach out.

■ Most babies love bath time. Kicking helps your baby strengthen his leg and abdominal muscles, which are important for crawling and walking. Encourage your baby to kick his legs in the bath. You can also hold your baby so that his tummy is in the water but his head and shoulders are supported above the surface, allowing him to splash with his arms and legs. |

FEEDING

Weaning your baby from milk to solids is an exciting time and a big step for both of you. After all, food is one of the most enjoyable parts of life. It may be messy and frustrating but remember that by one year your baby will be eating the same foods as you. Babies roughly double their weight at six months and treble it at one year. Your baby will grow more rapidly in the first year than at any other time in his life.

Introducing solids

Babies need a high-calorie, nutrient-rich diet to cope with this rapid level of growth and to give them energy. For the first six months of your baby's life, however, breast milk or infant formula should be the main source of nourishment.

Babies' and young children's needs are different from an adult's as under-fives need significantly more fat and concentrated sources of calories and nutrients to fuel their rapid growth. Babies and young children should not be given too much fibre as it tends to be bulky and filling and they may not be able to eat enough food from other groups to supply all the energy and nutrients needed for healthy growth and development. Excess fibre can also deplete the body of valuable minerals and can cause other problems like diarrhoea.

Eating habits and tastes are formed in early childhood, so by introducing your baby to a wide range of fresh flavours you will help establish a healthy eating pattern for life. Poor nutrition causes problems that will plague our children for the rest of their lives. As parents of young children, one thing we do have some control over is what our children eat and that is vital as one-third of us will die from a diet-related illness like heart disease or cancer.

My recipes are quick and easy to prepare and most are suitable for freezing so that you don't have to cook every day and you can also prepare menus ahead using the menu planners provided (e.g. pages 180–1).

Children are exacting critics and while they are rarely interested in whether their food is healthy, they do care if it tastes good. All the recipes in this book have been tested by a panel of babies and toddlers to ensure they are designed to combine 'child appeal' with sound nutritional principles. I hope that many of these recipes will become firm family favourites and that you and your child will enjoy many happy meals together.

First stage

Don't be in a hurry to wean your baby onto solids because milk provides all the nutrients he needs for the first six months or so. The current medical advice is not to give solids until at least 17 weeks after your baby's due date. A very young baby's digestive and immune system is not sufficiently developed before this time and there is a greater risk of food allergy occurring. Giving solids too early may also strain a baby's kidneys, which can increase the risk of dehydration. Giving food too early may bring on colicky symptoms and may also cause constipation. Bear in mind, too, that if your baby was born prematurely, you will need to wait longer before introducing solids.

While sucking is a natural reflex, babies need to be ready to learn the new skill of moving food with their tongues from the front to the back of their mouth and swallowing. Young babies have a 'tongue thrust reflex' which causes them to push their tongue forwards, thereby pushing food out of their mouth, and this is something they need to learn to override.

If weaning is delayed until after six months, some babies can have difficulty eating foods with lumps. Also, as your baby gets older he will need more iron and nutrients than milk alone can provide.

Signs that your baby is ready for solids:
- He is still hungry after a full milk feed.
- He was sleeping through the night but has started to wake feeling hungry.
- He demands feeds more often.
- Your baby begins to reach for and show interest in the food you are eating.

Choosing first foods

First foods must be easy to digest and unlikely to provoke an allergic reaction. Baby rice is easily digested and its familiar milky taste makes an easy transition to solids. Choose one that is sugar free. You can mix baby rice with water, breast or formula milk. It also combines well with fruit and vegetable purées. It's good for thickening runny purées like pear or peach.

Dairy products

You can use cow's milk in cooking and with cereals from the start of weaning. However, it is low in iron

---

The best first foods

■ **First fruits: apple, pear, banana, papaya and avocado:** It's important that you choose fruits that are ripe and have a good flavour, so it's a good idea to taste them yourself before giving them to your baby. Banana and papaya do not need cooking if they are ripe, and can be puréed or mashed on their own or together with breast or formula milk. Bananas are not suitable for freezing.

■ **First vegetables: carrot, potato, swede, parsnip, pumpkin, butternut squash and sweet potato:** Root vegetables and winter squash like pumpkin and butternut squash tend to be the most popular with very young babies due to their naturally sweet flavour and smooth texture once puréed.

---

and vitamins A, C and D so babies should continue with breast or formula milk for the first year as their main drink. You can give dairy products such as pasteurised whole-milk yoghurt and fromage frais, cream cheese and mild hard cheeses such as Cheddar or Edam – these provide a good source of calcium.

Between six months and one year, babies should have between 500 and 800 ml (16 and 25 fl oz) of milk each day, mostly in the form of breast or formula milk. However, a proportion can come from dairy products.

Judging quantities

It's impossible to be precise about the amount of food babies should eat as all babies' appetites and needs are different. As a rough guide you will probably find that at the beginning your baby will only take 1 or 2 tsp of purée so allow 1 tbsp (15ml) or one ice-cube portion. As your baby develops and if he loves to eat, don't restrict the amount of food when the food being offered is good quality. Quite a few babies seem to eat really well up to one year old only to lose interest after that time. Providing your baby is gaining weight and has plenty of energy, rest assured he is doing fine. If your baby has an insatiable appetite and you are worried he is overweight, then seek professional advice.

Starting off

Try to make feeding a special time to share with your baby rather than a chore and pick a time of day when you are not rushed or liable to be distracted. Try to feed him around the same time every day, if possible, to establish some kind of routine. In the first week, offer one meal of solids each day, probably at lunchtime, and work towards three meals of solids: breakfast, lunch and supper by four to six weeks after weaning.

Texture

To begin with, purées should resemble the consistency of a super-smooth thick soup. They should only be made with the water from the bottom of a steamer or the cooking liquid if boiling vegetables in a saucepan. Thin purées by adding cooking liquid or milk and thicken them by stirring in some baby rice.

What temperature?

A baby's food should be given at room temperature or lukewarm. If re-heating in a microwave, heat until piping hot all the way through, allow to cool and then stir thoroughly to get rid of any hot spots and check the temperature before giving it to your baby. A baby's mouth is more sensitive to heat than ours are.

Sitting comfortably

When you feed your baby you can either hold him comfortably on your lap or sit him facing you in his baby chair. It would be best if both of you are protected against spills.

Foods to avoid up to six months

■ **Cow's milk (or goat's, sheep's, etc.):** Don't give this as a main drink. However, cow's milk can be used in cooking. Dairy foods, e.g. yoghurt or cheese, can be introduced once first weaning foods are accepted.

■ **Foods containing gluten:** Wheat, rye, barley and oats can be introduced from six months.

■ **Lightly cooked eggs:** Eggs cooked until the yolk and white is solid can be included once first foods have been accepted.

■ **Honey:** Very occasionally honey can contain a type of bacteria which, if eaten by a baby under the age of one, can result in a potentially serious illness called 'infant botulism'.

■ **Salt:** Babies under a year should not have any salt added to their food as a baby's kidneys are too immature to cope.

■ **Sugar:** Unless food is really tart, don't add sugar. Adding sugar is habit forming and will increase the risk of tooth decay. If you must sweeten, use dried apricots or dates.

■ **Peanuts:** In the case of peanuts and peanut products which can induce a life-threatening allergic reaction – anaphylactic shock – it is best to err on the side of caution. In families with a history of any kind of food allergy, it is advisable to avoid all products containing peanuts, including peanut oil, until the child is three years old and then seek medical advice before introducing peanut products into the diet. Peanut butter and finely ground nuts, however, can be introduced from six months, provided there is no family history of allergy. Whole nuts should not be given to children under the age of five because of the risk of choking. (See also Allergies, page 177.)

■ **Other foods:** The other most common foods that should not be fed to babies before six months are spicy and smoked food and shellfish.

Food rejection

Learning to eat food from a spoon is a tricky skill for a baby so don't worry if he makes a fuss and refuses to eat to begin with. Try re-introducing food after a couple of days and perhaps prepare a runnier purée that is easier for your baby to swallow or mix it with a little baby rice and milk for a more familiar taste. Try dipping a clean finger into the purée and let your baby suck the food off your finger.

Methods of cooking

Steaming or microwaving

This is the best way to preserve the fresh taste and vitamins in vegetables and fruits. Vitamins B and C are water-soluble and can easily be destroyed by overcooking, especially when fruits and vegetables are boiled in water. When microwaving, chop the vegetables or fruit and put them in a suitable dish. Add a little water, cover, leaving an air vent, and cook on full power until tender. Purée to the desired consistency but take care to stir well and check that it is not too hot to serve to your baby.

Boiling

Use the minimum amount of water and be careful not to overcook the vegetables and fruits. Add enough of the cooking liquid to make a smooth purée.

Baking

If you are cooking a meal in the oven for the family, you could use the opportunity to bake a potato, sweet potato or butternut squash for your baby. Wash and prick the chosen vegetable with a fork and bake until tender. Cut in half (removing the seeds from the squash), scoop out the flesh and mash together with some water or milk.

Homemade food

■ By making baby food yourself, you can be sure of using only the best-quality ingredients without the need for thickeners or additives. It also works out more economical. Introducing a wide range of foods is important in establishing a varied and healthy diet, and you have the choice of organic fruit and vegetables if you prefer.

■ Homemade purées have a much fresher taste than commercial jars of baby purée that often have a shelf life of two years. Natural variations in the taste of fresh food rather than the uniform bland taste of commercial baby food help to integrate your baby into family meals. You can prepare vegetables for your baby's purée alongside those you are preparing for the rest of the family. Many of the baby purées in my books are so tasty that they will also make delicious soups for the rest of the family with the addition of extra stock and seasoning.

■ However, commercial baby foods are a convenient option when you and your baby are away from home. One of the best ways of using them is to mix them with fresh food – for example, you could mash a banana and mix it into some apple or pear purée or mix some baby rice with carrot purée.

Puréeing

Mouli: This is a hand-turned food mill and is ideal for vegetables like potato or sweet potato. Puréeing potato in a food processor tends to break down the starches and produces a sticky glutinous pulp so potato is much better puréed using a mouli. A mouli is also good for foods that have a tough skin, like peas or dried apricots, as you can then produce a smooth purée and discard the indigestible bits.

Sieve: If you don't have a mouli, press food through a sieve to remove any tough fibres or seeds, but it is much more labour intensive. Use the underside of a ladle to push the food through.

Electric blender: This is ideal for making baby purées and can handle quite small quantities.
Food processor: This is good for puréeing larger quantities when making batches for freezing. Many food processors have mini bowl attachments, which will work better with smaller quantities.

Preparing and freezing

Preparing tiny amounts of purée is difficult. It is much better to prepare more than you need and freeze extra portions in ice-cube trays or small pots. You can then also plan your baby's meals in advance so that you probably only need to cook for your baby once a week.
■ Freeze food as soon as it has cooled down. Speed up the process by placing a bowl of the food in iced water.
■ Freezer temperature should be −18/−20°C.
■ Baby food can be kept in the freezer for six weeks.
■ If you freeze purées in ice-cube trays, knock them out once they are frozen and transfer them to plastic freezer bags. Label and date the contents.

  Thaw food by taking it out of the freezer overnight or several hours before a meal and re-heating in a saucepan. If using a microwave, stir the food thoroughly to remove hot spots.

Your baby's drinks

Milk: Cow's, goat's or sheep's milk isnot suitable as your baby's main drink before one year as it does not contain enough iron and other nutrients for proper growth. Whole cow's milk can be used in cooking or

Weaning is a messy business. Plastic bibs save on the washing.

with cereal when weaning but should not be given as your baby's main drink before the age of one year.
Water: The only drink apart from breast or formula milk that your baby should have in the first six months is water. For babies under six months, take water from a mains tap and boil it, then allow to cool. Bottled natural mineral water can contain high concentrations of mineral salts that are unsuitable for babies.
Baby drinks: Babies are more vulnerable to tooth decay than older children or adults. Fruit and herbal drinks manufactured for babies sometimes contain quite large amounts of sugar, which can lead to tooth decay. Labels that state 'no added sugar' do not mean that the drink is sugar free; it may contain a different type of sugar, like fructose, glucose, dextrose or maltose. If you want to give your baby fruit juice, it is much better to squeeze your own fruit juice or choose one that contains only natural fruit sugars. Orange juice is a good source of vitamin C, which will help your child to absorb iron. All juices should be diluted (one part juice with five parts cooled, boiled water) as even natural fruit sugars can cause tooth decay and drinks other than water or milk are best confined to mea times.

  It is important not to let your baby continually sip at any fluid except water. Even diluted natural fruit juices and milk contain sugar that can cause decay if the teeth are continually exposed to them.
Feeding cups: It's best not to put anything into a bottle apart from formula or breast milk; comfort sucking on sweetened drinks is the main cause of tooth decay in young children. It is a good idea to start using a lidded cup with a spout from the age of six or seven months and eventually move on to a cup. Try to dispense with bottles, apart from perhaps a bottle at bedtime, by the time your baby is one year old.

Food allergies

An allergic reaction generally occurs when the immune system wrongly perceives a harmless substance as a threat. Food allergy tends to begin in childhood and can trigger a wide range of symptoms from vomiting, persistent diarrhoea and abdominal pain to eczema, skin rashes, runny nose and swelling. It is often hard to be sure that food is to blame or to find out which food. A young baby's immune system is not fully matured and babies can become ill very quickly so always call a doctor if you are worried.

Many children outgrow early allergies to food by the age of three. But there is no cure for some allergies and the only way to remain healthy is to avoid the problem food. The foods that carry the highest risk of allergic reaction or food intolerance are cow's milk and dairy products, nuts, eggs, wheat-based products, shellfish and chocolate. Berry and citrus fruits can trigger a reaction but rarely cause a true allergy.

Food intolerance

A food intolerance, sometimes called a 'false' food allergy, is a condition whereby the body is temporarily incapable of digesting certain foods. It is generally short-lived and not the same as a true food allergy, which involves the immune system. If you suspect your child is allergic to a common food like cow's milk, consult your doctor before changing milk formula. It is possible that your baby's reaction is only temporary.

Do not remove key foods from your child's diet without first consulting a doctor. If you suspect that your child is allergic to a common food such as milk or wheat, you should seek expert advice.

Weaning your baby

Unless there is a family history of allergy, food allergies are fairly rare. But if your family has a history of food allergy or atopic disease (e.g. asthma, eczema, hay fever), the risk of developing an allergic disorder more than doubles.

▓ If possible continue to breastfeed exclusively for at least four and preferably six months.
▓ Do not start weaning before six months .
▓ Start with low-allergen foods like baby rice, root vegetables, apple and pear.
▓ Introduce new foods one at a time for two or three days so that any adverse reactions can be traced.
▓ Avoid high-risk foods such as wheat, egg, nuts, fish and citrus fruits until nine to 12 months of age.
▓ Avoid cow's milk and dairy products if you are breastfeeding – there is no point if your baby is drinking formula as he is already exposed to milk proteins.
▓ If there is a family history of allergy to a particular food, avoid that food until your child is at least one year old, and if you are breastfeeding avoid that particular food in your diet.

Gluten intolerance

Gluten is found in wheat, rye, barley and oats and gluten sensitivity can cause coeliac disease which, although rare, can be serious. Symptoms of gluten intolerance include loss of appetite, poor growth, swollen abdomen and pale, bulky, frothy and smelly stools. Foods containing gluten, i.e. bread or pasta, should not be introduced before six months.

Baby rice is the safest to try at first for babies under six months, and thereafter there are plenty of alternative gluten-free products. Some supermarkets have a gluten-free section.

Developing new tastes

To begin with babies prefer fruits and vegetables with a mild taste, which can be made into very smooth purées. Foods with a stronger taste and which are more difficult to make smooth are better introduced after a few weeks once a baby has got used to eating solids. Then, by six months, your baby should have doubled his birth weight and be eating three meals a day. Milk alone may not be enough to supply all his needs. It is important to include foods like red meat, which provide a good source of iron and zinc.

Your baby is now able to eat all vegetables, including onions, leeks, spinach, sweetcorn, mushrooms, green beans, sweet peppers and tomatoes. If the flavour of certain vegetables like spinach or broccoli is too strong for your baby, you could try mixing them together with cheese sauce or root vegetables like sweet potato, carrot or potato. Steamed vegetables, like carrot sticks or cauliflower florets make good finger food.

Your baby should also be able to eat all fruits. Take care to remove stones and do not give whole grapes to young babies as they may choke on them. Citrus and berry fruits provide a good source of vitamin C, but ensure you remove the pith and seeds from them. To begin with use berries in small quantities as they can be indigestible. Combine them with other fruits like apples, bananas, pears or peaches. Some babies can be allergic to citrus fruits so watch carefully for any reaction. Fruit is also good mixed with yoghurt, porridge or baby rice.

Hygiene in the kitchen

■ Always wash your hands thoroughly before preparing or offering food to your baby.

■ Sterilise weaning spoons for the first six months but after that there is little point in sterilising anything

Vegetables and fruits

Courgettes: These are best steamed and mixed to a purée with another vegetable like sweet potato, carrot, butternut squash or potato.

Cauliflower or broccoli: Steam broccoli or cauliflower florets and purée with sweet potato, pumpkin or a cheese sauce.

Peaches and nectarines: Skin and chop, discarding the stones and then purée. Mix the fruit pulp with baby rice to thicken.

Plums and apricots: To skin the fruit, cut a shallow cross on the skin, submerge in boiling water for 1 minute and then plunge into cold water. Cut into quarters and discard the stone. Steam for a few minutes until soft and then purée.

Melon: Take a small wedge, scoop out the seeds and discard. Peel away the skin and cut the flesh into chunks. Purée until smooth. Melon is good with mashed banana.

Dried apricots and peaches: Simmer ready-to-eat dried apricots or peaches in a little water until soft, then purée in a mouli to get rid of the skins and add a little of the cooking liquid to make a purée. Dried apricot purée is good mixed with pear, apple or banana, baby rice and milk.

other than bottles and teats. Your baby's bowls can be washed in a dishwasher or very hot water (80°C). Always use a clean tea towel or paper towel for drying.

■ Do not re-heat food more than once.

■ Use baby food stored in the fridge within 24 hours.

■ Do not save your baby's half-eaten food as bacteria-carrying saliva will have been introduced.

Other new foods

Breads and cereals: Once your baby has passed the six-month stage and is eating bread and other foods containing gluten, you can use adult cereals like porridge, Weetabix or Ready Brek. Choose a cereal that is not highly refined and is low in sugar and salt. You can also give wholemeal bread but avoid large amounts of high-fibre foods such as high-fibre bread or cereals – these are too difficult for babies to digest and can deplete the body of vital nutrients.

Eggs: Eggs are an excellent source of protein and contain iron and zinc and can be introduced after first tastes are accepted. Do not serve raw or lightly cooked eggs to babies under one year as there is a risk of salmonella. The white and yolk should be cooked until solid. Hard-boiled eggs, omelettes or scrambled eggs are fast to cook and nutritious.

Red meat: On average, babies are born with sufficient iron reserves for approximately the first six months of life only. Iron deficiency is the most common nutritional problem for young children and red meat, particularly liver, provides the best source of iron for your baby. Lean ground beef, lamb or liver can be sautéed with a little onion and combined with mashed potato. Slow-cooked lamb or beef casseroles also make good purées.

Chicken: An excellent source of protein and rich in B vitamins, chicken is popular with babies because of its mild taste. It combines well with root vegetables and fruits like apple and grapes and also goes well with rice or couscous.

Fish: This remains one of the healthiest foods that you can eat so it is important to try to encourage your baby to enjoy the taste of fish. Introduce fish fillets like cod, plaice or salmon. Plaice is good to begin with as it has a very soft texture. Fish also combines well with mashed potato or a home-made cheese sauce. Always check carefully to make sure there are no bones before serving fish to your baby.

Pulses: You can now introduce pulses – peas, beans and lentils. They are a good source of protein and iron and are especially valuable for vegetarian babies. However, they can be difficult to digest and may cause flatulence and loose stools so only give them in small quantities. If they cause a problem, leave them out for a few weeks and then try again. They are good combined with root vegetables. Tofu is also a good source of protein for vegetarian babies and soft tofu can be mixed with fruit or vegetables.

Rice: Flaked rice can be mixed with sweet or savoury foods and it's quicker to cook and easier for babies to swallow than ordinary rice.

When you re-heat your baby's food make sure it is piping hot throughout because tepid food provides a breeding ground for bacteria. Allow the food to cool and test the temperature before giving it to your baby.

Time-saving tips

By using a multi-layered steamer you can prepare three different purées at once and so save time.

Even busy working mums can give their baby the best start in life since foods like mashed banana, avocado or papaya make excellent no-cook baby purées.

Much of your baby's food can be prepared alongside your own. For example, if you are having vegetables for your supper, simply prepare extra vegetables, leave out the seasoning and blend to a purée for your baby's meal. This is the first step towards sharing family meals.

If you have lots of single-ingredient purées in the freezer, you can mix flavours to make new combinations, e.g. apple and pear or sweet potato and broccoli.

Frozen vegetables and fruits often contain more nutrients than fresh because they are frozen within hours of being picked. It can be handy to mix and match fresh and frozen vegetables together, like carrots and peas, for example. Once frozen vegetables have been cooked, they can be re-frozen.

Meal planners

In this and the following chapters I have devised meal planners to help you through weaning. Every baby develops at his own pace so these should be used as a guide only since timings will vary depending on individual babies. In the first couple of months babies should be fed on demand and may want more feeds than indicated here, especially if they are breastfed. I have given as wide a choice as possible although, in reality, meals that your baby enjoys will no doubt be repeated many times and there is nothing wrong with giving the same food on two consecutive days. Adapt the recipes according to seasonal fruits and vegetables.

First tastes

Weeks 1 and 2	On waking	11–11.45am	2–2.30pm	6–6.30pm	11pm	Middle of night
Days 1 and 2	Milk	Milk and solids: give half of milk feed first, then solids, then finish with milk: baby rice mixed with formula or breast milk	Milk	Milk	Milk	In the first couple of months, babies will almost certainly need a feed in the early hours of the morning
Days 3 and 4	Milk	Milk and solids: First vegetable purée, e.g. carrot (p.182)	Milk	Milk	Milk	
Day 5	Milk	Milk and solids: First fruit purée, e.g. pear purée mixed with baby rice (p.184)	Milk	Milk	Milk	
Day 6	Milk	Milk and solids: First fruit purée, e.g apple (p.184)	Milk	Milk	Milk	
Day 7	Milk	Milk and solids: First vegetable purée, e.g sweet potato or butternut squash (p.182)	Milk	Milk	Milk	
Weeks 3 and 4	**On waking**	**11-11.45am**	**2–2.30pm**	**5.30–6.30pm**	**11pm**	**Middle of night**
Days 1–7	Milk	Any of the vegetable first weaning foods puréed on their own or mixed with baby rice, e.g. carrot, sweet potato, parsnip or pumpkin	Milk	Any of the fruit first weaning foods puréed on their own or mixed with baby rice	Milk	In the first couple of months, babies will almost certainly need a feed in the early hours of the morning

After first tastes are accepted

	Breakfast	Lunch*	Mid-afternoon	Supper**	Bedtime
DAY 1	Milk Cereal and fruit purée, e.g. Trio of fruits (p.185)	Milk Vegetable purée, e.g. Creamy butternut squash (p.188)	Milk	Milk Mashed avocado and banana (p.186)	Milk
DAY 2	Milk Cereal and baby yoghurt or fromage frais	Milk Vegetable purée, e.g. Sweet potato, carrot and parsnip (p.184)	Milk	Milk Trio of fruits (p.185) and rusk or rice cake	Milk
DAY 3	Milk Cereal and fruit purée, e.g. Peach delight (p.185)	Milk Vegetable purée, e.g. Carrot or butternut squash (p.184)	Milk	Milk Apple purée with mashed banana	Milk
DAY 4	Milk Cereal and fruit purée, e.g. Nectarine, pear and blueberry (p.186)	Milk Vegetable purée, e.g. Vegetables with cheese sauce (from six months) (p.190)	Milk	Milk Pear, peach and apple crumble (p.190)	Milk
DAY 5	Milk Pear and cinnamon with baby rice (p.188)	Milk Chicken purée with carrots and apple (p.221)	Milk	Milk Sweet potato and pear purée	Milk
DAY 6	Milk Cereal and mashed banana	Milk Vegetable purée, e.g. Sweet potato and broccoli (p.189)	Milk	Milk Pear, peach and apple crumble (p.190)	Milk
Day 7	Milk Cereal and fruit purée, e.g. sieved cantaloupe melon and strawberry	Milk Tasty fish with sweet potato and orange (p.224)	Milk	Milk Baked butternut squash or baked potato with a knob of butter and a little milk	Milk

Babies of this age may need extra feeds. It is quite a long time between breakfast and lunch.
Many babies will also continue to wake in the early hours of the morning for a milk feed.
* At lunch, you can also give fruit for dessert from six months.
** At supper, you can offer savoury food and fruit from six months.

Recipes

● First vegetable purée

This method of puréeing food will work for any other root vegetables, e.g. sweet potato, potato, swede and other good 'first' vegetables like pumpkin or butternut squash. Cooking times will differ depending on which vegetables you choose.

First weaning food
Makes 8 portions
✳ Suitable for freezing
350 g (12 oz) carrots, peeled and chopped

■ Put the carrots in a steamer set over boiling water and cook until tender (15–20 minutes). Alternatively, put the carrots in a saucepan and pour over just enough boiling water to cover. Cover with a lid and simmer until soft (15–20 minutes).
■ Purée until very smooth together with some of the water in the bottom of the steamer or some of the cooking liquid. The amount of liquid you add really depends on your baby; you may need to add a little more if your baby finds the purée difficult to swallow.
■ Spoon some of the purée into your baby's bowl and serve lukewarm.

TIP When puréeing potato, purée in a mouli or press through a sieve. Do not use a food processor as this breaks down the starches and produces a sticky pulp.

● Creamy vegetable or fruit purée

You can give vegetables and fruit a more creamy mild taste by combining them with some baby rice and milk. This can make a good introduction to new tastes.

First weaning food　　　　　　　　3 tbsp your baby's usual milk
Makes 1 portion　　　　　　　　　4 tbsp fruit or vegetable purée
1 tbsp baby rice

■ Mix the baby rice and milk together according to the packet instructions and stir into the vegetable or fruit purée.

First fruit purée

Choose only sweet ripe fruit for your baby. Pink Lady apples are a very sweet variety, for instance, whereas Coxes can be quite tart. Ripe Conference pears have a good flavour.

First weaning food
Makes 6 portions
2 medium dessert apples or 2 pears,

peeled, cored and chopped
1–2 tbsp water or pure unsweetened apple juice (optional)

■ Put the chopped fruit into a thick-based saucepan and, if using apples, add the water or apple juice; ripe pears will not need any extra liquid.
■ Cover with a lid and cook over a low heat until tender (about 6–8 minutes for apples and 4 minutes for pears).
■ Blend the fruit to a purée. Spoon a little into your baby's bowl and serve lukewarm.

Sweet potato, carrot and parsnip

Vegetables like sweet potato, pumpkin and butternut squash are easy to digest, which makes them good weaning foods. Sweet potato is delicious when baked in the oven so if you are making a roast, simply prick the skin of the sweet potato and cook in the oven the same way you would a baked potato. You can then mash or purée it together with a knob of butter and a little of your baby's usual milk and freeze the remainder.

First weaning food
Makes 5 portions
✷ Suitable for freezing

175 g (6 oz) sweet potato, peeled and chopped
175 g (6 oz) carrot, peeled and chopped
100 g (4 oz) parsnip, peeled and chopped

■ Put the vegetables into a saucepan and cover with 300 ml (½ pint) boiling water. Cover with a lid and cook over a medium heat until tender (about 20 minutes). Blend the vegetables to a purée. If you want a thinner consistency, you could add a little of your baby's usual milk.
■ Alternatively, steam the vegetables until tender, blending to a purée using some of the boiled water from the bottom of the steamer. You could also add some of your baby's usual milk. Spoon a little into your baby's bowl and serve lukewarm.

Trio of fruits

When buying dried apricots, choose a semi-dried variety as they are nice and soft. Sometimes dried apricots are treated with sulphur dioxide (E220) to preserve their rich orange colour and prevent fungal growth. It is best to avoid these, as this substance can trigger an asthma attack in susceptible babies.

First weaning food
Makes 6 portions
✳ **Suitable for freezing**
75 g (3 oz) ready-to-eat dried apricots
2 apples, peeled, cored and chopped

75 ml (3 fl oz) water
1 large ripe pear, peeled, cored and chopped
2 tbsp baby rice
2 tbsp your baby's usual milk

■ Put the apricots and chopped apple into a small saucepan and pour over the water. Bring to a gentle simmer and cover and cook for about 7 minutes. Add the pear and continue to cook for 2 minutes. Purée the fruit in a blender. Mix together the baby rice and milk and stir into the fruit purée. Spoon a little into your baby's bowl and serve lukewarm.

Peach delight

For now, always cook any peaches, nectarines, melon, apricots, mangoes or plums that you want to give to your baby but after six months you can try mashing the peeled fruits without cooking them. Give uncooked food to your baby soon after it is prepared.

First weaning food
Makes 1 portion

½ ripe peach, peeled, stoned and chopped
½ ripe pear, peeled, cored and chopped
4 slices of a small banana

■ Put the fruit into a steamer, set over boiling water, and cook for 2–3 minutes, then purée in a blender. Spoon a little into your baby's bowl and serve lukewarm.

TIP To peel a peach, put boiling water in a bowl and add the peach to the water for 1 minute. Drain the water and pour cold water over the peach. The skin should then peel off with ease.

SUPERFOODS
DRIED APRICOTS are very good for you. In fact, they formed part of the diet of American astronauts during some of their space flights. The drying process increases their concentration of betacarotene, iron and potassium.

PEACHES are a rich source of vitamin C and their soft flesh is easy to digest.

Instant no-cook baby food

Avocado, banana or papaya make good first-stage weaning foods. After first tastes of food have been accepted, you can give your baby uncooked peaches, nectarines, melon, apricots, mangoes or plums. Always choose fruit that is sweet and ripe and peel it. Don't give your baby too much uncooked raw fruit as it can cause loose stools.

Each recipe makes 1 portion First weaning foods and after first tastes
Avocado and banana
First weaning food
■ Mash a quarter of a small avocado together with half a small ripe banana and 1–2 tbsp of your baby's milk.
Papaya and banana
First weaning food
■ Cut a small papaya in half, remove the black seeds and purée or mash together with half a small ripe banana.
Mango and banana
After first tastes
■ Purée or mash the flesh of a quarter of a small mango with half a small ripe banana.
Peach or nectarine and pear
After first tastes
■ Skin and stone a ripe peach or nectarine (see page 185) and skin and core a ripe pear. Purée or mash together. If the purée is too watery, stir in some baby rice to thicken.

Nectarine, pear and blueberry purée

This purée could also be made with a peach instead of a nectarine.

After first tastes
Makes 3 portions
✳ **Suitable for freezing**
1 ripe nectarine, skinned (see page 185),

stoned and chopped
1 ripe pear, peeled, cored and chopped
40 g (1½ oz) blueberries
2–3 tbsp baby rice

■ Put the fruit into a small saucepan, cover and cook over a low heat for about 3 minutes to soften the fruit. Purée in a blender and strain through a sieve. Mix together with the baby rice. For a very smooth purée you can blend in the baby rice using an electric hand blender. Spoon a little into your baby's bowl and serve lukewarm.

SUPERFOODS
PEARS **are easy to
digest and one of the
least likely foods to
cause an allergy so
they are good for
weaning your baby.**

BUTTERNUT **squash is
pear-shaped with
smooth beige skin. To
prepare, top and tail
the squash then, with
a sharp knife, cut
away the skin and cut
in half and remove
the seeds. Butternut
squash is rich in
betacarotene which,
when the squash is
cooked with a little
fat, is more easily
absorbed by our
bodies. Butternut
squash is easily
digested and rarely
causes allergies.**

Pear and cinnamon with baby rice

Cinnamon adds a new flavour for your baby to try and goes well with apples or pears.

After first tastes	2 large ripe pears (approximately 450 g/
Makes 6 portions	1 lb), peeled, cored and cut into chunks
✻ **Suitable for freezing**	generous pinch of cinnamon
	4 tbsp baby rice

■ Put the pears and cinnamon into a small saucepan, cover with a lid and cook over a medium heat for 2 minutes. Blend to a purée and stir in the baby rice. Spoon a little into your baby's bowl and serve lukewarm.

Creamy butternut squash

If you can't find butternut squash, this is also good made with pumpkin or orange-fleshed sweet potato. Butternut squash can also be baked in the oven. Pre-heat the oven to 180°C/350°F/Gas Mark 4. Cut the squash in half, scoop out the seeds and brush with some melted butter. Cover with foil and bake in the oven until tender (about 1½ hours). Scoop out the flesh and mash or purée with a little milk.

After first tastes	chopped
Makes 4 portions	40 g (1½ oz) French beans, topped and
Suitable for freezing	tailed and cut in half
25 g (1 oz) butter	150 ml (¼ pint) unsalted vegetable stock or
40 g (1½ oz) leek, carefully washed and	water
finely sliced	40 g (1½ oz) frozen peas
300 g (11 oz) butternut squash, peeled and	3 tbsp cream cheese or mascarpone

■ Melt the butter in a thick-based saucepan and sauté the leek until softened (about 3 minutes). Stir in the butternut squash and cook, stirring for 1 minute. Add the French beans and pour over the vegetable stock or water. Simmer, covered, for 10 minutes.
■ Add the frozen peas and cook for 4 more minutes. Purée the vegetables and then stir in the cream cheese or mascarpone. Spoon a little into your baby's bowl and serve lukewarm.

Sweet potato and broccoli or peas

After first tastes
Makes 4 portions
✳ Suitable for freezing

200 g (7 oz) sweet potato, peeled and cut into chunks
60 g (2½ oz) broccoli or frozen peas
a knob of butter

◾ Steam the sweet potato for about 5 minutes. Add the broccoli and continue to cook for about 6 minutes. If using peas, cook these for about 4 minutes.
◾ Purée together with a little of the water from the bottom of the steamer to make a good consistency for your baby and stir in the knob of butter until melted. If using peas, purée in a mouli to give a smooth texture.

TIP If your baby is not keen on certain foods, try mixing them with familiar tastes – perhaps some baby rice and milk or some puréed potato, to make a more gentle introduction.

Cauliflower cheese purée

You can also make this using 150 g (5 oz) cauliflower and leave out the broccoli, and you can try using a different cheese like Gruyère or maybe a combination of Gruyère and Cheddar cheese.

From six months (contains gluten)
Makes 4 portions
✳ Suitable for freezing
150 g (5 oz) cauliflower, cut into florets or
75 g (3 oz) each of broccoli and cauliflower cut into florets

Cheese sauce
15 g (½ oz) butter
15 g (½ oz) flour
200 ml (7 fl oz) milk
pinch of nutmeg
50 g (2 oz) Cheddar or Edam cheese

◾ Steam the cauliflower for about 8 minutes or until tender. Meanwhile, for the sauce, melt the butter over a gentle heat in a heavy-bottomed saucepan and stir in the flour to make a smooth paste. Gradually whisk in the milk and the nutmeg, bring to the boil and simmer for a couple of minutes. Stir in the cheese until melted.
◾ Blend the cooked broccoli and cauliflower together with the cheese sauce. Purée for younger babies and mash or chop into little pieces for older ones.

SUPERFOODS
BROCCOLI is king of the healthy vegetables. It is rich in antioxidants, which are believed to reduce the risk of cancer. Broccoli should be steamed as boiling it in water almost halves its vitamin C content. Broccoli also contains iron in a form that is quite well absorbed by the body because broccoli is also a rich source of vitamin C.

CAULIFLOWER provides a good source of vitamin C. It's best to steam cauliflower as boiling in water nearly halves the vitamin C content. Like broccoli it is also high in cancer-fighting antioxidants.

189

Vegetables with cheese sauce

If your baby isn't too keen on eating his vegetables, try mixing them with a tasty cheese sauce. From six months you can use cow's milk in cooking.

Suitable from six months
Makes 4 portions
✳ **Suitable for freezing**
75 g (3 oz) cauliflower, cut into florets
50 g (2 oz) broccoli, cut into florets
1 medium carrot, peeled and sliced

50 g (2 oz) frozen peas
Cheese sauce
15 g (½ oz) butter
15 g (½ oz) flour
200 ml (7 fl oz) milk
40 g (1½ oz) Cheddar cheese, grated

■ Put the vegetables into a steamer set over a pan of boiling water and cook for 4 minutes. Add the frozen peas and continue to cook for 3 minutes.
■ To make the cheese sauce, put the butter, flour and milk in a small saucepan. Heat gently, and stir or whisk until the sauce is smooth and thickened. Stir in the grated cheese until melted.
■ Pour the cheese sauce over the vegetables and blend to a purée or chop the vegetables for older babies and mix with the sauce. For young babies you can add a little more milk to thin the purée, if necessary. Spoon a little into your baby's bowl and serve lukewarm.

Peach, pear and apple crumble

Another good combination of fruit for this crumble is peach, pear and strawberry. Substitute 3 strawberries for the apple and cook, covered, over a gentle heat for about 3 minutes.

Suitable from six months (contains gluten)
Makes 5 portions
✳ **Suitable for freezing**
2 ripe peaches, peeled (see page 185), cored and chopped

1 large ripe pear, peeled, cored and chopped
1 apple, peeled, cored and chopped
1 reduced-sugar baby rusk

■ Put all the fruit in a saucepan, cover and cook over a gentle heat for about 6 minutes, then blend to a purée. Crumble the rusk to a fine powder (this can be done buy putting it into a plastic bag and crushing with a rolling pin) and stir into the fruit purée. Spoon a little into your baby's bowl and serve lukewarm.

CHAPTER FOUR

GROWING UP
7–9 months

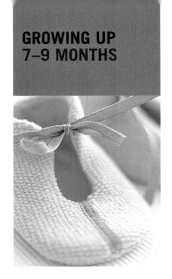

PRACTICALITIES

By now most babies are crawling and investigating their environment. They love to touch whatever their eye has taken a fancy to. Once they get hold of it they will mostly try to pull it down to look at it, and then it goes straight into the mouth. They have no way to work out what is safe and what is unsafe, so you have to help them by making their environment as safe as possible.

Making your home safe

There are a few key areas in the home where your baby is most likely to suffer from an accident – in the kitchen, on the stairs and in the bathroom. So read on and decide what you need to do to your home to keep your baby safe from harm.

In the kitchen

■ Remove all cleaning chemicals and other household poisons to a high cupboard where they will be out of sight and reach of your baby. By putting a lock on a cupboard door you might think your baby is safe but it is so easy to forget to lock it.

■ Fit baby locks on drawers and low cupboard doors.

■ Keep the kettle well out of reach. Choose a kettle with a curly flex if possible and keep the kettle well back on your kitchen worktop. If you have a cordless kettle, ensure you only use it over the kitchen worktop – do not carry it around when it contains hot water.

■ Keep hot drinks out of reach and never hold your baby and a hot drink at the same time. A cup of tea or coffee can burn your baby for up to 15 minutes after it has been made.

■ Put saucepans on the back rings of the cooker and turn their handles away from the edge so that your baby or toddler cannot reach up for them. Look for a guard that attaches to the front of the hob.

■ If you leave the iron out to cool, make sure it is well back from the edge of the kitchen worktop and that the flex cannot be reached by your baby.

■ If you are using a high chair, make sure your baby is strapped in using a five-point harness. The crotch strap alone is not enough to hold your baby safely in place.

■ Never leave a baby unattended in a high chair – especially if she is by a table. She could push herself back with her feet and topple over backwards onto the floor.

■ Stay with your baby while she is eating in case of choking.

> If you spend a lot of time in the kitchen, make one cupboard baby friendly with non-breakable bits and bobs, e.g. saucepan lids, wooden spoons. This allows your baby to pull things out safely and play at this cupboard while all the other low-level cupboards remain safely fastened.

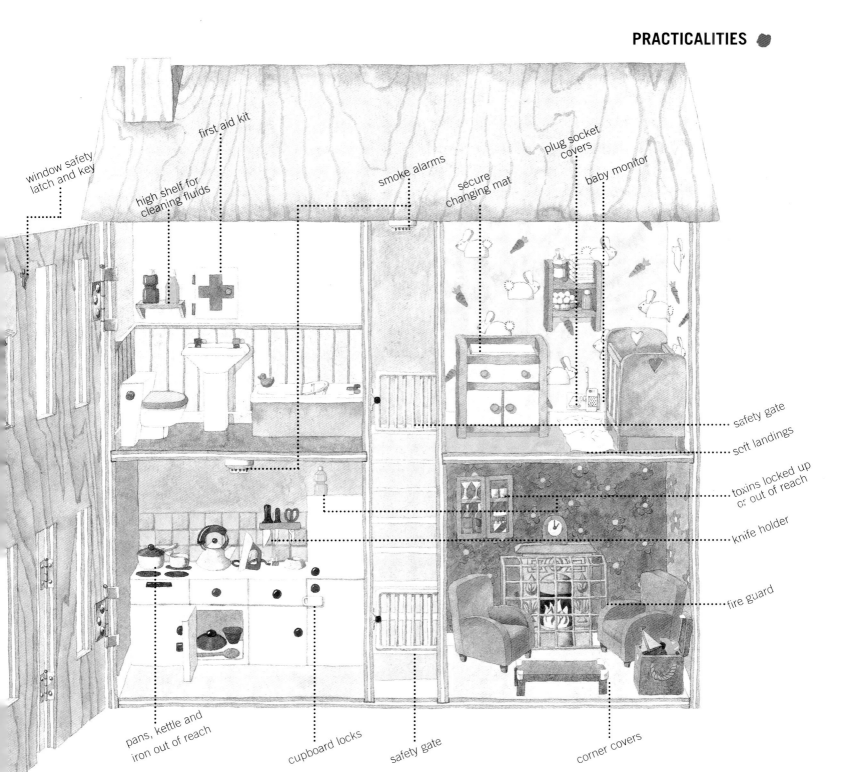

window safety latch and key

first aid kit

high shelf for cleaning fluids

smoke alarms

secure changing mat

plug socket covers

baby monitor

safety gate

soft landings

toxins locked up or out of reach

knife holder

fire guard

corner covers

pans, kettle and iron out of reach

cupboard locks

safety gate

What to do if your child has a burn or scald

Burns or scalds are the most common cause of serious injury in babies.

■ If a child has a burn or scald, cool the burn under a cold, running tap or immerse it in cold water for at least ten minutes.

■ If possible, also remove the clothing from the burned area immediately. If this isn't possible, wet the clothing with cold water and then try to remove it.

■ If material is sticking to the skin, carefully cut around the fabric.

■ Do not touch the skin or burst any blisters as this can cause an infection.

■ Cover the burn with non-fluffy material to prevent infection – all-purpose cling film is ideal or a clean tea towel or handkerchief.

■ Leave burns on the face uncovered.

■ Get advice from a doctor or accident and emergency department at your local hospital.

■ Keep knives and scissors well out of the reach of your baby.

■ Be very careful if your oven door is one that gets hot on the outside.

A safety gate across the door can be useful for keeping your baby out of the kitchen. If your kitchen is large enough, you could use a playpen to keep your baby safe and occupied while you are cooking.

■ Do not allow your baby to crawl about in the kitchen when the oven is on.

■ If you have any pets, pick up the food bowls immediately after use and make sure your baby is not left alone near your pet's water bowl.

On the stairs

■ Make sure you have safety gates at the top and bottom of the stairs. Babies love to climb stairs but cannot understand the dangers. Most often they can only go up the stairs at this age as they they don't yet know how to come down. The time will come, however, when you probably least expecting it so it is best to be prepared in advance.

■ The staircase should also be enclosed on both sides by walls or banisters. These banister rails should be vertical and have a gap of no more than 10 cm (4 in) at any point between them. This is so that your baby cannot fall through accidentally or get trapped between the rails.

In the bathroom

■ Never leave your baby unattended in the bath, even for a moment. Babies can drown in as little as 5 cm (2 in) of water.

■ Non-slip mats and bath rings can help you hold your baby in the bath but you should not rely on them – your baby still needs you there to support her.

■ To avoid scalding your baby accidentally, test the temperature of the bath water with your elbow or inner wrist before you put her in the bath. It's best to run the cold water first and then add the hot water to a comfortable temperature. Remember that a baby's skin is sensitive to heat so don't have the water too hot.

■ Do not leave your baby alone in the bathroom with a

toddler. The older child will not understand the risks and cannot be expected to take responsibility.

■ Empty the bath immediately after use.

■ Keep all medicines, razors and scissors out of reach – preferably in a locked medicine cabinet.

■ Move cleaning materials out of sight and reach.

■ Be aware that heated towel rails can get very hot to the touch and be careful if your baby is crawling.

■ Keep the toilet seat down.

In the bedroom

■ Make sure the cot you are using is safe. If you are using a second-hand cot, make sure it meets current safety guidance. It should be at least 49.5 cm (20 in) deep and bars should be between 4.5 cm and 6.5 cm (2 and 2½ in) apart. The mattress should be firm and flat with a gap of no more than 4 cm (1½ in) anywhere between the edge of the mattress and the cot.

■ Never use a duvet or pillow for a baby under a year old.

■ Cot toys should have strings no longer than 20 cm (8 in) and should be removed as soon as your baby can sit up or get on all fours.

■ Cot bumpers are not recommended. They can give your baby a foothold to climb out and can cause her to overheat.

■ Baby monitors are not a safety device. They can help give you peace of mind, but should not replace regular checking. Many accidents happen silently.

■ Use window locks in your baby's room. They can stop the window opening more than 10 cm (4 in) so that she cannot fall out. Keep the key somewhere handy in case of fire.

■ If you have blind or curtain cords in your baby's room, either tie them up well out of the reach of your

---

Once your baby can crawl

■ Place plug socket covers in all empty sockets.

■ Where possible fit child safety locks on drawers and cupboards.

■ Place plastic corner protectors on tables.

■ Don't leave cigarettes, alcohol, essential oils or perfume within reach – they can be poisonous.

---

baby or cut the loop so they cannot cause a strangulation hazard.

■ Babies should never sleep in clothes with ties or ribbons, nor in dungarees – they are strangulation hazards. Sleep suits or nighties are the safest option.

In the living room

■ Choose toys that are made for babies and toddlers. Toys that are marked unsuitable for children under 36 months contain small parts that could choke a baby or toddler. Keep older children's toys with small parts away from babies and throw away broken or damaged items immediately.

■ Fit a fireguard on all fires and heaters.

■ Never leave a baby unattended on a sofa or armchair – they can easily roll off.

■ Keep fragile objects out of reach.

■ Move alcohol, essential oils, cigarettes, lighters and matches well out of the sight and reach of your baby.

■ Avoid trailing flexes from lamps, the television, etc.

■ Move furniture away from windows where possible and use window locks to restrict opening.

■ Low windows or glass doors should be fitted with safety glass. If this is not possible, use safety film to reduce the risk of injury.

■ Use corner cushions on sharp edges such as coffee tables and bookcases to prevent injuries if your baby bumps in to them.

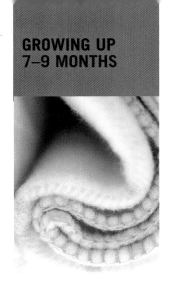

SLEEPING

All babies wake at night but you need your baby to be able to settle back to sleep herself so that she does not disturb you. A baby that relies on her mother or father to be rocked, fed or picked up cannot go back to sleep alone as these triggers have become the key to going to sleep. This then becomes very difficult for the parents because the baby may start to wake more and more often just to be close to her mum or dad, the ultimate prize being for her taken into her parents' bed.

Helping your baby to sleep well

If your baby has become accustomed to going to sleep when one or both of her parents is on hand you might want to consider trying the following:

■ Make bath time as relaxed and enjoyable as possible with plenty of bath toys and a warm towel afterwards.

■ Take your baby to a quiet bedroom after the bath to feed.

■ Put your very sleepy baby down into the cot to finish drifting off to sleep alone. Your baby may become more wakeful at this stage but leave her to settle.

You could then:

■ Leave the room going back in 10 or 20 minutes to reassure your baby.

■ Potter about the bedroom, tidying up but paying no attention to your baby – your baby will be reassured by your presence.

■ Stay by the cot holding your baby's hand or stroking her forehead and over her eyes. Don't look your baby in the eye and don't talk to her.

■ Use mobiles and music to distract her.

Separation anxiety may start at this stage (see page 200) so going to bed may become difficult. You need to keep to a routine and be loving but firm with her. All this will take time; you may be in and out of the bedroom for up to an hour each evening. But don't give in unless you feel your baby is not well or you just know it's one of those nights when nothing works. Eventually your baby will get the message that bedtime is for sleeping.

If your baby wakes at night, carry out the same routine adopted at bedtime but think of the following:

■ Watch daytime sleeps – she may have slept too much or too long in the day.

Possible routine

6.30–7am	Wake up and have milk and breakfast.
9–10am	Sleep.
10–12 noon	Playtime/outing/visitors.
12–12.30pm	Lunch and milk/juice or water.
12.30–2.30pm	Nap.
2.30–3pm	Milk.
3–5pm	Playtime.
5–5.30pm	Supper with water or juice.
6–7pm	Bath/massage, milk and bed.

■ Is she hungry, in which case you may need to adjust daytime eating.

■ Is she wet or uncomfortable?

■ Is she cold, in which case stretchsuits can be very helpful for her?

■ It is also possible that your baby is unwell or teething, in which case you need to take care of her. A sick baby may be less active than normal, breathing may be different (more rapid or irregular), she might hold or rub a painful area, e.g. her ear or tummy, or she may be floppy or pale (see page 163). Your baby will need to be comforted and cuddled. Sick babies need lots of extra love and attention. If your baby has a fever, you may need to apply a cold compress and remove some of the bedclothes to cool her down. You may need to give infant paracetamol suspension or rub a teething gel on her gums if she is teething. If you are at all worried, call a doctor.

If your baby has been unwell, don't wait until she has fully recovered to go back to your original routine – resume it as soon as she starts to get better.

Sleeping during the day

Your baby needs to rest during the day and will probably now have two naps, one in the morning and one in the afternoon. The average daytime sleep for this age is about three hours. If your baby misses out on sleep during the day it is likely that she will become over-tired and difficult to handle, not eat properly and not settle to sleep well at night.

If you can, it is best to keep to a routine and have set nap times. That doesn't mean you have to be tied to the house during these periods as your baby can sleep in her pram or car seat if you need to be out and about. Whatever you are doing, it is probably best not to allow

---

● *Q What should I do if my baby keeps on waking up early in the morning?*

A The normal waking time for a four- to six-month-old baby is 5–7am. If your baby wakes up early in the morning and she is used to being fed at 5am, it's likely that this will become a habit. It is hard to cope with the day ahead if you have been up since 5am, so try to train your baby to wake up later.

■ Make sure your baby isn't sleeping too long in the day; ensure she gets exercise and fresh air.

■ Try to ensure that light doesn't creep into the room in the early morning: use a blackout blind.

■ Put a lamp with a timer switch in the bedroom set it to come on at your baby's usual waking time and gradually set it to come on later. Your baby may associate the lamp with getting up and may drop off to sleep again if the light hasn't come on.

■ Put some toys into your baby's cot when she is asleep that she can reach out and play with when she wakes in the morning.

■ If all else fails and your baby is really hungry, take her into your bed in the morning, feed her and hopefully she may doze off again. This may work but don't spend two hours trying to get her back to sleep. If it's going to work, it will work fairly quickly. Otherwise, get up and try to catch up with a nap during the day.

---

your baby to sleep more than three hours during the day and also try to keep her awake for the three hours before bedtime.

Now your baby is spending more time awake you may worry how you are going to fit in the things you need to do during the day. But you will soon find your baby enjoys being part of your life whether it's out shopping with you or watching you cook.

CRYING

As the months go by your baby will have settled down and not cried so much. But there will be new reasons why occasionally she may begin to cry a little more. This is due to teething, frustration at wanting to crawl and reach for toys (or similar) and separation anxiety. Thankfully, unlike the crying from the early months, this type of crying is generally easily fixed. Hopefully you will have learned by now to understand what your baby is crying about and know how to help her. Food can also be used at this stage as a distraction.

Separation anxiety

A new type of crying becomes obvious at this stage: it is the one of separation anxiety. These cries are fixed as soon as the mother or father picks up the baby or takes the baby from the other person. The best approach is to hold your baby while you talk to this person; your baby will be guided by you and in return feel more relaxed and take to the person with greater ease. As cries reduce, smiling and giggling increases.

Equally, your baby may cry because either you or your partner is out of sight, has turned away from her, put her down, handed her over to another adult to hold, put her in the buggy/car seat or put her to bed. This constant pressure to be ever present seems like an unnecessary demand. From the baby's point of view, she just can't bear to be away from her Mummy or Daddy. She may feel that she doesn't know how to get her/him back. Of course, as an adult a parent knows they will be back but the baby has not worked this out yet. As time goes by, however, she will become less anxious when you are away.

At about six months a baby begins to feel separate from her mother and with the understanding of independence comes this fear of separation. It is common for babies to feel anxious and cry when you go away,

which can be very upsetting. Your baby needs to learn that her mother will return and all will be well. If you are going out, make sure that your baby is familiar with her surroundings and the people looking after her. When you do leave, say goodbye and go quickly as staying around too long increases the pain and confusion. At this age you would expect your baby to cry for 10–20 minutes after you have gone, then settle to play happily until you return. The more emotional support you give your baby at this stage, the more confident and independent she will become later.

A crying baby is always difficult for a parent to cope with, especially in public. When tired even the most patient parent can reach the end of her tether and the cry of separation is particularly hard to cope with. This cry can wear down the most patient person because it can seem to be without reason.

Rows and unpleasant situations will also upset your baby at this age. If she is exposed to this, hold her close to you and comfort her. Gently tell her that everything will be all right, there's nothing to worry about. If there are any sudden loud noises and your baby is frightened, pick her up and comfort her. Babies are often frightened of pets like dogs or cats, and bigger children can seem very noisy and active to a small baby – keep your baby close and give her the reassurance that she needs.

Crying at bedtime

Because your baby has started to feel anxious when she is separated from you, you may find that she becomes unsettled at bedtime. If your baby cries, reassure her, tuck her in, stroke her back and then say goodnight. Hopefully her crying will not last long and she will drift off to sleep. It might help to settle her down to sleep and then spend a little while with her in the room tidying up so that she settles down and relaxes, knowing that she is not alone. A comforter like a familiar blanket or soft toy is a good sleeping aid and it will have its uses if your baby wakes in the middle of the night as she may find it reassuring to cuddle up with this in your absence.

Be prepared for the crying with firm, loving handling and you can expect the settling time to reduce or become less difficult as the weeks go by. Some babies will always find bedtime difficult but sometimes a mother just has to try to accept this and see it as normal for her.

Don't be tempted to slip out without your baby noticing even if you intend to return in five or ten minutes. If your baby looks up and finds you gone, she may feel anxious and find it difficult to settle down and play even when you do come back as she will be afraid that you will disappear again without warning.

Controlled crying

■ Controlled crying is probably the best way to help your child to learn to fall asleep.

■ Once your baby has been bathed and fed and you have finished your cosy bedtime routine, say your good-nights, put her in her crib or cot while still awake, then leave the room, even if she is crying.

■ If your baby continues to cry, wait for a certain amount of time before checking, rather than rushing in immediately. The amount of time you wait depends on how many days you have followed the programme of controlled crying and what your nerves can take. It's a good idea to change the time occasionally or your baby will get used to waiting for, say, 10 minutes – so sometimes go in after 8 minutes or maybe 12 minutes.

■ When you do go in, soothe your baby by talking gently to her or stroking her, but don't pick her up, feed her or rock her, and don't stay too long. If your baby knows that crying brings rewards, it will encourage her to cry more.

■ Gradually increase the amount of time between checking on your baby, but don't leave your baby to cry for more than 20 minutes on her own.

■ Resist all temptation to pick up your baby; the key to success is to be consistent.

■ If this still doesn't work after several weeks, you could try staying in the room with your baby as she falls asleep. Place her in her cot and remain in the room in her line of vision but don't pick her up and try not to make eye contact. If your child is upset, you can reassure her by stroking her, holding her hand or talking soothingly to her. For the first few days you may need to stay in the room for quite a while but as your baby gets used to this routine, you can move further and further away from her cot until eventually she falls asleep without you.

DEVELOPING

During these three months you are likely to see quite a difference in the way your baby gets around, although the age at which babies become mobile varies. Generally a baby starts to crawl at eight or nine months while some may not crawl until ten months and others may never crawl. Some babies get around on their tummies or pull themselves along with their arms. Some bottom shuffle, which can delay walking because it is an efficient way of getting around.

Greater movement

Some babies seem to progress from sitting to walking without ever crawling and some early developers are cruising around the furniture at the age of ten months but most babies start walking at about one year. Most babies will walk without support by 15 months. If you are tempted to get a baby walker that your baby can sit in, think again. Health professionals do not recommend their use as they have been the cause of many serious accidents (see page 233). In addition, research has shown that rather than encouraging a baby to walk, they can delay independent walking.

Safety

Once your baby is mobile you will need to think seriously about safety around the house (see page 194). Most of your cupboards will need to have childproof catches but it's a good idea to have one small safe cupboard or some shelves where you can keep toys and objects that appeal to your baby. She can then take out the objects herself and explore them. Fit gates at both the top and bottom of the stairs, ensure there are safety plugs in all the electrical sockets and make sure that there are no small objects lying around that your baby might put in her mouth and choke on.

Toys

You will no doubt find you are accumulating a wide range of toys and books. Don't be tempted to stack a huge range in front of your baby – it is far better to choose one or two at a time and change them as she becomes bored with them, which may not take long!

Building bricks: These are great for developing hand and finger control. Soft building bricks are best for young babies, but at first your baby will only be able to knock them down.

Stacking toys: Stacking rings or beakers help your baby learn about size and you can have fun hiding toys under one of the beakers too.

Activity centre: Look for one with buttons to press, knobs to turn, spinners to spin, etc.

Toys that make a noise: e.g. soft rubbery toys that squeak when pressed.

Toy telephones: Your baby will love to mimic you on the telephone and some come with lights and sounds.

Books: Expand your range to include lift-the-flap, textural, plastic, board and those that make noises.

Balls: There are some amazing electronic balls with lights and sounds, which your baby will enjoy rolling about and playing with.

Your baby at 7 months

At seven months babies can bear their own weight for short periods if they stand supported. They will also start to anticipate what is going to happen next. For example, if you tie a bib around your baby's neck she will know that it is time to eat, or if she hears the bath water running she will know that it will soon be time for her bath. Once your baby is able to sit up comfortably and bend forwards to pick up her toys without toppling over, she will be able to keep herself amused for longer periods of time. Quite a few babies start teething at this age.

Movement	Hand-to-eye coordination	Language	Learning	What your baby enjoys	Stimulating play
■ Your baby can now roll from back to front and vice versa. ■ She likes to experiment with crawling. When on her tummy she can support her upper body with her arms and will sometimes tuck her knees up under her and will rock backwards and forwards on her knees. ■ Your baby needs both her hands to pick up an object. It is easier for her to	■ At this age babies begin to coordinate their two hands better and can do things like passing objects from one hand to the other. ■ Your baby can pick up a toy like a rattle. ■ She begins to reach for and grasp a toy or object using her fingers and thumb in a pincer movement. ■ As a result, she is better at holding	■ Your baby begins to understand the meaning of 'No'. ■ She becomes more responsive as you talk to her as she understands more of what you say, especially if accompanied by actions. ■ She is able to sense if you are cross or happy with her by the tone of your voice. ■ Your baby starts to use one object to	■ She knows how to make toys or objects move. ■ She anticipates playtime, bath time, bedtime by familiar routines. ■ She searches the floor for an object that she has dropped. ■ Let her feel and recognise different textures, such as touchy-feely books, the grass outside, different fabrics like velvet or silk, or	■ Exploring toys by banging, sucking, shaking them or dropping them over the side of the high chair. ■ Swinging in a baby bouncer suspended from the doorway. These are great at this age for short periods of time. ■ She feels secure with a familiar routine. ■ Having a tug of war with you: give	■ Demonstrate how to pull a toy towards you that is attached to a string and see if your baby will copy you. She will become aware that her actions produce certain results. ■ When you are playing, bathing or changing your baby make a comment that requires a response, e.g. 'Look at the train', and see if she responds. ■ Roll a ball towards your baby and get

Movement	Hand-to-eye coordination	Language	Learning	What your baby enjoys	Stimulating play
play if she is supported in a sitting position, leaving both hands free for playing with the toys or objects on a tray or table in front of her. ■ Lying on her front, she may be able to wriggle forwards or backwards with her tummy raised. ■ She can bear her own weight when supported under her arms and can bounce up and down on her feet. ■ She is now able to sit up unsupported. ■ She likes to bring her foot into her mouth to suck on her toes.	objects and less likely to drop them. ■ She feeds herself finger food, more accurately. Give your baby food that she can pick up with her fingers, like toast soldiers, pasta shapes, etc. (see page 211).	get another, e.g. if a toy she wants is on a towel or the carpet but out of reach, she may pull at the cloth to bring the toy closer and within reach. ■ She enjoys making sounds like blowing raspberries. ■ Your baby now uses double syllable sounds, e.g. 'ad-ah', 'ga-ra', 'ah-goo'.	household items such as a sponge, cooked spaghetti, or a toothbrush. ■ She remembers the faces of people that she has seen before, e.g. a friend or the babysitter. ■ She clearly recognises facial expressions such as anger or fear.	your baby one end of a scarf and pull gently on the other. ■ Pulling funny faces or making sounds at her reflection in a mirror. ■ Playing with bubbles that you blow through a wand and delighting in trying to catch them in her hands.	her to stop it using her hands. She will not be ready yet to roll it back to you. ■ Show your baby how to play the drums holding a wooden spoon and a selection of upturned saucepans or plastic bowls. ■ Your baby's main interest in toys is in holding them, looking at them and exploring them with her mouth. At this age, apart from shaking or banging them, there is not much more she can do with them so she will soon want to explore new objects. There are many everyday objects that make great playthings such as measuring spoons, empty plastic bottles, scrunchy paper. Remember that everything your baby plays with must be safe for her to put in her mouth so make sure there are no sharp edges or small parts that she could choke on.

Your baby at 8 months

At this age your baby will be looking for a new challenge and may try getting up and standing in her cot by holding on to the bars. There's one problem, though: she won't know how to lower herself down again. She is also good at picking up small objects with her thumb and forefinger. Your baby starts to be able to plan ahead a little: for example, if there is a toy on the end of a piece of string she will pull on the string to get hold of the toy. She may now be quite clingy when other people are around and feel anxious with strangers.

Movement	Hand-to-eye coordination	Language	Learning	What your baby enjoys	Stimulating play
■ Your baby can sit up unsupported with her legs out in front of her and can lean forwards and sideways without toppling over.	■ She is able to lean forwards and pick up objects with her fingers and thumb in a pincer movement. She may be able to do this so well now that she can pick up very small objects like peas.	■ She may be able to say 'Mama' and 'Dadda'. When you start to hear distinguishable sounds like these, point to Mummy and Daddy and repeat what she's saying. She then starts to link the sounds she's making with words and their meanings.	■ She begins to copy some of your actions like nodding her head or waving bye-bye.	■ Holding onto something for support and bouncing up and down.	■ To encourage your baby to crawl, put a favourite toy a short distance in front of her.
■ She can take her own weight and may be able to stand when holding on to a piece of furniture or a person.	■ She points to things that she wants which are clearly in her view.		■ She tries to get hold of objects that are out of reach.	■ Bouncing up and down on your lap in time to music.	■ You can also crawl beside your baby and see if she mimics your movements.
■ She may be able to pull herself to a standing position. Encourage your baby to stand a few times during the day	■ She may be able to hit two toys together and will soon learn to clap her hands.	■ Talk to your baby whenever you can and tell her what you are doing and the names of things around you. She can then start to associ-	■ Pop-up toys that burst out when a button is pushed encourage finger control – the element of surprise will delight your child.	■ Action games and rhymes like 'Pat-a-Cake', 'Incey Wincey Spider', 'This little piggy went to market', 'One, two, buckle my shoe'.	■ When you have a cluster of toys in front of your baby, demonstrate how they work and let your baby choose the one she is interested in. After she has chosen, simplify
				■ Playing with toys that come apart and fit together. She can take them apart but	

Movement	Hand-to-eye coordination	Language	Learning	What your baby enjoys	Stimulating play
by gripping on to a low table or heavy chair. Be ready to catch her if she loses her grip and falls over, and give her lots of cuddles and encouragement. Make sure there are no flimsy pieces of furniture that might topple over if your child tries to hold on to them for support. ■ Your baby may start to crawl, which will involve alternating between two pairs of diagonal limbs, moving one pair first, e.g. right hand and left leg, and then the other pair. Some babies will crawl on their hands and knees and some on their hands and feet. Others will shuffle around on their bottoms and some babies never crawl at all before walking.	■ Play 'Follow My Leader' – bang on a drum, clap your hands, etc., and see if your baby copies your actions.	ate objects and actions with words. ■ Try to face your baby as you talk so that she can see how your lips move. ■ She likes to imitate sounds you make. ■ She likes trying to make animal noises – make animal noises yourself and see if your baby can mimic you. ■ She may shout to gain your attention. ■ Try to use short sentences as this helps your baby understand the request better, e.g. say, 'Look – it's your teddy,' and she may turn to look at it. ■ Don't flood your baby with information, instead use repetition, e.g. 'Where is the ball?' 'Here is the ball', 'What colour is the ball?' 'The ball is red'.		is not yet able to fit them back together again. ■ Listening to music and you singing nursery rhymes to her. She may even try to join in. ■ Chewing, banging and shaking objects and toys. ■ Playing with noisy or musical toys, e.g. a toy drum, maracas, xylophone. ■ Playing with stacking rings or colourful blocks. She may not be able to assemble these by herself but she will enjoy knocking them over. ■ Watching and being with other babies. ■ Playing alongside other children although she does not interact with them yet.	the scene for your baby by moving away the other distracting toys. ■ Loosely wrap some old toys in newspaper and colourful paper and put them in a large carrier bag. Your child will delight in having to figure out how to unwrap them and find out what is inside. ■ Hide a wound-up musical toy under a blanket and see if your baby can find it. ■ Static exercisers, – in which the baby sits in the centre of the unit and is surrounded by a circle of interactive toys – are great for a baby at this age, and she can rotate the seat to play with all the toys. These are good for keeping your baby occupied in a small space.

Your baby at 9 months

Your baby may be able to climb upstairs but she won't be able to climb down yet. At this age, your baby has no sense of danger so she musn't be left alone near steps. Once your baby is able to crawl, she eagerly explores and investigates everything to which she has access. You need to be vigilant about safety, putting dangerous objects out of reach and safety gates on the stairs. Check that there aren't any unsteady pieces of furniture that could topple over if your baby tries to pull herself up on them. Don't hurry your baby through any phase of becoming mobile; she will develop at her own pace. Early walking is not a sign of a brighter baby!

Movement	Hand-to-eye coordination	Language	Learning	What your baby enjoys	Stimulating play
■ Your baby may now be able to crawl backwards and forwards and may also be able to turn around. It's a good idea to dress her in clothes that cover her knees. ■ She should be able to stand if she is holding on to something, but she will be a bit wobbly. ■ Your baby may well look for help once she manages to stand as she cannot yet let go and sit	■ Your baby now has more coordinated hand movements. She may now be able to build a tower of two bricks. ■ She masters picking up small objects like raisins or peas with her thumb and index finger. ■ She may start to use one hand more than the other (usually the right hand). ■ She may be able to place stacking rings on a spindle.	■ It's really good if you can name lots of things as you go about your day with your baby, either at home or when out and about. If you see your baby looking with interest at something, tell her what it is. ■ She can understand simple instructions with gestures, e.g. 'Give me the ball' as you hold out your hand at the same time. ■ She babbles	■ She may help you when you dress her – putting her arm through a sleeve or giving you her foot for you to put on a sock. ■ She may be able to pull off her socks. ■ She likes to explore and feel different textures. Occasionally it is a good idea to let your baby experiment with her food, like feeling jelly or cooked pasta shapes. Let her	■ Playing with sand. You can give her a mini sandbox to play with, either in the kitchen or somewhere outside. Let her experiment with a shovel and bucket, trying things like digging, emptying, etc. ■ Walking holding onto someone or pieces of furniture. ■ Putting objects or toys inside a box or bucket and then taking them out again. ■ Reaching for	■ Playing with stacking rings and beakers is a good way to get your child to improve her hand-to-eye coordination and teaches her how to order objects according to size. ■ Sit a little way from your baby, roll a soft ball towards her and see if she can roll it back to you. ■ Play games like hiding your baby's favourite toy behind

Movement	Hand-to-eye coordination	Language	Learning	What your baby enjoys	Stimulating play
down again. Rather than just dumping her on her bottom, teach her how to do this by gradually lowering her into a sitting position and encouraging her to have the confidence to let go. ■ The stage between standing and walking is called 'cruising'. This involves holding on to pieces of furniture that are close together, moving along with a side-step motion. A long sofa, a line of small chairs in a row and a low table would be ideal so that she can edge her way along from one end to the other. About 25% of babies will be able to cruise around furniture by the age of nine months. ■ Encourage your baby to cruise by putting a favourite toy at the end of a line of furniture so that she can see it. If she manages to reach it, give her lots of praise.	■ She may be able to point to an object that she wants and may be able to wave goodbye. ■ She should be able to drink from a beaker with a spout. ■ Your baby can see almost as clearly as an adult.	continuously, using two-syllable words like 'Mama' and 'Dadda' and makes up her own words for familiar objects like 'Oom-pah' for Grandpa. Encourage her by imitating her voice sounds and then make a new sound and see if she can copy it.	experiment with a variety of textures, like crumpling up tissue paper or tearing up newspaper. ■ If you wave to your baby, she may wave back to you. ■ Your baby may be able to offer you a toy but she may not be able to let go of it very well. ■ It's good to read the same story to your baby several times – and more – as repetition helps her to learn new vocabulary. It's also good not just to read the story but also ask questions like 'Who's that?' or 'I wonder if baby bear takes a teddy bear to bed with him,' and then answer the questions yourself. As your baby learns to talk, she'll be the one to answer the questions. ■ Her memory is improving – if you hide a toy under a bucket she will remember it is there.	objects that are placed high on, say, a coffee table or sofa. You can take the seat cushions off the sofa to make her play area lower. ■ Playing with an activity centre that has buttons to press, spinners to spin, knobs to turn and bells to ring. This could be free standing or attached to the cot.	your back, bring your hand out without the toy and see if she will try to crawl behind you to find it. ■ Games like Peek-a-boo are great, helping your baby to understand that if you disappear out of view you will be coming back. ■ Turn toys upside down in front of your baby and encourage her to turn them the right way up. ■ If your baby is good at pulling herself up but can't quite figure out how to get down again, you can let her practise by holding on to the end of a pole or broom handle so that you can help ease her down to a soft landing.

FEEDING

Between seven and nine months is a period of rapid development and because your baby is growing very fast she will need plenty of calories. She should be eating three meals a day and is ready to enjoy a wide variety of tastes. Half her daily intake of calories should be from milk and half from solids. As well as vitamins, minerals, proteins and carbohydrates, she must get enough fat in her diet as this is crucial for growth and development. Babies and young children need proportionately more fat in their diet than adults do.

Exploring new tastes

Once your baby can sit unsupported (probably at around seven months), she can use a high chair. Try to make eating a sociable event by getting her to sit at the table with you whenever possible.

For breakfast you can now give your baby fruit and cereal or something like cheese on toast. Your baby will probably be desperate for milk first thing in the morning so give some milk first and then give cereal or fruit. You don't have to buy special baby cereals, Ready Brek and Weetabix are good as they are wholegrain cereals and are rich in vitamins and iron. You can also give these with mashed or chopped up fruit.

Introduce protein at lunchtime – e.g. fish, chicken, meat, cheese or lentils – because it takes longer to digest. Once your baby is eating protein at lunch you can give diluted juice or water at this feed. A vitamin

It's best not to give milk with lunch or supper and instead give diluted juice or water. Try to give juice after your baby has eaten most of her solids so as not to spoil her appetite.

Q How much milk should my baby drink?
A Babies of this age should have 600–800 ml (20–25 fl oz) of formula or breast milk each day up to the age of one year. If your baby is breastfed or if she is taking less than 600 ml (20 fl oz) a day of a fortified infant milk, she also needs supplementary vitamins A and D at least up until one year of age. A portion of the milk intake can come from dairy products like cheese and yoghurt or milk used in cooking such as a cheese sauce.

C-rich juice is good as this assists iron absorption (see page 212).

For supper give pasta, vegetable purées, finger foods, etc. Once your baby is around eight months old you can give protein for supper. As your baby gets older she will want to feed herself so mini sandwiches with nutritious fillings like peanut butter, egg mayonnaise, cheese, tuna or sardines are good (see page 215).

Each day, aim to offer:
Two mini portions of fruit and vegetables, e.g. a banana, small apple, pear, carrot.

■ Two to three mini portions of starchy foods, e.g. a small baked potato, portion of cereal or 25 g (1 oz) rice or pasta.
■ One mini portion protein rich food, e.g. 25 g (1 oz) meat, fish or cheese, 1 egg, 25 g (1 oz) lentils.

Foods to avoid
■ Whole or chopped nuts as children under five may choke.
■ Shellfish.
■ Undercooked eggs: the white and yolk should be solid.
■ Too much sugar. Sugar-free or reduced-sugar drinks can contain large amounts of artificial sweetener, which is not recommended for young children.
■ Unpasteurised cheese, including blue cheese.
■ Salt or stock cubes.
■ Honey: don't give this to babies under a year as occasionally honey can cause infant botulism.
■ Too many high-fibre foods like bran cereals, lentils and dried fruits.

Textures

Every baby develops at her own pace, but your baby's first tooth will probably be cut at around six to seven months. As teeth begin to emerge you can introduce slightly thicker purées and some mashed or grated food. Even with very few teeth, babies can be very efficient at chewing food with their gums.

For a gradual introduction you could mix some mashed or grated food with some of your baby's favourite purées. So, if your child likes carrots, for example, purée some of the carrots and mash some and mix the two together. You can slowly increase the proportions until all the food is mashed. Don't expect her to be thrilled by this change, as lumps take a bit of getting used to. Once your baby has got used to mashed food, you can try chopping food and mixing some of it with the mashed food. Some babies will cope very well with chopped food at nine months while others still prefer smoother textures. However, it is very important to persevere with getting your baby to eat lumps.

Another way to introduce texture is to prepare a fairly smooth purée and then add some tiny cooked pasta shapes. You can buy soup pasta like stelline, which looks like tiny stars, or orzo, which is pasta the size and shape of grains of rice. Some babies do not get on well with mixed textures of purée with soft lumps. They may do better with soft chopped foods such as chopped cooked carrots.

If your baby is not keen on lumpy food, it might be that she is still drinking a lot of milk. You may find that cutting down on the amount of milk she drinks will mean she is hungrier for her solids and therefore not so fussy about the texture. Replace milk with water or very dilute juice as your baby still needs the fluids.

Introducing red meat

Unless you choose to bring your child up as a vegetarian (see page 216), red meat is an excellent food as it provides the best source of iron, which is vitally important for both physical and mental development. The trouble is that meat can be very chewy, which can put babies off. So it is best to combine meat with root vegetables or pasta, both of which will help to produce a texture that is much smoother and easier to swallow. Even for older babies I find that, when cooking minced meat for a Bolognese sauce or a shepherd's pie, it really helps to chop it in a food processor for a few seconds so that it doesn't have a lumpy texture.

Iron

Iron is very important for your baby's mental and physical development. Iron deficiency is the most common nutritional problem in children in the Western world and can leave your child feeling run down and more prone to infection. Babies are born with a store of iron that lasts for about six months. After this it is important to make sure they get the iron they need from their food. Iron deficiency can lead to anaemia, which can affect your child's mental development as iron is an important factor in brain development. A baby's iron requirements are particularly high between six months and a year. Premature babies are especially at risk as their store of iron may last for only about six weeks and they will need an iron supplement plus a special low-birthweight formula milk that contains all the nutrients and calories they need.

Iron deficiency can be difficult to spot. It commonly remains unrecognised because of subtle symptoms such as pallor, listlessness and fatigue. Also growth and development may seem slower than normal. However, preventing iron deficiency is not difficult: it's a question of thinking about what our children are eating and trying our best to ensure that they have a balanced diet which provides all the iron they need.

How best to absorb the iron in the food we eat

Iron in foods of animal origin, like red meat or poultry, is much better absorbed than iron in foods of plant origin, like green vegetables or cereals. Fish does not contain much iron, but it helps the absorption of iron from other foods. Vitamin C also helps the body to absorb more iron from foods, so giving your baby plenty of vitamin C-rich foods, e.g. sliced kiwi fruit or a glass of orange juice with a fortified cereal or vegetables like sweet pepper or cauliflower with lentils, will help to increase the absorption of iron in non-meat sources.

> **Q What should I do if my baby chokes?**
> **A** If your baby chokes, do not try to fish for food in his mouth as you may only end up pushing it further down his throat. Tip him face down over your lap with his head lower than his stomach, and slap him between the shoulder blades to dislodge the food.

Protein-rich foods also aid iron absorption. By mixing lean meat, chicken or fish with dark leafy vegetables or lentils, you can assist the absorption of the vegetable sources of iron by about three times. Continue to give breast or formula milk to your baby as cow's milk is not a good source of iron.

Good sources of iron

- Red meat, particularly liver, is the best source of iron.
- Chicken or turkey, especially the dark meat.
- Oily fish (like salmon and mackerel).
- Pulses (like lentils, baked beans).
- Iron-fortified baby rice, fortified breakfast cereals.
- Bread.
- Egg yolk.
- Green leafy vegetables, e.g. broccoli, spring greens.
- Dried fruit, especially dried apricots.

Finger foods

As your baby develops better finger control (usually at around seven or eight months), introducing finger foods will help to develop the valuable skills of biting, chewing and self-feeding. Finger foods should be big enough for your baby to pick up, easy to hold and should not have any stones, pips or bones. Choose foods that either dissolve in the mouth or can be chewed with her gums. You should avoid relatively hard foods like raw carrots or apple or whole grapes, which might cause your baby to choke.

To begin with, as your baby learns to feed herself, she will probably drop a lot of her food on the floor. Invest in a plastic splash mat, which can be laid under her high chair so that the food falls on a clean surface and can then be recycled. The ability to pick up small objects with the thumb and forefinger in a pincer grip doesn't develop in most babies until about nine months.

It's best to place three or four finger foods onto the tray of your baby's high chair or put them into a plastic bowl in front of your baby – bowls with suction pads are good. Don't put too much food in front of your baby or she may just swipe it all onto the floor.

Remember never to leave your baby alone while eating as babies are quite likely to bite off a piece of food, try to swallow it whole and choke on it.

Making finger foods fun

■ Sticks of vegetables like carrots make good finger food but raw vegetables can be difficult to chew and your baby can bite a piece off and choke on it. So it is much better to lightly steam vegetables lightly or cook them in a little boiling water for a few minutes so that they are still crunchy but not quite so hard. When your baby seems to cope well with these, try introducing cucumber and then some raw vegetables.

■ Toast soldiers tend to work better than plain bread as they do not fall to pieces so readily. Bagels, pitta or naan bread are good too.

■ Fingers of wholemeal bread slowly dried in the oven make a healthy alternative to baby rusks, which can contain quite large amounts of sugar

■ Fruits make good finger food and if your baby finds it difficult to chew, give soft fruits that melt in the mouth like banana or peach. Slices of peeled softish apple are good.

■ For fun finger food you can cut sandwiches, cheese or large vegetables into shapes using cookie cutters. Good sand-

First finger foods

Below are some ideas for first finger foods. Offering a selection of these to your baby will get her used to chewing many different textures.

■ Banana, melon, apricot, peach, avocado, halved, peeled grapes, kiwi fruit, sliced apple, etc.

■ Dried fruits like apricots, apple or prune.

■ Rice cakes.

■ Steamed carrot sticks, small florets of steamed cauliflower or broccoli.

■ Sticks of peeled cucumber.

■ Cooked pasta shapes.

■ Fingers of toast, pitta bread, rice cakes, miniature sandwiches, dry breakfast cereals.

■ Hard-boiled egg cut into quarters or strips of well-cooked omelette.

■ Mild cheese, e.g. Edam, Cheddar, Emmenthal.

■ Slices or chunks of chicken or turkey.

■ Miniature meatballs.

wich fillings are mashed banana, cream cheese, Marmite, peanut butter, tuna mayonnaise, egg mayonnaise, hummus or mashed sardines.

Upset tummy

If you child is suffering from constipation or diarrhoea, see page 78. If she has an upset tummy, make sure she has plenty of fluids and you can try the American BRAT diet. Offer small amounts of the following foods:

■ **Bananas** settle an acid stomach and provide potassium to regulate the body's fluid balance.

■ **Rice** helps relieve diarrhoea and provides energy and protein.

■ **Apples**, especially stewed apples, are a traditional cure for gastroenteritis.

■ **Toast** (dry white) also helps to settle the stomach and provides carbohydrate for energy.

After 48 hours, if symptoms have improved, introduce potatoes, cooked vegetables (especially root vegetables) and a boiled egg. Leave out dairy foods for a while as an irritated gut can sometimes be aggravated by lactose in dairy foods.

Teething

Your baby will be teething from around six months to about two years and so gums may be sore and your child may be quite unsettled and not interested in food. Some babies sail through this period whereas others seem to suffer for the entire 20-tooth, two-year experience, becoming irritable and dribbling non-stop as each tooth cuts through the gums.

You may notice several symptoms that suggest a new tooth is on its way. There may be a change in your baby's sleep and feeding patterns and she may become restless and irritable. Some babies get red cheeks and sore patches around the mouth and dribble a lot. Others get a slightly raised temperature. Your baby may also be off her food for a little while, in which case you may need to give her more milk or go back to smooth purées.

How you can help

■ A chilled, gel-filled teething ring can help soothe gums.
■ Give chilled raw vegetables like sticks of carrot or cucum-

> Babies have a habit of chewing food and then storing it in their mouths without swallowing. If this happens try to get your baby to open her mouth and scoop out the food with your finger.

Q I have heard that children can get fluorosis, which can lead to mottled enamel, by swallowing too much fluoride. Is that true?
A If children take fluoride supplements in addition to using a fluoride toothpaste then it is possible to get too much fluoride and teeth may become mottled. However, if they don't take fluoride supplements and use only a small amount of toothpaste there is very little risk. It's a good idea to teach your child to spit out toothpaste rather than swallow it.

ber or use fruit like apple, a bagel or teething biscuits.
■ Put a banana in the freezer for a couple of hours and let your baby chew on that; it's good for sore gums.
■ Rubbing an infant teething gel onto the gums may help ease the pain as they contain a local anaesthetic or give infant paracetamol.
■ Teething often causes your baby to dribble, so it is a good idea to put a little aqueous cream or petroleum jelly all around her mouth and chin to help prevent it from becoming dry and red.

Your baby's teeth

You may wonder why you need to worry about the state of your child's teeth when they are going to fall out in a few years anyway. However, baby's milk teeth are very important for several things: speech development, chewing solid food and guiding permanent teeth into the correct position.

Tooth decay occurs because bacteria present on teeth uses sugar – either natural sugar in juices and milk or added sugar – to produce acid, which dissolves tooth enamel, leading to decay. Children run the greatest risk of decay because the enamel on erupting and newly formed teeth is especially susceptible to decay in the first three years. Also, in the first year or two, the immune mechanism in the mouth, particularly the saliva that is the mouth's natural defence, is not fully developed so young babies are more vulnerable to tooth decay than adults. Not only does the immune system become more active as children grow older, but other factors like regular brushing with fluoride toothpaste also helps to protect your child's teeth.

Plaque is a sticky layer that covers the teeth and is largely composed of bacteria. Every time you eat food or drink containing sugar, the bacteria turns the sugar into acid, which attacks the tooth surface. One of the best ways to prevent your baby getting tooth decay is to reduce her sugar intake and clean her teeth properly. The more frequently sugary foods and drinks are consumed, the more likely it is that damage to enamel will occur so it is best to confine sugary foods and drinks to meal times. Eating other foods at the same time dilutes the acid, reducing the harmful effects of the sugar.

In addition to tooth decay, children can suffer from dental erosion. This happens when teeth are constantly exposed to foods such as fruits, particularly dried fruit, fruit juices and fizzy drinks. The natural acid present in these foods directly attacks the enamel surface of teeth and causes it to become thin. This is another reason not to let babies and young children continually sip on anything other than water.

> **You should start brushing your baby's teeth as soon as the first tooth appears. Use a small baby toothbrush with soft fibres and a tiny pea-sized blob of children's fluoride toothpaste. Otherwise you could wrap a clean flannel around your finger and gently rub the teeth and gums.**

Baby-bottle tooth decay

■ Nursing-bottle caries (also known as baby-bottle tooth decay) occurs when a young baby or small child is allowed to suck frequently from a bottle containing milk or sugary drinks such as fruit juice. If your baby likes to suck frequently from a bottle, give water only in the bottle. Breastfed babies who are allowed to suckle very frequently can also get nursing caries, as the natural sugar in milk can affect teeth.

■ It is even worse to give a baby a bottle to suck at night when there is less saliva than usual, which results in sugar clinging to the teeth. It is better to give water between meals, reserving fruit juice for meal times only. If your child insists on a bottle for bed, then use water.

Ways to help prevent caries

■ Avoid bottle feeding from one year of age. Try to get your baby used to a cup from six months – perhaps just giving a bottle at bedtime.

■ Do not allow breastfed babies to comfort suckle throughout the night.

■ Put only milk or water in your baby's bottle.

■ Both added sugars and those naturally present in fruit juice can cause decay. Try to encourage your child to drink water rather than diluted fruit juice between meals.

■ Don't add sugar to weaning foods except when it is necessary to improve the palatability of sour fruit.

■ Brush your baby's teeth twice a day – especially at bedtime.

■ Once your baby is enjoying finger foods, try to avoid sugary snacks like biscuits between meals. Instead give banana, carrot, apple, mini sandwiches, crumpets or pikelets.

■ Cheese is particularly beneficial at the end of a meal as it raises the calcium concentration in plaque. Also, protein from cheese is absorbed onto the enamel surface and slows down the growth of dental caries.

A vegetarian diet

A balanced vegetarian diet can be very healthy for babies and young children but it's important not to give up meat without replacing the nutrients that it provides, particularly protein, iron, zinc and B vitamins.

Young babies need to have nutrient- and energy-rich foods like avocado, eggs, cheese and other full-fat dairy products. They must not have too much fibre as this can inhibit the absorption of minerals like calcium, iron and zinc.

All animal protein, including egg and milk, is a high-quality protein. Cereal and vegetable protein has a lower quality although the protein from pulses is almost as good as animal protein. Soya is the only plant-based food that contains all the amino acids.

For your baby to get enough high-quality protein from six months, at least two meals a day should include dairy food or eggs. It need only be a small quantity or combine different non-animal proteins, e.g. lentil and vegetable purée with cheese, or peanut butter sandwiches.

First tastes (after 17 weeks)
■ Breast or formula milk will provide all the nutrients that your baby needs.
■ Start introducing baby rice and simple fruit and vegetable purées.

After first tastes
■ You can now give solids more often, building up to three times a day. However, milk is still the most important food for your baby. Although breast or formula milk should remain your baby's main drink, you can use cow's milk with cereal or in cooking. Dairy foods like yoghurt and cheese provide a good source of calcium, important for strong and healthy bones and teeth.

■ Introduce nutrient-dense foods like avocado and mix stronger-tasting green vegetables like spinach or broccoli with root vegetables to make combinations like sweet potato, spinach and peas, or potato and broccoli.

7–9 months
■ Most babies will be eating three solid meals a day, but milk should still form a large part of their diet.
■ Solids should now provide the chief source of iron. Good sources include lentils, dark green leafy vegetables, fortified cereals, egg yolks and dried fruit. The absorption of iron is aided by vitamin C so give fruits like kiwi fruit or purées like strawberry and pear.
■ Stir sieved hard-boiled egg yolk into chopped or puréed vegetables to add protein and iron. You can also give well-cooked scrambled eggs and omelettes.
■ You can now introduce wheat and oat-based cereals like Weetabix, Ready Brek and porridge. Fortified breakfast cereals are also a good source of iron. Once your baby is able to hold food, fingers of wholemeal toast with spread with butter/margarine are good.
■ Provided there is no history of atopic illness in the immediate family, e.g. asthma, food allergy, eczema, food allergy or hayfever, smooth peanut butter can be introduced from six months. This is a wonderfully nutrious food, providing a valuable source of protein and minerals. Do not give whole nuts to children under the age of five as there is a risk of choking.

10–12 months
■ Make sure your baby's diet includes concentrated energy foods like lentils, avocado, eggs, cheese or smooth nut butter.
■ Finger foods become an important part of your child's diet – see page 212 for ideas.

Meal planner

7-9 months or when weaning is well established

	Early morning	Breakfast	Lunch*	Mid-afternoon	Supper**	Bedtime
DAY 1	Milk	Weetabix and milk Mashed banana	My first chicken casserole (p. 221) Apple, pear and blueberry purée (p. 227)	Milk	Vegetable purée with tomato and cheese (p. 220) Fruit, e.g melon, plum or peach	Milk
DAY 2	Milk	Ready Brek and milk Mango and papaya purée (p. 227)	Fillets of plaice with carrots, cheese and tomato (p. 222) Yoghurt or fromage frais	Milk	Mashed sweet potato, cauliflower and peas (p. 218) Pear, apricot and banana purée (p. 226)	Milk
DAY 3	Milk	Banana and fig porridge (p. 225) Yoghurt or fromage frais	Chicken liver with apple and creamy mashed potato (p. 222) Fresh fruit, e.g. strawberries, peach, plum	Milk	Mini sandwiches (p. 212) Fresh fruit with peach melba yoghurt dip (p. 228)	Milk
DAY 4	Milk	Oat cereal and finely chopped fruit Fingers of buttered toast	Chicken purée with carrots and apple (p. 221) Yoghurt or fromage frais	Milk	Steamed vegetables, e.g. carrot sticks, cauliflower florets, with a dip, e.g. humus Fruit	Milk
DAY 5	Milk	Weetabix and milk Fresh fruit, e.g. kiwi, peach or melon	Beef and vegetable purée (p. 224) Apple, pear and plum with cinnamon (p. 225)	Milk	Vegetable purée with tomato and cheese Grated apple and dried fruit	Milk
DAY 6	Milk	Trio of fruits (p. 185) Fingers of buttered toast	Lovely lentil purée (p. 220) Yoghurt or fromage frais	Milk	Mini sandwiches (p. 212) Fresh fruit and peach melba and yoghurt dip	Milk
DAY 7	Milk	Ready Brek and milk Fresh fruit, e.g. kiwi, peach or melon	Tasty fish with sweet potato and orange (p. 224) Yoghurt or fromage frais	Milk	Cauliflower cheese purée (p. 189) Pear, apricot and banana purée (p. 226)	Milk

Babies of this age will probably wake early and demand a drink before breakfast. It can be milk, diluted juice or water. Bigger, hungrier babies may also need a snack between meals, like fingers of toast (see Finger foods, page 212). By this stage, babies will also no longer need a milk feed during the night and if they wake, a drink of water will be enough

* Give water or diluted juice in a beaker or cup with lunch. ** Give water or diluted juice in a beaker or cup with supper.

Recipes

🟣 Sweet potato with spinach

When introducing stronger-tasting vegetables like spinach it's good to combine them with a sweet-tasting root vegetable or winter squash like pumpkin or butternut squash.

Makes 4 portions
✳ Suitable for freezing
225 g (8 oz) sweet potato, peeled and chopped

200 ml (7 fl oz) milk
100 g (4 oz) fresh spinach, washed and stalks removed
a generous knob of butter

■ Put the chopped sweet potato into a saucepan and pour over the milk. Bring to the boil, then cover and simmer for 10 minutes until tender. Meanwhile, place the spinach in another saucepan and cook for about 2 minutes until just beginning to wilt. The water clinging to the leaves should provide enough liquid but if necessary sprinkle with a little extra water.
■ Remove the spinach from the pan, gently press out any excess water, then return to the pan, add the butter and cook for 1 minute. Strain the cooked sweet potato, reserving the milk. Blend together with 6 tbsp of the milk used for cooking and the spinach. You can add extra milk if it is still too thick for your baby. Spoon some of the purée into her bowl and serve lukewarm.

🟣 Mashed sweet potato, cauliflower and peas

Now that your baby is older you can start mashing her food instead of always puréeing it.

Makes 6 portions
✳ Suitable for freezing
350 g (12 oz) sweet potato, peeled and chopped
100 g (4 oz) cauliflower, cut into florets

50 g (2 oz) frozen peas or sweetcorn
a generous knob of butter
50 g (2 oz) Cheddar cheese, grated (optional)
6 tbsp milk

■ Put the sweet potato and cauliflower in a steamer over a pan of boiling water and cook for 10 minutes. Add the peas or sweetcorn and continue to cook for 3–4 minutes. Add the butter and the cheese (if using) and stir until melted. Mash together with the milk. Spoon some of the purée into your baby's bowl and serve lukewarm.

TOMATOES are one of the best sources of lycopene, a powerful antioxidant that helps to prevent cancer and heart disease. Lycopene is absorbed more efficiently if the tomatoes have been cooked with oil or butter. This is good news for toddlers as it means that both tomato ketchup and pizza sauce are more powerful antioxidants than raw tomato!

LENTILS are bursting with nutrients for growing babies. They are a good source of B vitamins, protein, zinc, iron and other minerals and also provide fibre. In addition, they are rich in isoflavones, which help protect against cancer.

Vegetable purée with tomato and cheese

Mixing sautéed fresh tomatoes with grated cheese gives this purée a lovely taste. Instead of carrots you could also make this with sweet potato or pumpkin.

Makes 5 portions
* Suitable for freezing
1 tbsp vegetable oil
50 g (2 oz) chopped leek
1 potato, peeled and chopped
200 g (7 oz) carrots, peeled and chopped

200 ml (7 fl oz) boiling water
20 g (¾ oz) unsalted butter
2 ripe tomatoes, skinned, de-seeded and roughly chopped
50 g (2 oz) Cheddar cheese, grated

■ Heat the vegetable oil in a saucepan and sauté the leek until softened but not coloured. Add the potato and carrots, pour over the boiling water, then cover and cook for 20 minutes. Melt the butter in another saucepan and sauté the tomatoes until they turn mushy, then stir in the grated cheese until melted.

■ Blend the vegetables to a purée and mix together with the cheese and tomato sauce. For older babies you can mash together the vegetables and then mix with the sauce. Spoon some of the purée into your baby's bowl and serve lukewarm.

Lovely lentil purée

Mixing lentils with vegetables and cheese provides an excellent source of protein for babies who are being brought up on a vegetarian diet.

Makes 6 portions
* Suitable for freezing
1 tbsp vegetable oil
40 g (1½ oz) onion, chopped
25 g (1 oz) celery, chopped

50 g (2 oz) red lentils, washed and drained
275 g (10 oz) carrots, peeled and chopped
450 ml (15 fl oz) vegetable stock or water
50 g (2 oz) frozen sweetcorn
60 g (2½ oz) Cheddar cheese, grated

■ Heat the oil in a saucepan and sauté the onion, carrot and celery for 2–3 minutes. Mix in the lentils and pour over the stock or water. Bring to the boil, then reduce the heat and cover and cook for 20 minutes.

■ Add the frozen sweetcorn and cook for a further 5 minutes. Stir in the cheese until melted. Purée in a blender to the desired consistency and then spoon some of the purée into your baby's bowl and serve lukewarm.

Chicken purée with carrots and apple

This is a good recipe for introducing your baby to chicken. The carrots and apple add sweetness and flavour to the chicken and give it a smooth texture, which is easy to swallow.

Makes 5 portions
✻ Suitable for freezing
½ tbsp olive oil
½ small onion, peeled and chopped
350 g (12 oz) carrots, peeled and sliced

250 ml (8 fl oz) unsalted chicken stock
1 chicken breast (approximately 125 g/ 4½ oz)
1 small apple, peeled and chopped

■ Heat the oil in a saucepan and sauté the onion until softened. Add the carrots and pour over the stock. Bring to the boil, then reduce the heat and cover and cook for 10 minutes.
■ Cut the chicken into pieces and add to the carrots together with the chopped apple and continue to cook for 10 minutes. Purée in a blender and then spoon some of the purée into your baby's bowl and serve lukewarm.

My first chicken casserole

Chicken is very versatile and can be introduced after first foods have been accepted. You can buy fresh unsalted chicken stock in some supermarkets, otherwise you can make it yourself (see my book *The New Complete Baby and Toddler Meal Planner* for the recipe).

Makes 6 portions
✻ Suitable for freezing
1½ tbsp vegetable oil
50 g (2 oz) leek, carefully washed and sliced
1 chicken breast, cut into chunks
25 g (1 oz) celery, chopped
1 carrot, peeled and chopped

200 g (7 oz) sweet potato, peeled and chopped
1 medium potato, peeled and chopped
1½ tsp tomato purée
1 tbsp chopped fresh parsley
300 ml (½ pint) water or unsalted chicken stock

■ Heat the oil, add the leek and sauté for 2 minutes. Add the chicken and sauté for 2 minutes. Add the celery and carrot and continue to cook for 3 minutes and then add all the remaining ingredients. Bring to the boil, then reduce the heat and cover and cook for 20 minutes. Purée in a blender and then spoon some of the purée into your baby's bowl and serve lukewarm.

SUPERFOODS
CHICKEN is a good source of protein for babies and it's very versatile. Pieces of cooked chicken also make great finger food. It is good to give the dark meat of the chicken to your baby to eat as it contains twice as much iron and zinc as the light meat.

LEEKS belong to the same family as garlic and onion. They contain potassium, which helps to counteract the effects of salt in the diet. Like onions, eating leeks helps to prevent your blood clotting and reduces the risk of heart disease and stroke.

SUPERFOODS

LIVER is a wonderful food for babies as it is a very rich source of iron, which is a very important factor in brain development. Babies are born with only sufficient iron reserves for about the first six months of life, so iron-rich foods need to be part of their diet (see page 179).

FISH is packed with vitamins, minerals and protein so it is important to introduce tasty fish recipes at an early age. Although white fish such as plaice doesn't contain much iron, it helps iron absorption from plant foods.

Chicken liver with apple and creamy mashed potato

Liver is easy to digest and purées to a smooth consistency. The apple brings out a slightly fruity flavour that babies really like.

Makes 4 portions
* **Suitable for freezing**
150 g (5 oz) potatoes, peeled and chopped
a generous knob of butter
2–3 tbsp milk
1 tbsp vegetable oil

½ onion, peeled and chopped
100 g (4 oz) chicken livers, trimmed and cut into pieces
½ apple, peeled and thinly sliced
60 ml (2 fl oz) apple juice

■ Put the potatoes into a saucepan, cover with boiling water and simmer for about 12 minutes until tender. Drain and mash with the butter and milk.
■ Heat the oil in a saucepan and add the onion and and sauté for 2 minutes.
■ Add the chicken liver, sauté for 2 minutes and then add the apple. Pour over the apple juice and simmer, stirring occasionally, for about 4 minutes or until the liver is cooked. Purée the liver and apple and mix with the mashed potato. Spoon some of the purée into your baby's bowl and serve lukewarm.

Fillets of plaice with carrots, cheese and tomato

Plaice is one of the best fish to start with as it has a suitably soft texture for young babies.

Makes 5 portions
* **Suitable for freezing**
250 g (9 oz) carrots, peeled and sliced
225 g (8 oz) plaice fillets, skinned
2 tbsp milk

20 g (¾ oz) butter
2 ripe tomatoes, skinned, de-seeded and chopped
40 g (1½ oz) Cheddar cheese, grated

■ Put the carrots in a steamer over a pan of boiling water and cook for 20 minutes.
■ Meanwhile, place the fish in a microwave dish, add the milk, dot with butter and cover, leaving an air vent. Microwave on high for 2–3 minutes.
■ Melt the rest of the butter in a saucepan and add the tomatoes and sauté until mushy. Stir in the cheese until melted. Blend the carrots with the tomato mixture. Remove the fish from the cooking liquor and flake, making sure there are no bones. Mix the fish with the carrots and tomatoes. Spoon some of the purée into your baby's bowl and serve lukewarm.

SUPERFOODS

ORANGES **are a good source of vitamin C, which is important for boosting the immune system, and orange juice provides a particularly concentrated form of vitamin C. Freshly squeezed is best. When your child is a little older a glass of orange juice with a bowl of cereal is good for breakfast as vitamin C helps our bodies to absorb iron from wholegrain or fortified cereals.**

RED MEAT **is rich in protein, iron and zinc – essential for growth, healing and a healthy immune system.**

Tasty fish with sweet potato and orange

This may sound like a strange combination but it is very popular because it tastes so good. It is also bursting with vitamins and minerals.

Makes 4 portions
✳ Suitable for freezing
1 orange-fleshed sweet potato, peeled and chopped
175 g (6 oz) plaice fillets, skinned

juice of 1 orange (approximately 100 ml/ 3½ fl oz)
50 g (2 oz) Cheddar cheese, grated
a knob of butter

■ Place the sweet potato in a steamer over a pan of boiling water and cook for 10 minutes or until tender. Alternatively put the sweet potato in a pan, just cover with water and bring to the boil. Then lower the heat and cook until tender.

■ Meanwhile, place the fish in a suitable microwave-proof dish, pour over the orange juice and scatter over the grated cheese. Cover, leaving an air vent, and microwave on high for 3 minutes or until the fish flakes easily with a fork. Alternatively you could poach the fish with the orange juice in a saucepan for a few minutes until cooked and then stir in the grated cheese until melted.

■ Flake the fish with a fork, checking to make sure there are no bones. Mash the sweet potato with a knob of butter and combine with the fish. For young babies you can purée the fish together with the sweet potato. Spoon some of the purée into your baby's bowl and serve lukewarm.

Beef and vegetable purée

Often babies don't like eating meat due to its chewy texture rather than because they don't like the taste. Fillet steak is very tender so this makes a good introduction to beef for your baby.

Makes 6 portions
✳ Suitable for freezing
1½ tbsp vegetable oil
1 onion, peeled and finely chopped
150 g (5 oz) green beans, cut into short lengths

100 g (4 oz) beef fillet steak, sliced
150 g (5 oz) carrots, peeled and chopped
200 g (7 oz) potatoes, peeled and chopped
400 ml (13 fl oz) boiling water or unsalted beef stock

■ Heat the oil in a saucepan, add the onion and sauté for 2 minutes. Add the green beans and continue to sauté for 2 minutes, stirring occasionally.

■ Add the beef, carrots and potatoes and cook, stirring occasionally, for 1 minute. Pour over the boiling water or stock and simmer, covered, for 15 minutes. Then purée in a blender. Spoon some of the purée into your baby's bowl and serve lukewarm.

🍎 Apple, pear and plum with cinnamon

The dried version of plums is prunes and these are good to give your baby if she is constipated. You could substitute 4 ready-to-eat stoned prunes for plums in this recipe.

Makes 4 portions
✳ Suitable for freezing
1 large ripe pear, peeled and cut into chunks

1 apple, peeled and cut into chunks
2 ripe plums, peeled
a good pinch of cinnamon
2 tbsp ricotta or Greek yoghurt (optional)

■ Put the fruit into a small saucepan together with a tablespoon of water and a good pinch of cinnamon. Cover and cook over a low heat for 4–5 minutes. Purée in a blender. If you wish, you can stir in the ricotta or Greek yoghurt and then spoon some of the purée into your baby's bowl and serve lukewarm.

🍌 Banana and fig porridge

Now that your baby is older you can include many different cereals in her diet. Porridge oats are good because they give long-lasting energy. Ready Brek is also a good cereal to give as it is fortified with calcium, vitamins and iron and contains no added salt or sugar.

Makes 1 portion
2 tbsp porridge oats
2 soft, ready-to-eat dried figs, chopped

175 ml (6 fl oz) water
1 small banana

■ Put the oats into a small saucepan with the chopped figs, pour over the water and bring to the boil. Reduce the heat, cover and simmer for 5 minutes. Purée and press through a sieve. Mash the banana and mix with the porridge. Spoon some of the porridge into your baby's bowl and serve lukewarm.

SUPERFOODS
PLUMS are a good source of antioxidants. Peeled slices of plum also make good finger food.

DRIED FIGS are a good source of minerals as they contain potassium, iron and are very rich in calcium. Just 100 g (4 oz) of dried figs contains nearly one-third of the adult daily requirement. Including figs in your baby's diet is good if she suffers from constipation.

SUPERFOODS
One medium BANANA provides more than half the recommended daily requirement of potassium for children, which is essential for normal blood pressure and a healthy heart. If your baby has diarrhoea, then the BRAT diet of Bananas, Rice, Apple purée and Toast is good (see page 213).

BLUEBERRIES have a powerful antibacterial action, which may help urinary tract or intestinal infections. Eating blueberries can also improve eyesight.

CHERRIES stimulate the immune system and help to prevent infection. They are good for children who suffer from constipation.

Pear, apricot and banana purée

Bananas are an almost perfect 'fast food'. They come with handy, disposable skins, good for keeping pesticides and other chemical residues out of your baby's diet. They provide a good source of quick energy, which is why sportsmen and women often eat bananas before or even during a competition. Ripe bananas help with digestion.

Makes 1–2 portions
1 ripe pear, peeled, cored and cut into pieces

3 soft, ready-to-eat dried apricots, chopped
1 ripe banana

■ Put the pear and apricots into a small saucepan and cover and cook over a gentle heat for 3 minutes. Purée in a blender, and then mash the banana and stir into the pear and apricot. Spoon some of the purée into your baby's bowl and serve lukewarm.

Instant baby food

Some people might say that they just don't have the time to make their own baby food. If you only have a few minutes, you can still prepare delicious and nutritious food for your baby by simply mashing fruits together.

Banana and blueberry purée
Makes 1 portion
1 small ripe banana
40 g (1½ oz) sweet blueberries
■ Simply mash together the banana and blueberries.

Banana and cherry purée
Makes 1 portion
6 ripe cherries, halved and stoned
1 tbsp boiling water
1 ripe banana
1 tbsp baby rice
■ Put the halved and stoned cherries into a small pan together with the tablespoon of boiling water and simmer for 2 minutes or until softened. Purée and sieve. Mash the banana, mix with the cherry purée and stir in the baby rice. Spoon some of the purée into your baby's bowl and serve lukewarm.

Banana and kiwi purée
Makes 1 portion

1 small ripe banana
1 ripe kiwi fruit, peeled and cut into chunks

■ Simply purée the kiwi fruit with a fork and press through a sieve. Mash the banana and mix with the sieved kiwi fruit. Spoon some of the purée into your baby's bowl and serve lukewarm.

Mango and papaya purée
Makes 1 portion

½ small papaya, peeled and chopped
½ small mango, peeled and chopped
½ small ripe banana (optional)

■ Purée the papaya and mango in a hand-held blender. Serve the purée as it is or stir in a little mashed banana.

● **Apple, pear and blueberry crumble**

Both blueberries and apples are high in pectin – the soluble form of fibre – and have traditionally been used to treat diarrhoea. However, pears are a natural laxative so if your child has loose stools, make this using 2 apples and leave out the pear.

Makes 4 portions
✱ **Suitable for freezing**

1 large or 2 small ripe pears, peeled, cored and chopped

1 apple, peeled, cored and chopped
60 g (2½ oz) blueberries
1 reduced-sugar baby rusk

■ Put all the fruit into a steamer over a pan of boiling water and cook for about 5 minutes, then purée in a blender. Alternatively put the fruit in a saucepan and simmer for about 5 minutes. Crush the baby rusk and stir into the fruit purée. Spoon some of the purée into your baby's bowl and serve lukewarm

SUPERFOODS
KIWI FRUIT contain twice the vitamin C of oranges. Choose kiwi fruit that is soft enough to yield to gentle pressure as hard kiwi fruit can be very sour.

PAPAYA is rich in vitamin C and beta-carotene. Eating 75 g (3 oz) of papaya will provide a young child's daily requirement of vitamin C.

BLUEBERRIES have the highest antioxidant content of any fresh fruit.

Whole milk or full-fat yoghurt provides a good source of calcium, protein and phosphorus, which are all important for strong, healthy bones and teeth. Live yoghurt is especially good as it contains beneficial bacteria, which helps maintain the balance of good and bad bacteria in our guts and can help prevent illness.

Dried apricots are one of nature's great health foods as they are rich in beta-carotene and are also a good source of iron, potassium and fibre. Dried apricots also make good finger food for older babies.

🟤 Fresh fruit with peach melba yoghurt dip

It's good to sweeten natural yoghurt with fresh fruit purées. Remember that you don't need to wait for the arrival of teeth to start finger foods. Baby gums are hard and sharp and can mange to chew food quite well. Soft fruits also make ideal first finger foods.

Makes 3 portions
✳ Suitable for freezing
50 g (2 oz) raspberries
1 ripe peach, peeled and cut into chunks
approx. 1 tbsp icing sugar to sweeten

maple syrup
Greek yoghurt or live natural yoghurt
fresh fruit, e.g. apple, pear, banana, kiwi fruit, strawberries, mango, apricot

■ Put the raspberries, peach and icing sugar into a food processor and blend. Then press through a sieve to get rid of the seeds.
■ Mix 2 teaspoons of maple syrup with 50 g (2 oz) of Greek or natural live yoghurt and stir in 2 tablespoons of the raspberry and peach purée. Serve with a selection of cut-up fruit.

🟤 Flaked rice with dried apricots and sultanas

Flaked rice makes a good alternative to pudding rice as it is quick to cook.

Makes 4 portions
25 g (1 oz) flaked rice
1 split vanilla pod
350 ml (11 fl oz) milk
50 g (2 oz) soft, ready-to-eat dried apricots,

roughly chopped
1 tbsp sultanas
6 tbsp apple and mango juice (or apple juice)

■ Put the flaked rice into a saucepan together with the vanilla pod, pour over the milk and simmer for 5 minutes, stirring occasionally. Add the apricots to the pan together with the sultanas and scrape out the seeds of the vanilla pod. Add these to the pan with the pod.
■ Bring to the boil and simmer, covered for 7–8 minutes, until thickened.
■ Remove the vanilla pod and stir in the apple and mango or apple juice. Purée in a blender and then spoon some of the purée into your baby's bowl and serve lukewarm.

CHAPTER FIVE

MOVING ON
10–12 months

PRACTICALITIES

In the final quarter of his first year, your baby becomes more independent but he will need lots of support and patience from you. It is during this period that your child will probably say his first distinct words and may take his first steps. The more mobile your toddler becomes, the more you will need to watch him. Lots of your safety mechanisms will be in place already but you now need to become aware of a greater determination in most toddlers to explore and try to get hold of objects that attract their eye.

Safety and the mobile baby

Climbing may begin at this stage. It's not unusual to find a toddler climbing up on a chair to get onto the tabletop, for example. Also, if you leave a tablecloth over the table you may find that your toddler pulls on the tablecloth and there is a danger that everything on the table could fall on top of him. If your child visits other people's homes, look around the room for potential dangers and keep an even more watchful eye on your child.

■ As your child will be unsteady on his feet, it is a time of lots of falls so look out for sharp edges and corners at your child's height.

■ Changing tables may become too unsafe to use as a child may be able to wiggle and move very quickly.

■ A mat that attaches with suckers to the bottom of the bath may be helpful as your child may spend a lot of time pulling himself up and standing in the bath.

■ The toilet can be a wonderful place to investigate so make sure the lid is down. Not only is there a risk of infection but your baby may also drown.

■ Check the height of the mattress in your baby's cot. It may need to be lowered to prevent your toddler from being able to climb out. If you are worried, put some cushions under the cot to give a soft landing.

■ Take care that your baby doesn't try to pull himself up using unsteady objects like wobbly chairs or standard lamps. Also try to make sure there are no small objects around that your baby might choke on. An open handbag can be a danger, especially if it contains pills.

■ Watch out for open water, e.g. paddling pools and ponds. If you have a pond in your garden, consider putting heavy-duty mesh over the top or simply emptying it until your baby understands the danger.

Helping your baby to walk

To begin with your baby will probably pull himself up and cruise around the furniture. You can help by arranging stable pieces of furniture around the room quite close together and remove any that might tip over. Once your baby is adept at this he might be ready to take a few steps – you can steadily increase the spaces between the furniture so your baby has to let go and lunge for the next piece of furniture for support.

A baby's head is big in comparison to his body and until his legs strengthen, finding a good balance can be tricky. Babies tend to walk with feet wide apart and toes pointing out to improve their balance. There is no right age at which babies start to walk; they all come

Baby walkers

■ **Baby walkers** cause more accidents than any other nursery equipment and should not be used. In the UK in 1999, just over 3300 babies were taken to hospital with injuries associated with baby walkers. They give babies mobility, speed and height that can easily get them into danger. A baby in a walker can move very quickly towards dangers such as stairs and fires. Added height allows a baby to reach hazards such as hot drinks, household poisons or sharp objects. Most injuries associated with baby walkers are caused by falls. Baby walkers can tip over and the baby may be thrown down stairs or steps, crash into sharp furniture or fall into fires, heaters or hot ovens. The combined weight of the baby and walker hitting the floor, steps, stairs or other object increases the likelihood of the injuries being severe.

■ **Baby bouncers** (doorway bouncers) are fine as long as there is adequate head support for young babies. They should be used only for short periods and securely attached to the door frame exactly following the manufacturer's instructions. Bouncing cradles are also fine but should never be put on a high surface such as table or kitchen worktop.

to it in their own time and most babies are able to walk by the age of 15 months. Walking requires not only good balance and coordination but also lots of confidence. It is often the lack of self-belief that keeps a child from taking his first solo steps so you need to give lots of support and encouragement. You can help your baby gain confidence with some of the following ideas:

■ A stable toy like a push-along trolley is good practice for improving walking skills.

■ Hold his hands and walk slowly with him between your legs, or you and your partner could walk with your baby between you, each holding a hand.

The first birthday party

■ A first birthday is a very special event and is as much for the parents, grandparents and friends as for the guest of honour.

■ Try to choose a time when your baby doesn't usually take a nap. Your home is probably the best venue as your baby will be more relaxed but don't overwhelm him by inviting too many people. It is best to invite family and just a few friends with babies roughly the same age. Babies can become bored and fractious quite quickly so for maximum enjoyment keep the party quite short – 2 hours at the most.

■ If you are thinking of hiring an entertainer, be warned that one-year-old babies can sometimes find clowns and magicians quite terrifying. A puppet show, however, usually captures their attention but most babies and toddlers prefer to do their own thing. Clear a space and have a selection of toys for the babies to play with. Babies also like playing with bubbles that you blow and balloons.

■ Ordinary objects can also provide great entertainment – fill an old handbag with interesting objects that the babies can then remove and explore, or arrange some upturned saucepans and bowls in an area and give the babies wooden spoons to make a 'kitchen drumkit'. Sing and all join in with some action rhymes like 'Incey Wincey Spider' and the 'The wheels on the Bus'.

■ Don't be surprised if the babies don't play together – it is not until the age of two that a baby starts to understand the concept of sharing.

■ Finger foods are good, e.g. sandwiches cut into novelty shapes using cookie cutters, pizza cut into pieces and chopped-up vegetables like carrots, sweet pepper, cucumber served with a dip. Cut-up fresh fruit is usually popular as well as dried fruit like apricots, apple rings and raisins. Jelly with fresh fruit, cupcakes (see page 260) or ice cream are good for dessert.

SLEEPING

Between nine and 12 months your baby will probably sleep 13–14 hours a day, of which 11 or 12 hours are at night and about 2 to 2½ hours during the day. However, all babies vary, so if your baby sleeps more in the day, for instance, then don't worry – unless, of course, it affects his night-time sleeping. The routine below has the baby taking a long sleep in the morning but some babies take only a half an hour nap during the morning and then sleep in the afternoon between about 12.30 and 2pm.

The ever-changing routine

The dilemma around the age of one is often how much sleep your baby can have during the day without it affecting his night-time sleep. This is something you will need to judge for yourself. Too much sleep in the day can mean your child is not tired when it comes to bedtime. This includes sleeps in the car or buggy, especially late in the day. However, it doesn't follow that babies who don't sleep much during the day will sleep longer at night. Giving up naps can mean a very tired and bad-tempered baby and over-tired babies also have trouble sleeping at night.

Sometimes a wilful toddler simply won't nap and ends up exhausted by late afternoon and may begin to nod off then. Try your very best to avoid this happening or your toddler will wake up and get a second wind just around the time he's supposed to go sleep. It's best not to let your baby sleep after four in the afternoon. At around 12 months some babies may drop their afternoon nap altogether.

Bedtime routine

It's important to continue a calm, quiet bedtime routine to settle your baby at night. Bath time followed by baby massage (optional), then a story, bottle/breast and bed forms a very comforting routine that helps a baby remain settled and sleep well.

If your baby starts to fall asleep and comfort sucks rather than feeds properly, stop feeding and put your baby to bed before he falls asleep. Consistency remains as important, so it's good to keep bedtime around the same time each night. In fact, it may be an idea to read the same story or sing the same goodnight song each night until your baby settles into a routine so that nothing changes.

As you leave the room it's a good idea always to say the same thing along the lines of that comforting favourite: 'Night, night, sleep tight.'

Possible routine

6.30–7am	Wakes up.
7am	Breakfast time, e.g. milk and cereal.
10am–12 noon	Sleep.
12.30pm	Lunch.
2.30–3pm	Nap (maybe in the pram, car, etc.).
5pm	Supper.
6pm	Bath/massage.
6.30pm	Milk.
7pm	Bedtime.

CRYING

As your baby gets older he will spend more time awake and therefore there is more chance that he will become bored and express this through crying. Your baby will cry much less if you keep him with you as much as you can and involve him in the things that you are doing. He will enjoy shopping trips to the supermarket or banging with a wooden spoon on pots and pans while you are in the kitchen preparing a meal. But even with the freedom to move around, your baby will get bored if left alone too much.

Helping your baby

The attention span of babies is quite short – probably about ten minutes – so have a selection of playtime activities to hand. It's a good idea to take out just one or two toys at a time, let your baby play with these and then, as you see him lose interest, take them away and bring out something else, like a box with coloured bricks that he can empty out and put back into the box once again.

On your marks

As your baby grows up he will want to become more mobile and will crawl, or pull himself up on pieces of furniture and try to cruise around the room. He may well become frustrated because his desire to do things may well outstrip his ability. If this is the case, he will fall and knock himself or not be able to reach the toy he can see and he will cry in frustration. This is no bad thing on the whole as babies need to strive for themselves and they will learn from their frustration and become even more determined to succeed the next time.

Once your baby is good at crawling or he is able to walk holding on to convenient pieces of furniture, he will be much happier as he will be more able to get to the things he wants.

Q When my baby starts crying I want to rush to her immediately but I'm not sure this is always a good idea. What do you think?
A Unless you sense that it is a cry of distress or you know something needs to be done to make your baby comfortable, you are right – it is good for her to learn that crying will not always get her what she wants. This is important, especially as you will want her to drop off back to sleep at night by herself if she wakes up.

Once your baby has experienced his new-found freedom, he may well cry with frustration and anger if you stop him from doing something that he wants to do, like emptying out the contents of your handbag and playing with your brand new lipstick. Unfortunately, once your baby is mobile you will need to find a balance between letting him have the freedom to develop and keeping him safe. It is important to try to create a suitable environment at home where your baby can explore without harming himself, so ensure that you are rigorous about implementing safety measures (page 194).

DEVELOPING

Now that your baby is becoming far more active, you might want to consider involving him in more physical activities such as at Gymboree and Tumble Tots groups (see Useful addresses, page 268), which take babies from six months of age. Swimming, too, will help develop your baby's muscle tone and coordination. The earlier you introduce your baby to swimming, the less likely he is to develop a fear of the water.

Exercising your baby

Gymboree helps to stimulate and encourage babies to use all their senses through playing and Tumble Tots classes are designed to develop children's physical skills, agility, balance, coordination and climbing through the use of brightly coloured equipment.

You can start getting your baby used to the water with lots of splashing about in the bath but it is advisable for him to have had his combined triple vaccine DTP (page 267) before swimming in a public pool.

On your first visit, make sure that the water is warm – the ideal temperature would be 29°C (84°F) – and take some floating toys for him to play with. Your baby should wear swim pants as nappies swell up and disintegrate in the pool. You or/and your partner should get into the water with your baby and then keep him on the move with bouncing and swimming games – to keep him warm: 15 to 30 minutes is probably long enough. Make sure your baby feels secure as you support his torso and let him splash about with his arms and legs. You can get a special rubber ring designed for small babies to sit in or you can buy a costume with removable floats. Once your baby is confident in the water, you could take him to a swimming pool where they hold classes for babies and toddlers (see page 268).

Toys

During this period, freedom to move and explore is more important than specific toys so try to find a safe and uncluttered area for your baby to play. But try:

Push-along toys: These range from the traditional sturdy wooden trolley with colourful bricks to an electronic activity walker. Make sure that it has a wide base so won't topple over easily.

Sit-and-ride toys: Look for a low seat height so your baby's feet can rest securely on the floor. Some of these toys start out as a rocker and then, as your baby grows and develops, can transform into a toy with wheels.

Posting boxes and shape sorters: Choose a simple one to begin with: just three basic shapes and colour coding are enough. Also, choose rounded shapes so they fall in when placed over the right hole.

Musical instrument toys: e.g. keyboard, trumpet, xylophone, drum, maracas.

Puzzles: Wooden inset shapes are good first puzzles.

Balls or anything that rolls along: e.g. toy cars, trains – especially if they make a noise.

Wax crayons: By the time your baby in a year old he will be able to hold crayons. Look for bright colours and make sure they are chunky and so easier to grip.

Your baby at 10 months

Most babies of ten months are able to crawl and pull themselves up to standing. Some babies will even be able to stand by themselves for a short time. Practising standing will help your baby build up his muscles and get a sense of balance. As your baby gains independence, he will become more assertive. He may become more difficult to feed and will prefer to feed himself with finger foods. If you take something away from him, he might throw a tantrum. Luckily his memory is still very short and he will soon forget why he is crying and you can probably distract him with something new.

Movement	Hand-to-eye coordination	Language	Learning	What your baby enjoys	Stimulating play
■ Your baby can crawl or shuffle quite fast.	■ Your baby likes exploring inside drawers, cupboards and boxes. He enjoys putting toys like colourful plastic bricks into a container and then taking them out again.	■ There is now a better level of concentration so your baby is able to play with a more challenging toy.	■ Your baby is able to say a few words clearly like 'Dadda' or 'Bye Bye'.	■ Surveying the world in an upright position.	■ Put your baby in a crawling position at one end of the room with you at the opposite end. Get his attention and see if you can encourage him to crawl towards you.
■ He can pull himself up and stand on his own two feet holding onto something; the bars of a playpen or crib are ideal. He needs to learn how to sit down by falling flat on his well-padded bottom. Your baby's legs are only about one-third of his body length whereas in adults they account for about half the body length.	■ He likes to play with toys that move along the floor.	■ He can understand and follow simple instructions like 'Give me the banana'.	■ He recognises his name and may be able to recognise the names of familiar objects like bottle, teddy, nappy, etc.	■ Playing with toy telephones and mimicking Mummy or Daddy's conversations.	
	■ He likes to play with toys that fit together such as a very simple puzzle.	■ If your baby drops an object, he now starts to look to see where it might fall; he is beginning to understand how things behave when he can't see them.	■ He looks at you when you call his name. Try to use your child's name as much as possible when speaking with him to affirm what he is doing and keep his attention.	■ Playing with a pull-along toy on wheels.	■ Pretend to chase your baby. Start crawling slowly after your baby saying, 'I'm going to get you', and then gently grab him , give him a kiss and a cuddle and put him down so that you can continue the chase.
	■ He is able to drink from a cup.			■ He shows interest in a favourite doll or teddy and likes giving it a hug or kiss.	
				■ Playing in the bath filling up	

Movement	Hand-to-eye coordination	Language	Learning	What your baby enjoys	Stimulating play
■ He should be able to climb up a few stairs and possibly slide down them. It is never too early to teach your baby to turn around at the top of the stairs so that he climbs down feet first. ■ He is able to cruise around the furniture. ■ He can push simple shapes, e.g. square, circle, triangle, through a shape sorter. ■ Encourage him to pull himself up to a standing position by holding a favourite toy above him just out of reach.	■ He manipulates toys or objects with prolonged interest, transferring them from one hand to the other and turning them over and over. ■ Your baby enjoys playing with colourful stacking rings. Start by showing him how to take off the rings as this is easier than putting them onto the pole. Learning to stack the rings in order of size will not come until your baby is older. ■ Use lots of encouraging and praising words, e.g. 'Mummy opens the box', 'Tom opens the box', 'Good boy', 'Tom's opened the box'.	■ Your baby is really curious about the world so encourage him to touch and smell flowers, scrunch up fallen leaves, turn on a light switch, ring a doorbell, etc. ■ He helps you when you dress him. ■ He asks for things by pointing at them. ■ If you talk to your baby all the time, he learns to associate words with actions. ■ By dropping objects from his high chair he will be learning about object permanence, e.g. over the side equals gone, and then he gradually starts to realise it has not gone completely and looks for it. ■ Your baby loves trying to copy simple words that you say and will like it when you make words sound funny, e.g. 'splish, splash splosh' at bath time.	■ He uses a variety of consonant and vowel sounds. ■ He will babble away without making much sense but if you listen to him attentively, it will encourage him to talk more and eventually he will make sense. ■ He enjoys joining in with interactive rhymes like 'Row, row, row the boat' or 'Ring-a-ring-a-roses'. ■ Your baby uses body language to express what he wants as he is not always able to make you understand him. For example, he may grab your hand and pull you over towards the toy box if he wants you to open it so that he can play with the toys. It's a good idea if you put his request into words, e.g. 'Open the toy box?' and point.	containers like plastic cups or jugs and then transferring water from one container to another. ■ Playing with toys that make a noise like horns, musical instruments and toys that squeak when they are squeezed. ■ Looking at photos of himself and his family. ■ Tearing up pieces of paper like old wrapping paper or old newspapers. ■ Crawling through a plastic play tunnel. Start by shortening the tunnel so he can almost reach you, then extend it as he gets more confident. ■ Playing with balls. Roll a soft ball to your baby and see if he rolls it back. ■ Being held under his arms so you can swing him to kick a ball. This game is really fun if there is another person to roll the ball back.	■ Place a toy behind him to encourage him to learn how to twist his body around. ■ Stand with your legs apart and let your baby crawl through them. ■ Let your baby play with the zip on your coat or bag, pulling it by the tab. ■ Play hide and seek either with some toys or you could find somewhere to hide, like behind a chair or curtain, and call to your baby so that he can find you. ■ Your baby will enjoy a toy that he can ride along on like a toy tractor or car. Make sure that his legs are long enough to reach the ground and eventually he will learn to push himself along.

Your baby at 11 months

At 11 months your baby is quickly becoming a mobile and curious explorer. The problem with cruising or crawling is that a baby uses his hands as well as his feet, so it's difficult to hold anything. Some babies will have mastered walking by 11 months but most will get from place to place by crawling or cruising around furniture. Lifting each foot alternately, stepping forward while the other foot pushes down and takes all the weight and keeps your balance, is something we take for granted but it's a difficult skill for your baby to master. Your baby's progress will depend on his determination and lack of fear of falling over. Give him lots of praise.

Movement	Hand-to-eye coordination	Language	Learning	What your baby enjoys	Stimulating play
■ Encourage your baby to walk by helping him stand, then hold his hands and forearm to keep him steady and try to get him to step forwards as you gradually edge back. ■ Try holding your baby a few steps away from the sofa, facing it, and seeing if he will take the steps to a favourite toy on the sofa in front of him. ■ Often it is a lack of confidence that	■ Your baby can successfully turn the pages of a book. ■ He tries to pull lids off boxes to find out what is inside them. ■ He has a firmer grasp and can hold two things in one hand. ■ Your baby is getting better at feeding herself. He may be able to carry a spoonful of food to his mouth but his wrist action is still	■ Your baby can follow simple instructions like, 'Give it to me', 'Wave bye-bye'. ■ He may point to an object in a book when you name it. ■ He starts to use a few proper words to name familiar objects or people, e.g. 'Daddy' and 'teddy', in the right context. To encourage your baby, put toys or objects in a box and as you take them out introduce	■ At this age your baby has better concentration so he will be able to operate more complex activity boards, shape sorters, spinning tops, etc. ■ He can find an object hidden under another object. ■ He imitates more of your actions. ■ He begins to learn what is good and bad behaviour. He seeks praise and is likely to repeat an	■ Playing with push-along and pull-along toys. ■ Drawing with wax chunky crayons. ■ Cuddling soft toys and dolls. ■ Dropping and throwing things – rolled-up socks make a good soft ball. ■ Getting around without your help. ■ Being swung while supported	■ Make an obstacle course on the floor using cushions and pillows. Place your baby in the crawling position on one side while you go on the other and get him to crawl over them to reach you. ■ Make a tunnel by draping a sheet between chairs and encourage your baby to crawl through it. You can also make an exciting tunnel by opening up two sides of a large cardboard box.

Movement	Hand-to-eye coordination	Language	Learning	What your baby enjoys	Stimulating play

keeps a child from making his first independent step. If your baby likes cruising around the furniture, gradually increase the distance between the furniture to encourage him to walk without holding on.

■ You can also encourage him to stand by himself by holding him steady and then gently letting go for a couple of seconds to see if he can remain standing.

■ Your baby can walk pushing a sturdy trolley. Push-along toys range from the traditional wooden walker to electronic activity walkers with flashing lights. Your baby may need help changing direction.

■ He can climb downstairs backwards.

■ He can slowly and gently lower himself to the floor from a standing position.

developing and some of the food may be spilled on the way. It is therefore best to give non-runny food that stays on the spoon.

him to the concept of 'in' and 'out'. You can do the same with other concepts like 'big' and 'little', sitting a large teddy beside a small teddy.

■ This is also a good time to talk about colours. You could collect objects of the same colour or say things like 'Look at that balloon. It's blue, just like your jumper.'

■ Keep instructions simple using one step at a time, so rather than say, 'Please pick up the ball and give it to Daddy', it is better to say, 'Please pick up the ball', and when your baby has picked up the ball then say, 'Please give it to Daddy.'

■ He will act in response to simple questions like 'Where's the ball?'

■ He is a good mimic and will try to copy some of the words that you say.

action if he is praised.

■ For six months and under, 'out of sight is out of mind'. Even at eight months your baby won't remember that there is something he wants if it is hidden for very long and he is easily confused. But at 11 months, your baby is starting to realise that something that is out of sight can still exist. So look for hidden objects together – for example, if you hide a toy under a blanket or bucket he will try to lift it up to look for it.

under his arms. He also likes to be swung from side to side in a blanket held between two adults so that it forms a hammock.

■ Ride-on toys, although he won't yet be able to figure out how to use his legs alternately but he should be able to move backwards and forwards using both feet at once.

■ Being bounced up and down on your knee so that it feels like riding. You can recite rhymes like 'Ride-a-cock horse' or 'Horsey-horsey' at the same time.

■ Watching finger puppets acting out nursery rhymes or little stories.

■ Picture books; your baby will love to sit on your lap while you read to him. You can ask questions like 'Where's the dog?' and see if your baby can point to the dog on the page.

■ Half hide behind a sofa or curtain and call across the room to your baby. He'll soon crawl over to where you are and you can be ready with a big hug and lots of praise.

■ If your baby can walk at 11 months, let him try to push his own buggy provided it is stable. It would be a good idea to weigh it down by putting something on the seat.

■ Beat out a rhythm with a wooden spoon on an upturned pan and see if your baby can copy you.

■ Tie a length of string to one of your baby's toys and hide it under a bed or a sofa and see if he will pull on the string to retrieve the toy.

Your baby at 1 year

A magical milestone for every parent is when your baby starts walking. On average babies take their first independent steps sometime around one year and most babies are walking by 15 months. They will often fall when learning to walk and it is good for your baby's confidence to practise walking with a push-along toy like a sturdy trolley. He will also enjoy walking while holding onto your hands for support. Don't forget to give your baby lots of cuddles and praise for his efforts. It's best not to put socks or shoes on your baby's feet indoors; he will have a much better grip and balance when his feet are bare.

Movement	Hand-to-eye coordination	Language	Learning	What your baby enjoys	Stimulating play
■ Your baby may take his first steps. ■ He will want to be mobile and will probably use a combination of crawling, cruising along furniture and walking to get around. Crouch in front of your baby with your arms out and see if he can walk towards you. Gradually increase the distance so that he has further to walk each time. ■ A push-along toy with wheels and a	■ Your baby is more accurate at feeding himself with a spoon as he has learned to rotate his hand to get the spoon into his mouth. ■ He likes to play with toys that move, e.g. cars and trains. ■ He is getting better at building towers with blocks or stacking cups. ■ He may be able to make lines and scribbles with a chunky wax crayon.	■ Your child's ability to understand language continues to increase and he can follow simple instructions like 'Give me the ball' or 'Point to the teddy'. ■ Your baby's vocabulary increases and starts to include names of familiar people and objects. ■ Talk and listen to your baby, be interested and try to understand what your baby is saying. Don't interrupt him	■ Your baby enjoys playing with water to see if objects sink or float. ■ He mimics how you use objects, e.g. a toy steering wheel or telephone. ■ He may be able to stir with a spoon. ■ He loves to 'read' books, particularly interactive books with flaps to lift, pop-up pages, buttons to press that make noises. If you name a familiar object on	■ Twisting and turning things such as an activity board with lots of knobs, dials and buttons. ■ Drawing on paper with coloured crayons. ■ Pushing toy cars or trucks along the floor. ■ Building a tower of blocks and then knocking it down – he will need help to stack blocks one on top of another but will enjoy knocking	■ Put water into a washing-up bowl and let your baby play with toy boats, plastic ducks or plastic containers like watering cans or cups. ■ Toys like push-along trolleys, baby bouncers and balls, which he can chase after, will all help to build on your baby's walking skills. ■ Play make-believe together. Your baby will enjoy it if you take an active role

Movement

heavy base is good for helping your baby gain confidence in walking. He will probably use the handle to pull himself up to standing; ensure the toy is stable enough not to topple over.

■ Ride-on toys where your baby can propel himself along by pushing with his feet on the floor are good for developing leg muscles.

■ He is getting better at climbing stairs and sliding down.

■ He can sit down on a small, child-sized chair.

■ He pulls himself up on furniture and is more confident at lowering himself onto his bottom.

■ He starts to be able to climb onto furniture like a low sofa, but less keen on climbing down.

■ Swimming is a good activity for him (see page 236).

Hand-to-eye coordination

■ He is more adept at using a shape sorter.

■ He learns to twist things with his hands. Toys that pop up when your baby turns a knob will be popular.

■ He may be able to assemble very simple inset puzzles.

■ His preference for using his right or left hand is becoming more apparent although this won't be fixed for several years.

Language

to make him say things properly – this will come naturally in time.

■ Point to parts of your body and say things like 'Show me your nose.' See if your baby copies you and eventually you can just say the words without the actions and see if your baby can still point to the parts of the body that you name.

Learning

the page, your baby may be able to look at the picture and point to it.

■ He likes to climb inside and under things to see how he fits – this is good for spacial awareness but if he climbs under a table, take care that he doesn't bang his head.

■ Sometime during the first year your child may be able to group objects that look the same. For example, if you give him his daddy's shoes and his shoes, he may be able to group them together in pairs.

■ He likes to find out how things come apart and how to put them back together again.

■ He is able to do more things for himself, like pulling off his socks, putting his toys back in a box.

What your baby enjoys

them down. Your baby won't be capable of building a tall tower of blocks by himself until about 17 months.

■ You may find that your baby is quite keen to investigate the contents of your handbag. However, many of the items might be dangerous for him to play with so why not put a selection of small toys and objects inside an old handbag and let your baby have fun rummaging around and taking the things out one by one?

Stimulating play

too. For example, if he is playing with a toy telephone, help your child dial the number and then ask to speak to Daddy and hand the telephone back to him so that he can have a make-believe conversation. Or play together with a miniature plastic tea set, pretending to eat and drink.

■ Encourage your baby's interest in the adult world by giving him baby-sized versions of adult toys like brooms, rolling pins, cars and prams to play with.

■ Wooden inset puzzle trays and very simple jigsaw puzzles are great for developing hand-to-eye coordination and spacial awareness.

■ Toys like shape sorters are good for improving manual dexterity too and for learning that some objects are the same shape and some are different.

FEEDING

The final quarter of a baby's first year is a time of growing independence and, during this stage, many babies refuse to be spoon-fed and insist on feeding themselves. This particular stage can be a very challenging period in your baby's development. Towards the end of the first year, a baby's weight gain tends to slow down quite dramatically and sometimes babies who have been good eaters become fussy and difficult.

Encouraging self-feeding

Meal times are as much about exploring food and finding out about textures as eating. Squeezing a banana into a gooey mess and getting physical with a bowl of spaghetti are all part of the learning process. While you may not want to inhibit your baby's experimentation, it might be worth limiting the damage by using a bowl with suction pads and a spill-proof cup. The former is a good idea because it means that your baby is less likely to push the bowl around the tray in frustration as he tries to get a spoonful of food. This is bound to be a messy stage but the more you allow your baby to experiment, the quicker he will learn to feed himself.

Your baby will probably be following a more predictable sleeping pattern, which should help to make meal times more regular. Whenever possible, let your baby sit in his high chair close to the table and enjoy eating with the rest of the family.

Your baby's milk

Your baby may be drinking less milk as he will be eating more solid food, but he still needs 600 ml (20 fl oz) of his usual milk each day. Milk is particularly important for a growing child as it provides calcium, which is necessary for strong bones and healthy teeth. To help keep your baby's teeth in good condition, try to ensure that he takes all his drinks in a beaker or cup by the age of one. Gradually wean your baby off the bottle; the last bottle to go is generally the one at bedtime.

Once a bottle is no longer available, some babies don't seem too keen on drinking milk. If your baby's milk intake drops below 600 ml (20 fl oz), try to make sure that you give cereal with milk at breakfast and include dairy foods like yoghurt and cheese in his diet. You can also give foods like cauliflower cheese, cheese on toast or milk puddings like rice pudding.

Follow-on milks

Follow-on milks are designed for older babies (over the age of six months). They contain more protein, iron and

If more of his food ends up on the floor or on his lap than in your baby's mouth, you could use a two-spoon system. Give him a spoon to hold so he can attempt to feed himself and use another spoon yourself to get some of the food into his mouth at the same time.

Milk replacements
Foods containing the same amount of calcium as 300 ml (10 fl oz) milk

Fromage frais	175 g (6 oz), approx. three small pots
Yoghurt	80 g (2½ oz), approx. one pot
Vanilla ice cream	130 g (4–5 oz), approx. two scoops
Cheddar or Edam	20 g (¾ oz)
Cottage cheese	200 g (7 oz)
Cream cheese	175 g (6 oz)
White bread	3 large slices
Dried apricots	200 g (7 oz)
Dried figs	73 g (3 oz)

vitamins and can be useful in certain situations. Between the age of six and 12 months, if your baby is reluctant to take much formula or if he is breast fed, taking a follow-on milk means he is more likely to receive adequate amounts of vitamins A and D and iron. After the age of one year, if your child is fussy and eats only a small variety of foods, continuing with a standard infant milk or a follow-on milk instead of cow's milk might be beneficial.

Which foods to choose
By this age, your baby should have gained some teeth and graduated to a high chair. Babies who continue too long on puréed foods can become very lazy and reject lumpier textures. It's important to introduce coarser textures in order to encourage your baby to chew. Try to give some food mashed, some grated, some diced and

At this age it is normal for babies to be quite chubby. As soon as your baby starts crawling and walking, he will lose this excess weight.

Daily nutrition
At this age, and each day, your baby should be eating:
■ Three to four mini portions of starchy food, e.g. bread, pasta, potatoes.
■ Three to four mini portions of fruit and vegetables.
■ At least one serving of approximately 50 g (2 oz) of meat, chicken or fish, or two servings of a vegetable protein, e.g. eggs, cheese, lentils.

Good foods for your baby
■ Starchy foods, including bread, pasta, rice, cereal and potato.
■ Lean red meat, which provides the best source of iron.
■ Calcium-rich foods like cheese and yoghurt. These are important for healthy bones and teeth.
■ Eggs, which are a good source of protein.
■ Plenty of fresh fruit and vegetables.
■ Oily fish like salmon, tuna and sardines contain essential fatty acids, which are important for brain and visual development.

Foods to avoid
■ Lightly cooked egg.
■ Peanuts, whole nuts.
■ Shellfish.
■ Blue and unpasteurised cheese like Brie and Camembert.
■ Salt.
■ Honey.

some whole. It is surprising what a few teeth and strong gums can get through.

When a baby is first introduced to solids, he doesn't miss salt or sugar because a child's palate is a clean slate and he hasn't yet developed a taste for it. Try to

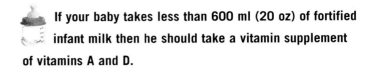

give as much fresh, unprocessed food as possible.

Be adventurous, too – children tend to be less fussy eaters if they are introduced to a wide variety of foods when they are young. The early years are important for instilling healthy eating habits. Many of the recipes in this chapter can be enjoyed by the whole family. Simply leave out salt from your baby's portion. Remember, too, that children are very impressionable so if there is some particular food that you aren't keen on (for example, liver), try not to show your dislike to your child.

Try to make foods look appealing – most babies prefer brightly coloured foods, such as fingers of chicken and little piles of broccoli florets and carrot sticks, rather than a mushy mess. Cut sandwiches into shapes using cookie cutters, make mini portions of foods like fish pie or shepherd's pie and don't overwhelm your baby by putting too much food on his plate.

Breakfast

Now that you are in a good routine of three meals a day, breakfast takes on a greater significance and it is good to vary what you give your baby to eat.

As well as baby cereals, you can give some whole-grain, low-sugar adult breakfast cereals, such as Weetabix, porridge or Ready Brek and add chopped

Remember that low-fat, high fibre dietary guidelines for adults do not apply to babies and young children. Babies and young children need more of their diet to come from energy-rich fats and dairy products so foods like macaroni cheese, shepherd's pie, baked potato and cheese and rice pudding are good.

If your baby takes less than 600 ml (20 oz) of fortified infant milk then he should take a vitamin supplement of vitamins A and D.

fresh or dried fruits and maybe some toasted wheatgerm for a nutritious meal. Many breakfast cereals are fortified with iron so it is good to give some vitamin C-rich food or drink at the same time, like kiwi fruit or orange juice, to boost iron absorption.

If your baby refuses cereal, you could try offering fingers of cheese on toast, fruit and yoghurt instead. Eggs are also a good food for breakfast but you must make sure that the yolk and white are cooked until solid. Poached eggs and soft-boiled eggs are not suitable for babies under the age of one.

Travelling with your baby

As far as feeding is concerned, from a year old it will become much easier to travel with your baby. You won't need any cumbersome sterilising equipment and all you will really need is some baby cutlery, a plastic bowl (preferably with suction), a beaker or cup and a bib. You might want to invest in a small plastic booster seat which straps onto any chair and then your baby can join you at the table, wherever you are eating.

Q Should I use only organic fruit and vegetables for making food for my baby?
A Organic farming is an environmentally friendly option but organic produce is expensive and parents should not feel that a non-organic diet is unhealthy. There is no evidence that pesticide levels in ordinary fruit and vegetables are harmful to babies and young children.

Meal planner

10–12 months

	Breakfast*	Lunch	Mid-afternoon	Supper	Bedtime
	Give breast milk or milk in a cup	Give water or diluted fruit juice with lunch	Give milk from a cup	Give water or diluted fruit juice with supper	Can give milk in a bottle but aim to dispense with a bottle by one year
Day 1	Milk Scrambled egg with cheese, tomato and ham, fingers of buttered toast	Turkey balls in a sweet and sour sauce (p. 256) Fruit	Milk	Mini muffin pizzas (p. 249) Yoghurt or fromage frais	Milk
Day 2	Milk Cereal and fruit	Meatballs with spaghetti and tomato sauce (p. 258) Fruit	Milk	Mini sandwiches (p. 212) Ice cream or jelly	Milk
Day 3	Milk Eggy bread (p. 248) Yoghurt or fromage frais	Mini fish pie (p. 250) Purple fruits (p. 259)	Milk	Tomato sauce with carrots and basil (p. 252) Fruit	Milk
Day 4	Milk Fruity muesli (p. 248) Yoghurt or fromage frais	Chicken or fish with sweet and sour sauce (p. 254) Fruit	Milk	Cheese on toast, crudités and dip, e.g. hummus Maple bananas	Milk
Day 5	Milk Cereal and fruit	My first shepherd's pie (p. 257) Ice cream or jelly	Milk	Mediterranean pasta (p. 250) Fruit	Milk
Day 6	Milk Scrambled egg with fingers of buttered toast Yoghurt or fromage frais	Stir-fried rice with chicken (p. 252) Fruit	Milk	Mini muffin pizzas (p. 249) Purple fruits (p. 259)	Milk
Day 7	Milk Cheese on toast or toast with peanut butter Natural yoghurt with maple syrup	Milk Mild korma curry with chicken, squash and couscous (p. 255) Fruit	Milk	Tomato sauce with carrots and basil (p. 252) Ice cream or jelly	Milk

* Babies of this age may wake early and demand a drink before breakfast. It can be milk, diluted juice or water. Bigger, hungrier babies may also want something to eat like a finger of toast before breakfast.

Recipes

Fruity breakfast muesli

This is very simple to prepare and you can add many different chopped fresh fruits like peach, banana or mango to the mixture or chopped, dried fruits.

Makes 1–2 portions
20 g (¾ oz) porridge oats
½ tbsp wheatgerm (optional)

75 ml (3 fl oz) apple and mango juice (or apple juice)
½ small apple, peeled and grated
4 grapes, peeled, seeded and chopped

■ Put the oats and wheatgerm, if using, into a bowl and pour over the apple and mango juice. Leave to soak for 1 hour or overnight. Before serving stir in the apple and grapes.

Scrambled egg with cheese, tomato and ham

Raw or lightly cooked eggs should not be given to babies or young children.

Makes 1–2 portions
2 eggs
1 tbsp milk
15 g (½ oz) butter
1 tbsp Cheddar cheese, grated

1 small ripe tomato, skinned, de-seeded and chopped
1 wafer thin slice of ham, shredded
salt and white pepper (for babies over 12 months)

■ Beat the eggs together with the milk. Melt the butter in a thick-bottomed saucepan and add the egg mixture. Cook slowly, stirring all the time. When the eggs are almost set stir in the cheese, tomato and ham. If your baby is over 12 months, add a little salt and pepper. Make sure the eggs are well cooked and serve immediately.

Eggy bread

Makes 1 portion
1 slice white or brown bread
1 egg

15 g (½ oz) butter
a little sugar

■ Cut the bread into four triangles. Crack the egg into a dish and whisk with a fork. Add the bread to the mixture and turn it over so that it gets soggy. Heat the butter in a frying pan and when it starts to foam, fry the eggy bread until golden on both sides. Transfer from the pan to a your baby's bowl and sprinkle with a little sugar.

Maple bananas

Makes 1 portion
a knob of unsalted butter
1 small ripe banana, peeled and sliced

1 tbsp maple syrup
1 slice raisin bread or ½ fruit muffin

■ Melt the butter in a small frying pan. Add the sliced banana and cook, stirring occasionally, for 1 minute. Add the maple syrup, cook for 1 minute more and then transfer to a bowl. Toast the raisin bread or muffin, lightly butter and cut into fingers. Serve with the sliced bananas.

Mini muffin pizzas

Makes 4 portions
1 tbsp olive oil
1 small onion, peeled and finely chopped
3 ripe tomatoes, skinned, de-seeded and chopped
1 tbsp tomato purée

½ tsp brown sugar
½ tsp mixed dried herbs
salt and pepper (for babies over 12 months)
2 white or wholemeal muffins, halved
40 g (1½ oz) mozzarella cheese, grated
40 g (1½ oz) Cheddar cheese, grated

■ Heat the oil in a small saucepan, add the onion and sauté for 5–6 minutes. Add the tomatoes together with the tomato purée, sugar and herbs and cook for approximately 8 minutes or until the mixture is thick enough to spread. Season with a little salt and pepper if your baby is older than 12 months.
■ Toast the muffins, divide the tomato sauce between them and top with the grated mozzarella and Cheddar cheese. Place under a pre-heated grill until golden and bubbling. Cut the muffins into quarters and serve.

SUPERFOODS
BANANAS are full of slow-release sugars, which provide sustained energy for several hours. The starch in bananas is not easily digested which is why children should eat only ripe bananas in which the starch has turned to sugar. Ripe bananas are easily digestible and contain soluble fibre that is good for the treatment of both constipation and diarrhoea.

CHEESE is a great food for growing children as it is rich in protein and calcium, important for strong bones and teeth.

Mini fish pie

If you want your child to grow up liking fish then you have to try this delicious mini fish pie. If you make them in ramekin dishes they will be just the right size for your child to enjoy.

Makes 3 mini fish pies
375 g (13 oz) potatoes, peeled and diced
1½ tbsp milk
25 g (1 oz) butter
salt and pepper (for babies over 12 months)
15 g (½ oz) butter
25 g (1 oz) onion, peeled and finely chopped
1 ripe tomato, skinned, de-seeded and chopped
1 tbsp flour
125 g (4½ oz) cod fillet, skinned and cubed
125 g (4½ oz) salmon fillet, skinned and cubed (or use 225 g/8 oz cod)
1 tsp chopped fresh parsley
1 bay leaf
100 ml (3½ fl oz) milk
40 g (1½ oz) Cheddar cheese, grated
a knob of butter

Decoration
cherry tomatoes
chives
red pepper
basil leaves
cooked green beans
rosemary

■ Bring a pan of lightly salted water to the boil, add the potatoes, reduce to a simmer and cook until tender (about 20 minutes). Drain the potatoes and mash together with the milk and butter until smooth and season to taste (for babies over 12 months).
■ Melt the butter in a saucepan, add the onion and tomato and sauté until softened. Add the flour and cook for 30 seconds, stirring. Add the fish to the onion and tomato together with the parsley and bay leaf. Pour over the milk and season to taste (again, for babies over 12 months). Simmer for about 4 minutes until the fish is cooked through. Remove the bay leaf and stir in the cheese until melted.
■ Divide the fish between three glass ramekin dishes (approximately 10 cm/4 in diameter) and top with the mashed potato. Heat through and then dot with a little butter and finish off for a few minutes under a pre-heated grill until golden.
■ If you like, you can decorate each mini fish pie with a cat's face. Cut the cherry tomatoes in half, place a short strip of chive in the centre of each to make the cat's eyes. Cut out a triangle shape from the pepper for the nose. Make the mouth using short lengths of fine green beans and finish off with basil leaves for the ears and rosemary for the whiskers.

Tomato sauce with carrots and basil

Tomato sauce with pasta is usually a firm favourite with children. It's a good idea to enrich the sauce by adding some extra vegetables. Here I have added carrot and courgette but there are other vegetables you could add like sweet peppers or mushrooms. You can then blend them into the sauce so the confirmed veggie haters can't pick them out!

Makes 4 portions
✳ Suitable for freezing
200 g (7 oz) carrots, peeled and sliced
3 tbsp tiny pasta shapes
15 g (½ oz) butter
½ small onion, peeled and chopped
1 tsp olive oil

1 medium courgette, topped and tailed and sliced
4 ripe tomatoes, skinned, de-seeded and cut into pieces
4–5 basil leaves, shredded
50 g (2 oz) Cheddar cheese, grated

◾ Put the carrots in a steamer over a pan of boiling water and cook for about 20 minutes or until tender. Cook the pasta according to the packet instructions.
◾ Meanwhile, melt the butter together with the oil, add the onions and sauté for 2 minutes, stirring occasionally. Add the courgette and sauté for 3 minutes, stirring occasionally. Add the tomatoes and torn basil leaves, cover and cook for about 5 minutes, stirring occasionally until mushy. Stir in the cheese until melted. Blend together the tomato sauce and the cooked carrots. Drain the pasta, stir into the sauce and serve.

Stir-fried rice with chicken

Stir-fried rice is a popular dish with children. Try this fluffy basmati rice with tender chunks of marinated chicken flavoured with soy sauce and spring onion.

Suitable from 12 months
Makes 6 portions
Marinade
1 tbsp soy sauce
2 tsp brown sugar
½ tsp sesame oil

1 chicken breast, cut into small chunks
175 g (6 oz) basmati rice
2 tbsp plus 1 tsp vegetable oil

1 egg, beaten
salt and pepper (for babies over 12 months)
60 g (2½ oz) frozen peas
60 g (2½ oz) frozen sweetcorn
1 small onion, peeled and finely chopped
1 clove garlic, crushed
60 g (2½ oz) red pepper, de-seeded and finely chopped
1 large spring onion, sliced

■ For the marinade, mix together the ingredients and marinate the chicken for at least 30 minutes. Cook the rice according to the instructions on the packet.

■ Heat 1 tsp of the oil in a small frying pan. Season the beaten egg (for babies over 12 months) and pour into the pan, tipping the pan to spread the egg evenly. Cook until set like a thin omelette. Remove from the pan, cut into strips and set aside.

■ Steam the peas and sweetcorn for about 4 minutes or until tender.

■ Heat the remaining oil in a large frying pan or wok, add the chopped onion, garlic and red pepper and cook for 2–3 minutes. Strain the marinade from the chicken and reserve. Add the strips of chicken to the pan and stir fry for 3–4 minutes or until cooked through.

■ Drain the cooked rice, add to the chicken together with the spring onion and reserved marinade and cook over a high heat for 2 minutes. Stir in the peas, sweetcorn and strips of egg and heat through before serving immediately.

Mild korma curry with chicken, squash and couscous

You might think it strange to introduce flavourings like curry to a baby, but in India nearly all babies will have enjoyed curry by the time they are a year old. The mild korma curry powder in this recipe combines well with the coconut to give the couscous a lovely flavour.

Makes 4 portions

½ tbsp olive oil
50 g (2 oz) onion, peeled and finely chopped
60 g (2½ oz) chicken breast, diced
½ tsp mild korma curry powder
100 g (4 oz) butternut squash, peeled and chopped
60 g (2½ oz) cauliflower, cut into small florets
350 ml (11 fl oz) chicken stock
100 ml (3½ fl oz) water
2 tbsp creamed coconut
100 g (4 oz) couscous

■ Heat the oil in a saucepan, add the onion and sauté for 2 minutes. Add the chicken and sauté, stirring until sealed. Stir in the curry powder and cook for 30 seconds.

■ Add the butternut squash, cauliflower and chicken stock. Cover with a lid and cook for 12 minutes.

■ Strain the stock into another saucepan and set the chicken and vegetables to one side.

■ Add the water and creamed coconut to the reserved stock and bring to the boil. Pour over the couscous in a bowl and stir to mix.

■ After 5 minutes fluff the couscous with a fork and stir in the vegetables and chicken.

SUPERFOODS

Couscous is a form of grain made from wheat and is popular in Middle Eastern cuisine. You can find it in most supermarkets next to the rice section. It is fairly high in minerals and vitamins and has a nice soft texture that is perfect for babies. It is also very quick and easy to prepare.

Chicken fingers with sweet and sour sauce

Many chicken nuggets contain artificial flavourings and colouring and more coating than chicken. However it's easy to make your own chicken fingers.

Makes 8 chicken fingers
Sweet and sour sauce
1 tbsp vegetable oil
½ onion, peeled and chopped
½ small red pepper, de-seeded and chopped
½ tbsp tomato purée
150 ml (¼ pint) chopped tinned tomatoes or passata
1 tsp dark brown sugar
60 ml (2 fl oz) pineapple juice

½ tsp soy sauce
½ tsp white wine vinegar
1 chicken breast
½ tbsp lemon juice
15 g (½ oz) flour
salt and pepper (for babies over 12 months)
1 small egg, lightly beaten
25 g (1 oz) fine breadcrumbs
½ tbsp finely chopped parsley (optional)
1 tbsp vegetable oil

■ For the sauce, heat the oil in a saucepan, add the onion and pepper and sauté for 6 minutes. Stir in the remaining ingredients, bring to the simmer and cook for 8–10 minutes. Transfer to a food processor and purée until smooth.

■ Cut the chicken breast into about 8 strips, gently bang with a mallet and marinate in the lemon juice for about 10 minutes. Remove from the lemon juice and coat in flour (season the flour for babies over 12 months), then dip in beaten egg and finally in the breadcrumbs and parsley, if using.

■ Heat the oil in a frying pan and fry the chicken for 5–6 minutes over a medium heat until golden. Serve the goujons on a plate with the sauce in small bowls so that your child can dip the goujons into the sauce.

Variation: Goujons of fish with sweet and sour sauce

Makes 8 goujons
75 g (3 oz) skinned plaice fillet
3 tbsp flour
salt and pepper (for babies over 12 months)

1 small egg, lightly beaten
25 g (1 oz) dried breadcrumbs
Vegetable oil

■ Cut the plaice into about 8 strips. Season the flour (for babies over 12 months) and toss with the fish until evenly coated (this can be done by putting the flour and fish in a plastic bag). Then dip the fish into the beaten egg and toss in the breadcrumbs. Shallow fry or deep fry in vegetable oil until golden (about 2 minutes) and drain on kitchen paper.

■ Serve on a plate with the sauce in small bowls for the goujons to be dipped into.

Turkey balls in a sweet and sour sauce

These turkey balls are a great favourite of mine and will make a delicious family meal. Serve them with rice and they are also good mashed with the sauce. You could also make these using chicken.

Makes 24 turkey balls (8 baby portions or 4 adult portions)
✻ **Suitable for freezing**
1 tbsp olive oil
1 onion, peeled and chopped
150 g (5 oz) carrot, finely grated
500 g (1 lb 2 oz) minced turkey
75 g (3 oz) fresh breadcrumbs
75 g (3 oz) crushed pineapple, drained
2 tsp soy sauce
1 tsp brown sugar
salt and pepper (for babies over 12 months)

flour
vegetable oil for frying
Sweet and sour sauce
1 onion, peeled and finely chopped
1 tbsp vegetable oil
1 x 400 g (14 oz) can chopped tomatoes
100 ml (3½ fl oz) pineapple juice
1 tbsp soy sauce
1 tbsp dark brown sugar
juice of ½ lemon
salt and pepper (for babies over 12 months)

■ Heat the oil in a small saucepan, add the onion and carrots and sauté for 3 minutes until softened. Remove from the pan and leave to cool. Once cold, mix with the turkey mince, pineapple, soy sauce, sugar and seasoning (for babies over 12 months). Transfer to a food processor and blend for a second or two. Shape into about 24 balls using floured hands.
■ Heat the oil in a frying pan, add the turkey balls and sauté for a couple of minutes over a high heat to seal. Then reduce the heat and cook for 6–8 minutes or until cooked through.
■ For the sauce, heat the oil in a small saucepan, add the onion and sauté for 5 minutes. Stir in the remaining ingredients and simmer, uncovered, for 10 minutes. Pour the sauce over the turkey balls and serve.

My first shepherd's pie

It's a good idea to make mini portions of shepherd's pie in small ramekin dishes for your baby. Combining minced meat with mashed potato and carrots gives it a nice soft texture.

Makes 4 mini shepherd's pies

125 g (4½ oz) carrots, peeled and sliced
450 g (1 lb) potatoes, peeled and chopped
1 tbsp vegetable oil
1 small onion, peeled and chopped
1 small clove garlic, peeled and crushed
300 g (11 oz) lean minced beef or lamb
200 g (7 oz) ripe tomatoes, skinned and
chopped
1 tbsp fresh chopped parsley
1 tbsp tomato ketchup
150 ml (5 fl oz) chicken stock
40 g (1½ oz) butter
2 tbsp milk
salt and white pepper (for babies over 12 months)

■ Put the carrots into a saucepan, pour over boiling water and cook, simmering, for 10 minutes. Add the potatoes and cook for 15 minutes more.

■ Meanwhile, heat the oil in a saucepan, add the onion and garlic and sauté until softened. Add the minced meat and sauté, stirring occasionally, until browned all over. Add the tomato, parsley, tomato ketchup and chicken stock.

■ Cover, bring to the boil and then simmer for 15 minutes. Uncover and cook for a few minutes until some of the stock has evaporated. Transfer to a blender and process for a couple of seconds (this gives the meat a much softer texture, which is more appealing to babies and toddlers).

■ When the potatoes and carrots are cooked, drain them and return to the saucepan together with half of the butter and milk and mash with a potato masher or potato ricer until smooth. Season to taste (for babies over 12 months).

■ Divide the meat between four mini ramekin dishes and top with the mashed potato and carrot. Dot with the remaining butter and place under a pre-heated grill until lightly golden. Allow to cool slightly and serve.

SUPERFOODS

RED MEAT contains iron in a form that is more easily absorbed than the iron in fruit, vegetables and grains. However, eating meat will help to boost the absorption of iron from plant foods such as these if they are eaten at the same meal.

Meatballs with spaghetti and tomato sauce

These tasty meatballs in tomato sauce are very easy to prepare and make a good meal for the whole family. They also make great finger food without the sauce and you could cook a batch of meatballs and freeze them. You can serve them with steamed vegetables such as carrot sticks and broccoli or cauliflower florets.

Makes 8 portions
2 slices of white bread (60 g/2½ oz)
2 tbsp milk
3 tbsp vegetable oil
1 small onion, finely chopped
½ apple, peeled and grated
225 g (8 oz) minced beef
1 tbsp chopped fresh parsley
2 tbsp freshly grated Parmesan
½ egg, lightly beaten

a few drops Worcestershire sauce
salt and pepper (for babies over 12 months)
flour
200 g (7 oz) spaghetti

Tomato sauce
2 tbsp olive oil
1 onion, chopped
1 clove garlic, crushed
500 ml (16 fl oz) passata
fresh basil, chopped

■ To make the meatballs, first tear the bread into pieces, put into a food processor and chop to make breadcrumbs. Soak the breadcrumbs in the milk for about 5 minutes. Heat 1 tablespoon of the oil, add the onion and sauté for about 3 minutes, until softened. Transfer to a food processor with the rest of the ingredients, not including the remaining vegetable oil. Briefly blend until mixed and then shape into about 16 meatballs using floured hands. If you have time, you can transfer them to the fridge to chill slightly but it is not absolutely necessary.

■ Heat the vegetable oil in a large frying pan and fry the meatballs over a high heat to seal, then reduce the heat and cook for 5–6 minutes, stirring occasionally.

■ Meanwhile, cook the spaghetti in a large pan of lightly salted boiling water according to the instructions on the packet.

■ To make the sauce, heat the olive oil in a saucepan, add the onion and garlic and sauté for 5–6 minutes. Stir in the passata and basil and season to taste. Simmer for 5–6 minutes. Add the meatballs and simmer for a few minutes. Serve with the cooked spaghetti.

Purple fruits

The blueberries turn this delicious fruit compote a wonderful deep purple colour. Serve this on its own or with vanilla ice cream.

Makes 6 portions
✳ Suitable for freezing
2 ripe peaches, halved and stoned
1 ripe pear, peeled, quartered and cored
2 ripe plums, halved and stoned

100 g (4 oz) blueberries
3 tbsp cranberry juice
2 tbsp caster sugar
1 small cinnamon stick
100 g (4 oz) raspberries

■ Cut each of the peach halves into four pieces and cut the pear quarters in half again to make eight pieces. Cut the plums into quarters. Put the peaches, pear, plums, blueberries and cranberry juice into a thick-bottomed saucepan together with the sugar and cinnamon stick. Bring to a gentle simmer, cover with a lid and cook for 10 minutes. Remove the cinnamon stick. Cut the larger pieces of fruit into small pieces and stir in the raspberries. Serve chilled.

Vanilla rice pudding with plum compote

A traditional rice pudding takes 1½ to 2 hours to cook but you can buy flaked rice in the supermarket that takes just 10 minutes to prepare.

Makes 3 portions
4 red plums
25 g (1 oz) butter
25 g (1 oz) brown sugar
25 g (1 oz) flaked rice

300 ml (½ pint) full cream milk
1 tbsp vanilla sugar or caster sugar
1 small vanilla pod split with the seeds
scraped out or a few drops vanilla essence

■ To make the plum compote, cut the plums in half, remove the stones and cut each half into 4 slices. Melt the butter in a saucepan, add the plums and cook for 2–3 minutes. Add the brown sugar and cook over a low heat for 10–15 minutes, stirring occasionally, until the plums are tender. Allow to cool a little and for young baibes remove the skin from the plums.
■ Meanwhile, put the flaked rice, milk, sugar and seeds from the vanilla pod or vanilla essence into a heavy-based saucepan. Bring to the boil and simmer gently for about 10 minutes, stirring occasionally.
■ To serve, mix the rice pudding with the plum compote.

SUPERFOODS
CARROTS **are a great
source of antioxidants
and raw carrot sticks
make a very healthy
snack. Their high fibre
and fluid content
means that eating car-
rots can help with
constipation. Equally,
eating boiled or
steamed carrots and
rice is a good remedy
for diarrhoea.**

Carrot cupcakes

These cupcakes are easy to make and look great for a special tea party or maybe even the first birthday party. Either use small cutters for the decorative shapes (see Useful addresses, page 268) or cut them out of the icing using a sharp knife. You could also ice the cake with pale pink icing and decorate with violet flowers, pink hearts and green leaves.

Makes 9 cupcakes
150 g (5 oz) self-raising flour
1 tsp baking powder
pinch of salt
100 g (4 oz) caster sugar
125 ml (4 fl oz) vegetable oil
2 eggs, beaten
1 tsp pure vanilla essence
60 ml (2 fl oz) pineapple juice

50 g (2 oz) finely grated carrot
Decoration
200 g (7 oz) white ready-to-roll icing
cornflour
pink, violet and green food paste colouring
150 g (5 oz) icing sugar
2 tbsp pineapple juice
yellow food colouring

■ Pre-heat the oven to 170°C/325°F/Gas mark 3. Mix the flour, baking powder, salt and sugar in a large bowl. Whisk together the vegetable oil, eggs, vanilla essence and pineapple juice and add to the dry ingredients with the grated carrots. Beat together until thoroughly mixed and then pour into 9 paper cases and bake in the oven for 20 minutes or until golden and firm to the touch. Transfer to a baking rack and leave to cool.

■ For the decoration, divide the ready-to-roll icing into three. Colour one piece pink, one violet and one green. Roll out each piece thinly on a work surface dusted with cornflour and stamp out tiny shapes using plunger cutters or mini cutter shapes. Leave to dry on a sheet of non-stick baking paper dusted with icing sugar.

■ Once the cakes are cool, you can make the icing. Sift the icing sugar into a bowl and stir in the pineapple juice to make a fairly thick, smooth paste. Colour it pale yellow with a little of the yellow food colouring and spread over the centre of each of the cakes using a palette knife. Arrange the heart, flower and leaf shapes on top. If necessary, dampen the underside of the cut-out shapes with water to attach them to each other.

YOUR BABY'S HEALTH

Your baby will be monitored at birth and then her growth and development will be monitored at 6–8 weeks and possibly at 8–9 months. These checks are a good opportunity to discuss any matters that are worrying you, for example if you are experiencing problems with colic, teething, sleep or feeding.

Development checks

Your baby will be given a series of routine health checks in the first few weeks of life. This can include a hearing screen, which uses a quick and simple test. In areas where this is not available at birth, hearing is usually tested at seven months. One baby in every 1000 is born with a hearing loss. It is not easy to identify that a young baby has a hearing loss and early identification is very important to the development of the child. It also means that support and information can be given to the parents. The screening may be done before you leave hospital and in some areas it will be carried out at home or at a health clinic.

The Apgar score
At birth your baby is given a simple medical examination to assess her condition. Her breathing, heartbeat, muscle tone, skin colour and reflexes are checked at

one minute old and again at five minutes and ten minutes. She is given a score of 0, 1 or 2 for each of the five checks, giving a maximum score of 10. This is called the Apgar score.

A score of 7 or over is normal. It is extremely rare for a baby to be given 10 at birth because almost all babies have bluish hands and feet even if they are in otherwise excellent condition at one minute old. The scoring is done as discreetly as possible so as not to disturb the moment of birth for you or your baby. You may not even notice it unless there is a problem. If the score is below 5, then your baby may need extra attention, possibly help with her breathing. Ask your midwife to explain the Apgar score to you if you have any concerns.

Vitamin K
Vitamin K is essential for normal blood clotting however in the UK about 65 babies a year suffer from bleeding related to a deficiency in vitamin K. Levels are low in the first weeks of a baby's life. Different maternity units have different ways of administering vitamin K at birth. There is a choice between oral and intramuscular vitamin K. If choosing oral administration, breastfed babies are usually given vitamin K by

You are observing your baby every day – if you have any concerns, however trivial, don't wait for your baby's scheduled development checks; contact your health visitor for advice.

mouth in three doses – at birth, at one week and again at four to six weeks – or they are given a single injection at birth. Bottle-fed babies only need two oral doses, one at birth and the other at one week because formula milk contains added vitamin K.

Heel prick test

Some time between six and 12 days of age a heel prick test is done on your baby by a midwife at home. The test involves pricking your baby's heel and soaking up spots of blood onto a special card. The card is sent away to a laboratory for testing. All babies are tested for a deficiency of thyroid activity, called hypothyroidism, which occurs in about 1 in 2500 babies. If levels of thyroid hormones are low, it could lead to slow brain and body development, which can be remedied with medication. Babies are also tested for phenylketonuria, another rare disease that affects about 1 in 75,000 babies and may affect brain development. This can be treated with a special diet. If the heel test is positive, a more accurate test will be done because the heel test often turns out to be a false alarm.

6–8 week check

This check-up is part of the service offered by the NHS and is usually carried out by a health visitor or sometimes by a GP. It is the first check-up your baby will

A hearing screen will only detect neurological hearing loss and parents must continue to watch out for any hearing loss as a result of conductive damage, e.g. glue ear, as this can delay speech development.

The red book

■ When your health visitor first comes to visit you at home she will give you a booklet known as the Red Book or Child Personal Health Record book. This is used as a record of your child's health, growth and development. It is important that you bring this with you whenever you visit the child health clinic or your doctor, or if your child goes to hospital. To begin with you can use the booklet to record your child's birth details, family history and any significant health problems.

■ The book includes information about your child's development and there are also pages for your health visitor and GP to fill in at the 6–8 week and 8–9 month checks plus later reviews up to school entry.

■ Included in the book is also a list of immunisations and at which age they should be given. There is space for you to record your baby's immunisations so that you will know when each one has been given and if there have been any adverse reactions. This information is often needed when entering nursery or school.

have had since the initial neonatal examination. Sometimes it can be combined with your baby's first set of injections at two months. The purpose of this check-up is to find out if there are any problems that might affect your baby's growth and development. Gross motor skills are checked as well as visual development and hearing. It is also a good opportunity for you to ask any questions that might concern you about your baby.

Your baby's ability to focus on an object with both eyes will also be checked. Her limbs will be moved around to check for flexibility and her hips will be checked for dislocation. Boys' testicles will be examined to see if they have descended. Your baby's reflexes will also be tested. Your GP will check your baby's heart and breathing. He will also feel your baby's fontanelles to make sure her skull is forming properly.

8–9 month check

If you haven't seen your health visitor for a while, she may contact you at around eight months to review your baby's progress. This is also a chance to ask her about anything that is worrying you. When you go to the health clinic you will need to take your Child's Personal Health Record book (see bo, page 263) with you. At the check your baby's length, head circumference and weight are measured and are compared to previous measurements to make sure her growth rate is normal. The health visitor will probably check the following:

■ **Is your baby's fontanelle closing?** The soft spot at the front of your baby's head will be checked as it should be getting smaller by six months and should have closed by about 18 months.

■ **Does she hear properly?** Your health visitor or GP does a simple hearing check to see if your baby can respond to a sound that she can't see. (This is not done if your baby has had a neonatal hearing test.)

■ **Does she see well?** Your baby's eyesight will be tested to make sure that she can focus on an object in the distance and follow it as it moves.

■ **Does she communicate with you?** Your baby's language development will be monitored – by this age she should be babbling away making sounds like 'ba-ba' or 'da-da'.

■ **Can she sit up by herself?** Your baby should be

> Your child's height and weight are a useful guide to general progress and development and you can have your baby weighed and measured regularly at your child health clinic or doctor's baby clinic.

Growth charts

■ At the 6–8 week and any future check on development your health visitor will measure your baby's weight, height and head circumference and these measurements are recorded on centile charts in your baby's Child Personal Health Record book, which assess her weight and length against her age. Each chart shows the range of weights or heights into which the vast majority of babies will fall. There are separate charts for girls and boys.

■ In each chart the bold line in the middle is what is called the 50th percentile. This represents the average. Your child's measurements should form a line roughly parallel to the central line. However, a baby's weight gain varies from month to month and sometimes individual measurements can worry parents. But provided your baby is growing steadily over the months there is nothing to worry about. Some weeks babies have growth spurts and other weeks they may hardly grow at all. A centile chart makes it easy to see if your baby's length and weight increase and match up and if her overall growth is at the expected rate despite some peaks and troughs.

■ If your baby is pre-term you will need to adjust her age accordingly and start plotting her measurements to the left of the zero, e.g. at 36 weeks. This adjustment continues until she is a year old.

starting to sit up by herself and by nine months should be able to sit up unsupported for at least a few seconds.

■ **Can she support her own weight when held in a standing position?** By nine months your baby should be able to bear her own weight on her feet if you hold her hands to help her keep her balance.

■ **Are her fine motor skills developing?** She should be beginning to reach and grasp a toy or object using her fingers and thumb in a pincer movement and eventually transfer objects from one hand to the other.

Immunisations

Babies inherit some natural immunity from their mothers while they are in the womb and also get natural protection from antibodies in breast milk. However, this eventually wears off and a child's immune system needs to develop and learn how to defend itself.

Immunisation using a vaccine protects a baby or young child against life-threatening diseases like diphtheria, meningitis C or polio. Vaccines are derived from components of the bacteria or weakened viruses and the vaccine ingredients have been treated so they do not cause the disease. When a child is given a vaccine, it stimulates the immune system to make antibodies. These stay in the system so that if the disease tries to attack again, the immune defence system will be able to recognise that it is harmful and the body's defences (the antibodies) fight it and prevent infection. Millions of children have been immunised without any problems and the benefits are enormous.

The normal programme of infant vaccinations is spread out over several months with many of the vac-

The BCG vaccine
The BCG vaccine protects against tuberculosis and is given to the following high-risk groups shortly after birth:
■ Babies born to families from countries with a high prevalence of TB, e.g. India and countries in Africa and the Far East.
■ Babies who will be staying for more than one month in a country with a high rate of TB.
■ Babies who could be in close contact with someone who has TB or has had TB in the past.
■ The BCG vaccine is routinely given to children between 10 and 14 years old.

Q Since many of these diseases are now very rare do I still need to immunise my child?
A As more children are being immunised, many of the diseases are becoming much more rare. It is easy to think that these diseases are no longer a threat but if children are not immunised, they can come back again. Also, what happens if your child travels to a country where some of the diseases that we routinely immunise against are still rife and what happens if someone from abroad brings the disease into the UK? Children who are not immunised grow up to be susceptible adults.

cines given in the first four months. The time scale for vaccinations is intended to increase your child's protection as her natural immunity wears off. It is important that your baby completes the course of vaccinations for maximum protection. Keep a record of your child's vaccinations in your baby's Red Book (see box, page 263).

If your child is unwell or has a fever, you will need to delay vaccination until she gets better. A common side effect of a jab can be a fever and even though infant paracetamol suspension shouldn't be given routinely before three months, many doctors suggest giving it after immunisation. Do not give aspirin to children under 12 years old. You will need to seek medical advice if your child has had any complications from any previous immunisations or is taking any medicine, particularly steroids.

Q Is there a normal reaction to a vaccine?
A Some babies and children develop a fever and feel slightly unwell for about 36 hours following a vaccine. There may also be a small tender area that is red and slightly swollen at the site of the vaccine. This can last for up to three months.

The MMR vaccine

Written in consultation with Professor Brent Taylor PhD FRCPCH (Royal Free Hospital, London). The decision to immunise your child is never easy, especially with all the controversy surrounding the MMR vaccine. Despite my first child Natasha dying from encephalitis at 13 weeks due to a viral infection, I still chose to immunise my three children. I believed the side effects from the actual disease outweighed the risks of the side effects from the immunisation.

There is an on-going debate about a link between MMR and the development of autism and Crohn's Disease but this has not been established by research. The controversy over the safety of MMR began in 1998 when Dr Andrew Wakefield and colleagues from the Royal Free Hospital in London published research in the *Lancet* of 12 cases of a new syndrome of autism and bowel disease, linked to the MMR vaccine given to children at 13 months. The paper describes the bowel condition of these children but concludes, 'We did not prove an association between measles, mumps and rubella vaccine and the syndrome described.'

In the media coverage that followed, Dr Wakefield said he believed the MMR vaccine overloaded the immune system and should be given to children separately at yearly intervals. This would mean children would not be fully protected until they were six years old. The DoH says there is no scientific evidence to link MMR with autism or bowel disease. There is also overwhelming evidence from many independent bodies, including the Medical Research Council, Joint Committee of Vaccines and Immunisation and the World Health Organisation (WHO) who all support the MMR programme.

In the US, the MMR vaccine has been in everyday use for about 30 years, and worldwide, 500 million doses have been used in over 90 countries since the early 1970s but no child has yet died as a result of the MMR vaccine. However, in the year before MMR was introduced in England, 86,000 children caught measles and 16 died. Following concerns about the MMR vaccine, fewer children are being immunised and the number of children contracting measles and mumps is already on the increase. In countries where the uptake of the MMR vaccine is not high due to poverty or social disruption, it is estimated that over one million children die each year from measles worldwide.

Even if not fatal, severe complications occur if a child catches the measles infection. It is the most likely childhood infection to cause inflammation of the brain, for instance, which can result in brain damage. It can also cause convulsions, meningitis or problems with blood clotting.

Mumps was the biggest cause of viral meningitis in children and the most common cause of acquired deafness. The damage rubella can do to unborn babies is devastating and pregnant women can catch it from their own child.

Some parents worry that a child's immune system is unable to cope with three vaccinations at once and that the MMR overloads the body with diseases. The DoH does not consider single vaccines to be in children's best interest. A child is often subjected to more than one infection at a time and the immune system copes. Also, the effects of the three viruses in the MMR vaccination start to work at different times, with about a week separating each one. A few doctors give single vaccinations, although nearly every independent expert group, including the WHO, support the use of MMR rather than single vaccinations. Having single vaccines puts your child at risk of catching measles, mumps or rubella in the gaps between vaccination. It also means six jabs instead of two (the MMR vaccine is given twice) and research shows that the more jabs a child needs, the less likely it is she will complete the course. Children who have an immune deficiency due to the treatment of cancer will be especially at risk. The single vaccine is as yet an unproven method of protection. Go to www.mmrthefacts.nhs.uk for more information and see Useful addresses on page 268.

The UK immunisation programme

Vaccination	Why it is needed	Possible side effects of the vaccine
Combined vaccine (DtaP/IPV/ Hib): protects against diphtheria, tetanus, pertussis (whooping cough), polio and *Haemophilus influenzae* type b (Hib). One injection given at **2, 3** and **4 months**. Booster dose (without hib) given at around **13 months**. Booster dose of hib only to be given at around **12 months**.	**Diptheria** causes breathing problems and can damage the heart. **Tetanus** is caused by germs from dirt getting into an open wound and attacks the nervous system, causing muscle spasms, which can affect breathing. It can be fatal. **Pertussis** (whooping cough) is prolonged coughing and possible vomiting over many weeks. May temporarily stop breathing and cause brain damage. **Polio** is an acute illness that can cause paralysis. If it affects the legs, they become weak or even permanently paralysed. **Hib**: Protects against *Haemophilus influenzae* type b (Hib), meningitis C.	▤ Swelling and redness at the site of the injection are common. ▤ Your baby may become fretful and slightly feverish within 24 hours of the injection.
Pneumococcal infection (PCV): one injection given at **2, 4** and around **13 months**.	Pneumococcal diseases can cause children to become ill very rapidly and in some cases they can be fatal. They are becoming increasingly resistant to antibiotics and their prevention by immunisation is therefore important.	▤ Swelling and redness at the site of the injection are common. ▤ Your baby may become fretful and slightly feverish.
Meningitis C (MenC): one injection given at **3, 4** and around **12 months**.	**Meningitis C** is a rare illness, but occurs more frequently in children under 5 years. It kills 1 in 10 babies affected and many of the survivors are left permanently brain damaged, epileptic or deaf. It can also cause blood poisoning.	▤ Swelling and redness at the site of the injection are common. ▤ Your baby may become fretful and slightly feverish.
MMR: a combined vaccine to protect against measles, mumps and rubella (German measles). Given at around **13 months** and again at **3 years 4 months** to **5 years**.	**Measles** can cause fits, encephalitis and pneumonia. **Mumps** may cause deafness and meningitis. **Rubella** contracted in pregnancy can cause serious birth defects.	▤ A week to ten days after the injection, may develop a mild fever and rash and lose her appetite. Should last no longer than three days. ▤ After about three weeks a few children get a swollen face and mild form of mumps. ▤ May have a febrile convulsion but it is more likely for a child to suffer a febrile convulsion if she were to contract the measles infection. ▤ A small flat scar on the upper left arm at the site of the injection.

NB The immunisation schedule is subject to change so check for the latest recommendations on www.immunisation.nhs.uk

Useful addresses

Support groups during and after pregnancy

Active Birth Centre
(Childbirth and parenting classes. Mail order service for pregnancy, childbirth and post-natal care.)
25 Bickerton Road
London N19 5JT
Tel: 020 7482 5554 (Mon–Fri, 9am–5pm)
www.activebirthcentre.com

Association of Breastfeeding Mothers
(Counsellors offering advice/information over the phone.)
PO Box 207
Bridgewater TA6 7YT
Tel: 020 7813 1481 (24-hours)

Breastfeeding Network Supporterline
(Independent support and information about breastfeeding.)
Tel: 0870 900 8787 (9.30am–9.30pm)
www.breastfeeding.co.uk/bfn

Cry-sis
See Serene, below

Family Planning Association (FPA)
(Trained staff providing confidential advice.)
2–12 Pentonville Road
London N1 9FP
Tel: 020 7837 5432
Helpline: 0845 310 1334 (Mon–Fri, 9am–7pm)
www.fpa.org.uk

Fathers Direct
(The national information centre for fatherhood.)
Tel: 020 7920 9491 (Mon–Fri, 10am–6pm)
www.fathersdirect.com

Foundation for the Study of Infant Deaths
(Support for bereaved parents and contact with local groups of other bereaved parents.)
Artillery House
11–19 Artillery Row
London SW1P 1RT
Helpline: 0870 787 0554 (9am–11pm)
www.sids.org.uk/fsid

Gingerbread Association for One-Parent Families
(Help, advice and contact with other lone parents.)
1st Floor
7 Sovereign Close
Sovereign Court
London E1W 3HW
Tel: 020 7488 9300
Helpline: 0800 018 4318 (Mon–Fri, 9am–5pm)
www.gingerbread.org.uk

Independent Midwives Association
(A central source for enquiries, data and information.)
1 Great Quarry
Guildford
Surrey GU1 3XN
Tel: 01483 821104
www.independentmidwives.org.uk

La Leche League
(Breastfeeding advice, breast pump hire.)
BM3424
London WC1N 3XX
Tel: 020 7242 1278 (Mon–Fri, 9am–6pm, answering machine at weekends)
www.laleche.org.uk

Maternity Alliance
(Information on maternity services, benefits and rights at work.)
45 Beech Street
London EC2P 2XL
Tel: 020 7588 8582
(Mon and Thurs, 10.30am–12.30pm; Tues, 6pm–8pm; Wed, 9.30–11.30am)
www.maternityalliance.org.uk

Meet-a-Mum Association
(Concerned with helping mothers who feel depressed and isolated when their babies are born.)
Waterside Centre
25 Avenue Rd
London SE25 4DX
Tel: 020 8768 0123 (weekdays, 7–10pm)
www.mama.org.uk

Miscarriage Association
(Advice and support for women who

have had or are experiencing a miscarriage. Contact with other local groups.)
c/o Clayton Hospital
Northgate
Wakefield
W. Yorks WF1 3JS
Tel: 01924 200 799 (Mon–Fri, 9am–4pm)
www.miscarriageassociation.org.uk

National Childbirth Trust (NCT)
(Organises antenatal classes. Offers breastfeeding advice. Post-natal depression counsellors.)
Alexandra House
Oldham Terrace
Acton
London W3 6NH
Tel: 0870 444 8707 (Mon–Thurs, 9am–5pm; Fri, 9am–4pm)
Breastfeeding Helpline: 0870 444 8708 (open every day, 8am–10pm)
www.nctpregnancyandbabycare.com

National Council for One Parent Families
(Provides free information and advice for people bringing up children on their own.)
255 Kentish Town Road
London NW5 2LX
Tel: 0800 018 5026 (Mon–Fri, 9am–5pm)
www.oneparentfamilies.org.uk

NHS Direct
(Providing nurse advice and confidential health information.)
Tel: 0845 4647 (24-hours)
www.nhsdirect.nhs.uk

Parentline Plus
(Help and information for parents concerning a range of topics.)
520 Highgate Studios
53–79 Highgate Road
Kentish Town
London NW5 1TL
Tel: 0808 800 2222
www.parentlineplus.org.uk

Pregnancy Crisis Centre
(Offering support and advice for those who are thinking about an abortion or have had one.)

Tel: 01474 534 404 *
www.btinternet.com/~DEvans_23/helparea.htm

Guild of Postnatal Exercise Teachers
(Classes run across the country.)
Tel: 01453 884268
www.postnatalexercise.co.uk

Serene (formerly known as Cry-sis)
(Provides emotional support and practical advice to parents dealing with excessive crying, demanding behaviour and sleep problems.)
Helpline: 020 7404 5011 (every day, 8am–11pm)
www.our-space.co.uk/serene.htm

Twins and Multiple Births Association (TAMBA)
(Provides information and mutual support networks for families of twins, triplets and more)
2 The Willows
Gardner Road
Guildford
Surrey GU1 4PG
Tel: 0870 770 3305 (Mon–Fri, 9am–4pm)
Helpline: 01732 868 000 (Mon–Fri, 7–11pm; weekends, 10am–11pm)
www.tamba.org.uk

Wellbeing
(Health research charity for mothers and babies.)
27 Sussex Place
Regent's Park
London NW1 4SP
Tel: 020 7772 6400 (Mon–Fri, 9am–5pm)
Sainsbury's/Wellbeing Eating for Pregnancy Helpline: 0845 130 3646 (Mon–Fri, 10am–4pm)
www.wellbeing.org.uk

Special care and special needs

Baby Life Support Systems (BLISS)
(A national charity offering support and information for the families of sick newborn babies.)
68 South Lambeth Road
London SW8 1RL

Tel: 0870 770 0337 (Mon–Fri, 9am–5.30pm)
Helpline: 0500 618 140 (Mon–Fri, 10am–5pm)
www.bliss.org.uk

The Osteopathic Centre For Children
(Tries to help provide paediatric osteo-pathy for all children.)
109 Harley Street
London W1G 6AN
Tel: 020 7486 6160
www.occ.uk.com

Tommy's The Baby Charity
(A charity that raises funds for research into prematurity and provides advice on pregnancy and premature birth.)
1 Kennington Road
London SE1 7RR
Tel: 020 7620 0188 (Mon–Fri, 9am–5.30pm)
www.tommys.org

Nappy cleaning services
National Association of Nappy Services (NANS)
Tel: 0121 693 4949
www.changeanappy.co.uk

Nappy Information Service
AHPMA
46 Bridge Street
Godalming
Surrey
GU7 1HL
www.nappyinformationservice.co.uk

Real Nappy Association
(Central source for information and advice on all nappy-related issues.)
PO Box 3704
London
SE26 4RX
Tel: 020 8299 4519
www.realnappy.com

Breast pump hire
Ameda Egnell Ltd
(Sells and hires hospital breast pumps.)
Tel: 01823 336362
www.ameda.demon.co.uk

Medela
(Sells and hires hospital standard breast pumps.)
Tel: 01538 386650
www.breastpumps.co.uk

National Childbirth Trust (NCT)
See Support groups, above
Breast pump hire: 0870 444 8707

Baby gym classes
Aquababies
(Teaching babies and young children to swim and to help aid their development.)
Aquababies Sport & Leisure Ltd
Suite G
Docklands Business Centre
10–16 Tiller Road
Docklands
London E14 8PX
Tel: 020 7702 4888 for nearest class
www.aquababiesltd.co.uk

Gymboree
(Interactive play and music programmes for babies.)
Tel: 0800 092 0911 for nearest class
www.GymboreePlayUK.com

Tumbletots
Tel: 020 8959 4261
www.tumbletots.com

Childcare
Au Pair and Student Agency
(A cultural exchange scheme for young people aged between 17 and 27.)
97 Monmouth Close
Valley Park
Chandlers Ford
Hants SO53 4SZ
Tel: 023 8026 1250
www.englishaupair.co.uk

The Child Accident Prevention Trust
(Charity focusing on safety issues for children.)
4th Floor
Clerks Court
18–20 Farringdon Lane
London EC1R 3HA
Tel: 020 7608 3828 (Mon–Fri,

9am–5pm)
www.capt.org.uk

ChildcareLink
(Links to childcare services in your area.)
Tel: 0800 096 0296
www.childcarelink.gov.uk

Childminders' Babysitting Service
9 Paddington Street
London W1M 3LA
Tel: 020 7935 2049
www.babysitter.com

Children's Information Service (CIS)
(Supplies a list of day nurseries in your area.)
Tel: ChildcareLink on 0800 096 0296

Daycare Trust
(Information on childcare options, where to find it and how to pay for it together with free information and advice for parents.)
21 St George's Road
London SE1 6ES
Tel: 020 7840 3350 (Mon–Fri, 10am–5pm)
www.daycaretrust.org.uk

National Childbirth Trust (NCT)
See Support groups, above

National Childminding Association
(For registered childminders. Dedicated to improving daycare standards.)
8 Mason Hill
Bromley BR2 9EY
Tel: 020 8464 6164 (Mon–Fri, 9am–5pm)
Helpline: 0800 169 4486 (Mon–Fri, 10am–4pm)
www.ncma.org.uk

National Council of Voluntary Child Care Organisations
(The voluntary childcare organisation.)
Unit 4
Pride Court
80–82 White Lion Street
London N1 9PF
Tel: 020 7833 3319
www.ncvcco.org

National Day Nursery Association
(Training and support programmes and provider of information and guidance to parents on choosing daycare.)
Oak House
Woodvale Road
Brighouse
West Yorkshire HD6 4AB
Tel: 0870 774 4244
www.ndna.org.uk

Parents at Work
(Provides information and advice regarding parenting and employment.)
45 Beech Street
London EC2Y 8AD
Tel: 020 7628 3565
www.parentsatwork.org.uk

Simply Childcare Magazine
(Listings magazine that also gives advice and information about childcare.)
16 Bushley Hill Road
London SE5 8QJ
Tel: 020 7703 7484
www.simplychildcare.com

Immunisation
Health Promotion England
www.immunisation.org.uk

MMR information
www.mmrthefacts.nhs.uk

The Informed Parent
http://www.informedparent.com/archives.html#immunizations

World Health Organisation
www.who.int/vaccines/

Cooking
Squires Kitchen
(Suppliers of flower blossom plunger cutters, mini heart and leaf shape cutters and paste food colouring. Mail order.)
Tel: 01252 734309

Index

Growing up with Annabel Karmel

Books for every stage of your child's development.

As a parent, giving your child a healthy start in life is a top priority. Annabel offers a cookbook for every stage of your child's development. As the UK's number one bestselling author on cooking for babies and children, Annabel's tried and tested recipes and meal planners have proved invaluable to families for over 20 years.

For more information go to **www.annabelkarmel.com**